W9-CKM-352

The Making of *Our Bodies, Ourselves*

NEXT WAVE

New Directions in Women's Studies

*A series edited by Inderpal Grewal, Caren Kaplan,
and Robyn Wiegman*

THE MAKING OF

Our Bodies, Ourselves

HOW FEMINISM TRAVELS ACROSS BORDERS

Kathy Davis

DUKE UNIVERSITY PRESS ✳ Durham and London ✳ 2007

© 2007 DUKE UNIVERSITY PRESS * All rights reserved * Printed in the United States of America on acid-free paper ∞ * Designed by C. H. Westmoreland * Typeset in Warnock Pro with Gill Sans display by Tseng Information Systems, Inc. * Library of Congress Cataloging-in-Publication Data appear on the last printed page of this book.

For my mother, Jan Davis,
who taught me the value of a good book

CONTENTS ✳

ACKNOWLEDGMENTS ✳

This is the book I have always wanted to write. Writing it, however, has taken considerably longer than any of my earlier books. The idea to write about *Our Bodies, Ourselves* (*OBOS*) and the group that wrote it began to form during a casual conversation with a colleague in 1997 and has gone on to span more than eight years, involving three prolonged sojourns in the United States. The book has been a long time coming in part because I had to finish other projects (the usual problem for busy academics) and squeeze in time to get back to the United States to do the fieldwork for the book. However, the main reason for this long genesis was not the usual problem of time and distance but rather a fateful eureka moment midway through my investigation that convinced me I had gotten it all wrong and needed to go back to the drawing board. What had started out as a history of one of U.S. feminism's most popular and successful projects had been transformed into a transcultural inquiry into how *OBOS* had "traveled" and the implications of its travels for how we think about feminist knowledge and health politics in a globalizing world. This shift in perspective added years to the project, making it more complicated (though also more interesting). It required excursions into several fields (translation studies, feminist activism in Latin America and postsocialist Europe, and postcolonial theory) that were relatively new for me. The result is, I hope, a better book—more timely, more forward looking, and more relevant for contemporary feminist scholarship.

Since I live and work in the Netherlands, this book would obviously have been considerably more difficult—if not impossible—to write without the chance to visit the United States at regular intervals.

From September 1998 to April 1999, the work was supported by a Rockefeller research fellowship at Columbia University. I am especially grateful to Mary Marshall Clarke and Ron Grele at the Oral History Research Office for introducing me—a dissident psychologist—to oral history as a discipline, methodology, and—they would argue—social movement. I thank them for making my stay in New York both inspiring and enjoyable.

In the summer of 2000, I received one of the last Berkshire Summer History fellowships offered by the Radcliffe Institute of Advanced Studies at Harvard University. In 2004–5, I returned to the Radcliffe Institute as a visiting fellow. I cannot thank the staff of the institute enough for making this such a stimulating and congenial place to do scholarly work. I would also like to thank the other fellows for making it a year I will never forget. Without the fellowship, finishing the book would have been a longer, much more arduous, and less pleasant process. During both fellowships, I spent many hours pouring over the Boston Women's Health Book Records (BWHBC) in the Schlesinger Library—a library not only unique for its collection on women's history but also for its commitment to women's scholarship. Many thanks to the members of its wonderful staff, who made working there such a treat, and, in particular, Kathy Kraft for her untiring help in tracking down "missing letters."

I am endlessly grateful to the members of the BWHBC who welcomed me with open arms and trusted me enough to tell me about their history. I arrived as the organization was in turmoil, and it is to their credit that they were willing to speak so candidly and thoughtfully about their experiences. Ruth Bell Alexander, Pamela Berger, Vilunya Diskin, Joan Ditzion, Paula Doress-Worters, Nancy Miriam Hawley, Elizabeth MacMahon-Herrera, Pamela Morgan, Judy Norsigian, Jamie Penney, Jane Pincus, Wendy Sanford, Norma Swenson, Sally Whelan, and Jennifer Yanco—thanks to all of you! I would especially like to thank Sally Whelan, one of the busiest people I know, for keeping me abreast of developments on the translation front, for reminding me why *OBOS* is not a thing of the past, and for her vision, which has helped create the transnational feminist community that *OBOS* has become. Jane Pincus, the "chronicler" of the collective, tirelessly answered all my questions, or pointed me in the direction of someone who could, not to mention reading several chapters. Judy Norsigian, Wendy Sanford, and Norma Swenson all met with me on several occasions, either alone or in groups, to discuss the history of the book and its translations.

I would have liked to speak with everyone involved in translating *OBOS*, but given the geographical distances this was a mission impossible. Nevertheless, my thanks go to those involved in the translations of *OBOS* for sharing their experiences and vision in interviews, group discussions, or online: Marlies Bosch, Irina Todorova, and Ester Shapiro, as well as the other participants of the Crossing Cultural Borders with *OBOS* conference, which was held in Utrecht in 2001: Codou Bop, Lobsang Dechen, Liana Galstyan, Toshiko Honda, Tatyana Kotzeva, Bobana Macanovic, Toyoko Nakanishi, Miho Ogino, Stanislava Otasvic, Jane Pincus, Lourdes Ruiz, Kornelia Slavova, Chantal Soeter, Norma Swenson, Malgorzata Tarasiewicz, Sally Whelan, and Alan West-Duran. This book could not have been written without the practical, intellectual, and personal support of the following people. Susan Reverby offered me a place to stay during my initial fieldwork and a sympathetic ear. She was also an invaluable source of information about the women's health movement in the United States and the importance of the BWHBC. Susan Bell provided generous support throughout this project. As longtime health activist, contributor to *OBOS*, and medical sociologist, she was the perfect conversational partner. Our monthly discussions while I was in Cambridge were invariably enjoyable and stimulating and helped keep me on track. Anna Aalten read various drafts of the manuscript, providing unfailingly sound scholarly and editorial advice. I appreciated her good-humored response to my desperate phone calls—sometimes trans-Atlantic—and willingness to help on short notice. Ah, yes, and three cheers for Bagels and Beans. I am grateful to Dubravka Žarkov for several insightful suggestions that changed the course of the book and for her unflagging support, especially at moments when I most needed it.

I was lucky enough to have three wonderful research assistants during this project. Elisabeth Yupanqui helped with the oral history interviews and offered critical perspectives from the "younger generation." Christina Ahn provided invaluable assistance doing Internet research and introduced me to Power Point. Daniel Morales did several Japanese translations and provided impromptu lessons on Japanese culture.

I will be forever grateful to Annique Boomsma and Jeff Gold, who not only commented on and proofread every chapter but provided me with a "home away from home" during my year as a solitary scholar in Cambridge.

I would also like to thank those friends and colleagues who read various drafts of chapters, provided background information, came up with translations for difficult words, stuck clippings in my mailbox, helped think of titles, and generally assisted me in getting "unstuck" at various moments in the past few years: Emily Abel, Jacqui Alexander, Piers Biernes, Sarah Bracke, Marsha Darling, Tine Davids, Roxanne Euben, Judith Ezekiel, Rachel Joffe Falmagne, Halleh Ghorashi, Nina Gregg, Barbara Henkes, Lena Inowlocki, Ynestra King, Sue Lanser, Gail Lewis, Helma Lutz, Barbara MacCaskill, Jenny Mansbridge, Susanne Maurer, Eun Kyung Min, Lorraine Nencel, Bode Omojola, Jane Pincus, Susan Reverby, Karin Rosemblatt, Sawitri Saharso, Cholthira Satyawadhna, Lynn Stephen, Francien van Driel, Gloria Wekker, and Sally Whelan. I am also indebted to the anonymous readers from Duke University Press for their excellent suggestions, which helped to sharpen my thinking on several points and generally contributed to making this a more readable book.

For help with the appendixes and invaluable assistance in putting titles in their appropriate alphabets, my heartfelt thanks go to Julia Bernstein, Arie Brouwer, Ayesha Chatterjee, Susan Ehrlich, Natalie Hanemann, Anissa Helié, Lena Inowlocki, Henk Latesteijn, Tal Litvak Hirsch, Vincent Lima, Daniel Morales, Irini Siouti, Gaye Tharawan, Irina Todorova, Kiki Zeldes, and "Kees" Chongua Zhang.

The final word of thanks goes to Willem de Haan for reading, commenting, and editing more drafts than either of us would like to remember, for putting up with my crankiness on Bad Writing Days, and for several memorable weekends when he put aside his own work and literally dragged me over the finish line. But, most of all, I am thankful to him for reminding me again and again why this was the book I had always wanted to write.

This is a book about a book: the feminist classic on women's health, *Our Bodies, Ourselves* (*OBOS*), and how it "traveled." The story begins in 1969. The country was in turmoil over the Vietnam War. Richard "Tricky Dick" Nixon had just been elected president after the riots at the Democratic National Convention in Chicago. Radical activism was everywhere: the civil rights movement and its offshoots— Black Power, La Raza, and the American Indian movement; antiwar demonstrations and draft resistance; radical student activism of the Marxist, socialist, or anarchist persuasion; hippies, yippies, and the "sexual revolution"; and, last but not least, a burgeoning women's movement. It was in this context that a small group of young women met at a workshop called Women and Their Bodies, held at one of the first feminist conferences in the United States, which took place in Boston. Some of the women had already been active in the civil rights movement or had helped draft resisters during the Vietnam War, but this was for many of them their first encounter with feminism. They talked about their sexuality (which was still, despite the sexual revolution, very much taboo), abortion (which was illegal— *Roe v. Wade* wasn't decided until 1973), their experiences with pregnancy and childbirth (several were young mothers), and their frustrations with physicians and health care. The group, which later evolved into the Boston Women's Health Book Collective (BWHBC), began to meet regularly. Its members collected information about health issues (which was, unlike today, scarce and hard to find) and wrote papers, which they discussed in meetings attended by increasing numbers of local women. These meetings were electrifying, leaving many of the participants irrevocably changed.

A year later the group assembled the discussion papers, and the first version of *OBOS* was born. Originally printed on newsprint by an underground publisher and selling for seventy-five cents, *OBOS* was a lively and accessible manual on women's bodies and health. It was full of personal experiences and contained useful information on issues ranging from masturbation (how to do it) to birth control (which methods were available and how to use them) to vaginal infections, pregnancy, and nursing. It combined a scathing critique of patriarchal medicine and the medicalization of women's bodies with an analysis of the political economics of the health and pharmaceutical industries. But, above all, *OBOS* validated women's embodied experiences as a resource for challenging medical dogmas about women's bodies and, consequently, as a strategy for personal and collective empowerment.

The book was an overnight success, and the group—to its surprise—found itself being wooed by commercial publishers. Since the first commercial edition was published in 1973, *OBOS* has sold over four million copies and gone through six major updates. The latest edition appeared in 2005. It occupied the *New York Times* best seller list for several years, was voted the best young adult book of 1976 by the American Library Association, and has received worldwide critical acclaim for its candid and accessible approach to women's health.

Often called the "bible of women's health," *OBOS* shaped how generations of women have felt about their bodies, their sexuality and relationships, and their reproduction and health. It has not only enjoyed a widespread popularity, unique for a feminist book, but has also transformed the provision of health care, helped shape health care policies, and stimulated research on women's health in the United States.[1] No family practice is complete without a copy of *OBOS* in the waiting room. Gynecological examinations have become more responsive to the patient's needs (e.g., by abandoning cold metal speculums in favor of more comfortable plastic ones), and hospitals have allowed women more control over the process of giving birth. As a result of *OBOS*, many women have been encouraged to enter medicine and midwives and nurse practitioners have been rehabilitated as respectable professionals in the U.S. health care system. The book has been a catalyst for myriad consumer and patient advocate organizations and campaigns for women's reproductive rights. It was instrumental in getting patient information inserts packaged with medications and has played an advocacy role in congressional hearings and scientific conferences on the safety of medications, medical devices, and procedures ranging from silicone breast implants to the injectable contraceptive Depo-Provera and the new genetic technologies. It has inspired research on women's health within the health sciences and medicine. Research protocols on—for example—heart disease no longer leave women out, and diseases that specifically effect women (such as breast cancer) have been given considerably more attention since the publication of *OBOS*. The recent study on the dangers of hormone replacement therapy (HRT), which exposed the negligence of the pharmaceutical industry and medical profession in indiscriminately promoting estrogen supplements for menopausal women, owes a debt to the pioneering work of *OBOS*.[2]

Personal Involvement

When *OBOS* was first published in the early 1970s, I was a college student in the United States and becoming active in the women's liberation movement (as it was then called). Like all of my friends, I had a copy of *OBOS*. I kept it on the floor next to my bed. When I look at it now, well underlined and full of notes, coffee stains, and other signs of wear and tear, it is clear that I pretty much read it from cover to cover. The exceptions were the chapters on pregnancy and menopause, which remained fairly pristine, holding less interest for me in those days than the chapters on sexuality, menstruation, and birth control. I remember discussing the book with friends and using it as a resource in self-help groups, where we experimented with many of the remedies it suggested for vaginal infections or menstrual cramps. I referred to *OBOS* before every visit to a gynecologist, and it was standard reading in many of the women's groups in which I participated throughout the seventies. As health activist, I used it in group discussions with women in my community and for advocacy work around women's health issues. For me, *OBOS* was like a wise friend, comforting and authoritative, a source of reliable health information and a stimulus for feminist activism.

By the 1980s, I had moved to Europe, had become a women's studies teacher, and was conducting research on women's bodies and health care issues. My copy of *OBOS* had moved from its place of honor at my bedside to one of the farthest corners of my bookshelves, where it remained unopened and collecting dust. While I invariably gave credit to *OBOS* in my writings, noting its centrality to any feminist critique of the health care system, it seemed far removed from the theoretical issues I was grappling with as a feminist scholar: debates about essentialism versus constructivism; how power and the cultural discourses of femininity are played out on women's bodies; or the political and moral dilemmas arising from women's active involvement in dangerous and ideologically problematic bodily practices such as dieting and eating disorders, cosmetic surgery, and reproductive technologies.[3] It did not occur to me to turn to *OBOS* for help in developing critical positions in what was increasingly being called the "body revival" by feminist and other cultural theorists in the academy. While I did continue to use *OBOS* in my classes on body politics, it was usually as a text to be contrasted with medical texts. I expected my students, who were well schooled in feminist theory and the methods of deconstruction, to look critically at the discourse, metaphors, and rhetoric of both texts. Interestingly, while my students had no trouble deconstructing medical texts, they were much less able to take an analytic stance toward *OBOS*, tending to either accept it at face value ("I love this text, it makes me feel good") or dismiss it out of hand as a relic of sixties feminism ("something for my mother"). In short, their responses replayed the same tension that I had been experiencing between contemporary feminist theory and feminist health activism—a tension that made a serious, analytic engagement with *OBOS* as a text difficult.

It wasn't until the end of the 1990s that I encountered *OBOS* once again, this time as a potential research object. I attended a conference in my hometown of Amsterdam on historical and sociological approaches to biographical research, where I met the woman who is now director of the Oral History Research Office at Columbia University, Mary Marshall Clarke. She mentioned that the program had recently been awarded a large Rockefeller grant to subsidize fellowships for oral history research on community organizations. She explained that she and her colleagues almost never got "something on the body" and even fewer proposals from sociologists. "Isn't there something you could do?" she asked. The prospect of spending six months at the Oral History Research Office in New York, not to mention returning to my country of origin after years spent living abroad, was, I must admit, the first thing that caught my attention. However, after thinking about ways to link my interest in feminism and "the body" to biographical research on community activists, the idea of doing a group history based on biographical interviews with members of the Boston Women's Health Book Collective seemed an obvious choice. After all, this was the group that had literally put women's bodies on the feminist agenda. Thus, I proceeded to write the proposal, was eventually awarded a fellowship, and packed my bags for a six-month sojourn in the United States, where I planned to interview the "founding mothers" of one of U.S. feminism's most famous (and favorite) projects.

At this point, I had every intention of writing a history of *OBOS* based on the collective memories of the women who wrote it. Situating myself in the tradition of oral history, I expected to use the interviews as a basis for explaining the success and longevity of the book, as well as its significance as a feminist icon. However, in the course of doing this research I made a rather momentous discovery—a discovery that completely changed the present inquiry, transforming it into something that is not quite a history.[4]

Not Quite a History

I discovered that the impact of *OBOS* was not limited to the United States but had extended beyond the country as well. From its inception, *OBOS* had been taken up, translated, and adapted by local groups of feminist activists, scholars, health providers, and health activists in different parts of the globe. By the late 1970s, it had already appeared in most Western European countries, as well as Japan and Taiwan. By the 1980s, it had moved south and east, with versions appearing in Hebrew and Arabic (the latter for Egypt). By the 1990s, it had been translated into Telegu (for India) and Russian and adapted in English for South Africa. In 2000, a Spanish adaptation for all Latin American countries, *Nuestros Cuerpos, Nuestras Vidas*, was published, and since 2005 the list has been expanded to include a French *Notre Corps, Notre Sante* for francophone Africa, a Tibetan translation, and translations for Eastern Europe (Poland, Bulgaria, Serbia, and Moldova), Armenia, China, Thailand, South Korea, and Indonesia. Moreover, the end is nowhere in sight; many more translation projects are waiting for start-up funding (in Brazil, Turkey, Nigeria, and Vietnam).

This impressive list indicates that *OBOS* has become one of the most frequently translated feminist books. It has sold more than four times as many copies as the international feminist best seller *The Second Sex*, written by Simone de Beauvoir.[5] And, while Eve Ensler's *The Vagina Monologues* (1998) may prove to have a similar global appeal,[6] *OBOS* remains U.S. feminism's most popular "export" to date.

The international trajectory of *OBOS* convinced me that a history of the book within the United States could not begin to do justice to its impact and significance. More important, however, the book's "travels" raise several questions that are irresistibly intriguing. How could such a distinctively U.S. book resonate with women in such diverse social, cultural, and geographic locations? What happened to the book when it traveled? How did it change in order to address the concerns of women in such different contexts? And, finally, what can the travels of *OBOS* tell us about how feminist knowledge and politics circulate transnationally? In what ways have these border crossings been shaped by, but also subverted, globally structured relations of power between what has critically been referred to as the "West and the rest" (Hall 1992)?

These questions are the focus of the present inquiry. Rather than writing a history of *OBOS* as a U.S. feminist project, I will be connecting the book's history within the United States to its travels outside the United States. I will use these travels to think about the book's impact, its changing content, and its significance for transnational feminist knowledge and body politics.

My approach to the history of *OBOS* will also deviate from recent feminist historiographies of what has been called—somewhat problematically—second-wave feminism.[7] Although *OBOS* emerged at this particular point in time and its history could be told as an example of this particular moment in U.S. feminism, I have opted for a different approach. Given the remarkable life of the book outside the United States, it is my contention that its history as a feminist project and cultural icon needs to be more forward looking. It must include how *OBOS* has been—and continues to be—taken up by women across the globe. Writing a history from the vantage point of its origins in the United States, as told from the perspective of its founders—as was my initial intention—would fail to do justice to what is arguably the book's most unique and remarkable feature, namely, its ability to speak to a wide variety of women at different times and in disparate circumstances and social, cultural, and political contexts. Thus, in line with Susan Sanford Friedman's (2001) warning that too much attention to history can submerge one's "geographical imagination" (16), I will be broadening my account of the history of *OBOS* to encompass its myriad and diverse border crossings, both inside and outside the United States.[8]

In order to analyze the production and reception of *OBOS* as traveling theory in a global context, I have drawn on and engage with recent debates within feminist scholarship on the "politics of location." I shall now turn briefly to these debates as they provide the theoretical and normative context in which the present inquiry is situated.

Feminism and the Politics of Location

Born of an engagement between feminist theory and multiculturalism, cultural studies and postcolonial theory, the politics of location recognizes the importance of location as the ground from which one speaks and as shaping one's identity, knowledge of the world, and possibilities for political action. Initially coined by Adrienne Rich (1986),[9] the politics of location has variously been referred to as "locational feminism" (Friedman 1998), "feminist conjuncturalism" (Frankenberg and Mani 1993), "postmodern geographies" (Kaplan 1996), "diaspora space" (Brah 1996), and "theory from the borderlands" (Anzaldúa 1987). In the context of the present inquiry, it is impossible to do justice to the complexities involved in all these debates about location and what the linkages between the "global" and the "local" might mean for critical feminist inquiry (Grewal and Kaplan 1994; Kaplan 1996; Alexander and Mohanty 1997; Mohanty 2003). I will limit myself to how a concern for the politics of location has generated fundamentally different views about feminist history, feminist knowledge and knowledge practices, and the possibilities and limitations in political alliances among women both within and outside the United States.

The politics of location introduces spatiality or geography as essential for understanding women's *history* as well as histories of feminist struggle. While U.S. feminism had tended to valorize history, emphasizing the retrieval of the "lost" voices of women and making women's accomplishments visible, a politics of location recognizes that "the social production of history takes place in a certain geographical location" (Friedman 2001, 17). Symptomatic of the centrality given to history was the preoccupation of U.S. feminism with its "origins" and its ubiquitous temporal rhetoric of "awakening, revelation, and rebirth" (18) as epitomized in the notorious "click experience," which represented a collective moment when women saw the light and became political subjects. The emphasis on the historical and temporal led many U.S. feminist historians to overlook the fact that feminism emerges in different forms in different places. Feminist ideas have a long and uneven history of being taken up and rearticulated in different locations across the globe throughout history, producing hybrid cultural formations that may bear only a passing resemblance to U.S. feminism in late modernity.[10] The assumption that feminism "began" (and "ended") in the United States separated women into the initiated and the uninitiated, a dualism that justified the view that U.S. feminists had achieved liberation while "traditional" or non-Western women were more severely oppressed and in need of salvation. The new emphasis on location involved a moving away from linear modernist histories of feminism to an exploration of how feminism "emerges, takes root, changes, travels, translates, and transplants in different spacio/temporal contexts" (15).

The politics of location has consequences for theorizing feminism as an *epistemological project*—that is, as a project that can generate knowledge and knowledge practices aimed at enhancing women's individual and collective empowerment. Initially, feminist epistemology employed a notion of location that referred to how an individual's (or group's) material position shaped her experiences, perceptions, and interactions with others. This particular conception of location provided the basis for feminist standpoint epistemology, which assumed that women use their material location not only as a resource for knowing what it means to be embodied as a woman in a particular social and cultural context but also as a place from which to construct a critical feminist subjectivity and perspective for social change.[11] Feminist standpoint epistemology has since generated considerable critical debate, most notably about the problems involved in privileging one aspect of women's experience—gender—while ignoring the ways in which race, class, and other categories of difference intersect in multiple and contradictory ways in women's everyday lives.[12] The issue of how to theorize intersecting identities, along with the implications this has for feminist epistemology, has been one of the most productive and highly developed areas of contemporary feminist scholarship.[13] An important outcome has been a shift from viewing location in terms of identity to viewing it as a context in which complex and shifting relationships are constituted within a dynamic field of historical and geopolitical forces (Mani 1989). Under the influence of postcolonial theory, this contextual understanding of location has been used to understand international exchanges of knowledge in a global-local nexus. Feminists have become increasingly concerned not only with the—often selective—reception of feminist texts in the United States (King 1994) but also with how feminist knowledge circulates through translation and dissemination of feminist texts across the globe (Spivak 1988b, 1985; Kaplan 1996). Feminism—both as theory and practice—is now viewable as a kind of "traveling theory" (Said 1983) that circulates globally and is rearticulated and transformed in the course of its relocation from place to place.

The politics of location makes it essential to imagine and implement *feminist political alliances* across lines of difference rather than through a shared identity as women. U.S. feminism has often had an international vision of a unitary world of women, bringing together women from different parts of the globe by virtue of their assumed shared experience of oppression and their common struggles as women (Morgan 1984). The danger of this version of "global feminism," however, was the centrality it tended to give to white women within what was a decidedly Euro-American version of feminism. In addition to being ethnocentric, global feminism often celebrated "cultural differences," whereby global power relations were mystified and a stance of cultural relativism was adopted that precluded the necessary discussions about feminist accountability and a more serious engagement with practices and politics in other parts of the globe (Lugones and Spelman 1983; Kaplan 1996; Narayan 1997, 1998). The problems inherent in global feminism were countered by integrating the feminist desire for transnational feminist alliances with a feminist, anti-imperialist culture critique (Mohanty et al. 1991; Grewal and Kaplan 1994; Alexander and Mohanty 1997; Mohanty 2003). This version of the politics of location entailed recognition of the myriad ways in which women across the globe are already linked in diverse and unequal relations through historical, global processes of domination produced by global capitalism, colonialism, imperialism, or slavery. These transnational and historically contingent relations of power—or "scattered hegemonies" (Grewal and Kaplan 1994)—provide, paradoxically, a location from which feminists can recognize the inequalities that separate them yet can also join forces, forming alliances around common concerns. This notion of international feminist politics is not based on women's biological identity or shared cultural identities. It takes as its starting point the tensions and divisions between women across divides of class, race, ethnicity, sexuality, and national borders (Mani 1989; Lugones 2003). It provides a vision of feminism that encompasses "imagined communities of women with divergent histories and social locations, woven together by the political threads of opposition to forms of domination that are not only pervasive but also systemic" (Mohanty 2003, 46–47).[14]

In conclusion, a politics of location identifies the grounds of historically specific differences and similarities among women in diverse and asymmetrical relations, creating alternative histories, knowledge practices, and possibilities for alliance. It opens up space for a new kind of critical feminist practice. Instead of being preoccupied with feminist history as a single story, multiple and diverse accounts of feminism in different places and at different points in time can be generated. It becomes possible to think about how feminism travels—that is, how feminist knowledge and knowledge practices move from place to place and are "translated" in different cultural locations. And, finally, we can consider how transnational feminist encounters emerge within a context of globally structured hierarchies of power and what this means for feminist encounters across lines of difference.

In the present inquiry, I will engage with these discussions about the politics of location in three different ways: in writing the *history* of *OBOS*, in analyzing it as a feminist *epistemological project*, and in understanding its significance for *feminist politics* in a global context.

First, the history of *OBOS* will encompass its trajectory inside as well as outside the United States. This means that the book's life outside the United States will not be treated as an afterthought to its "real" history or as an exotic footnote to the main story. On the contrary, the present inquiry will use the travels of *OBOS* as a lens through which the historical significance of the book can become visible. Its history will be presented as a transnational history situated in the context of a rapidly globalizing world.

Second, *OBOS* will be analyzed as a kind of feminist traveling theory. This will mean adopting the somewhat unorthodox approach of elevating what is commonly seen as "just" a popular book on women's health to the lofty-sounding status of a feminist epistemological project—that is, a project that generates feminist knowledge and knowledge practices. By analyzing the politics of knowledge that *OBOS* represents, I will be able to show how the book could be taken up in contexts very different from those in which it was originally produced. In other words, I will use the travels of *OBOS* to think about the production and reception of feminist theory in transnational cultures of exchange (Kaplan 1996).

Third, *OBOS* will be explored as a catalyst for feminist body/politics both within and outside the United States. Since the circulation of any U.S. or "First World" feminist text to postcolonial or "Third World" contexts raises potentially thorny questions concerning feminism as "cultural imperialism," I will engage with the "strange encounters" (Ahmed 2000) engendered by the revision of *OBOS* in the United States, as well as its translation and adaptation outside the United States among women in different social, cultural, and political locations.[15] In the present inquiry, I will use *OBOS* as a test case for addressing whether these encounters provide the conditions for a truly transnational feminism—that is, a feminism that joins a respect for difference with critical reflexivity and mutual empowerment (Grewal and Kaplan 1994).[16]

About the Book

The present inquiry spanned a period of several years, moving from a straightforward oral history to an analysis of the book as a transnational feminist epistemological project. It went through three phases. The first was concerned with mapping the history of *OBOS*. Initially, I conducted oral history interviews with the founders of the original collective.[17] From the fall of 1998 through the spring of 1999, I used my fellowship at the Oral History Research Office at Columbia University to travel back and forth between New York and Boston. With one exception, all of the interviews were face-to-face and lasted from one to three hours.[18] Since the BWHBC encompassed more than the founders, I also spoke with members of the then current staff, as well as with some who had left the organization under less than pleasant circumstances. I interviewed several members of the Board of Directors and talked to many women who had co-authored chapters of *OBOS* or been involved with editing or critically reading the book during its many revisions. In the course of my inquiry, I corresponded with many of my informants and, in some cases, conducted additional interviews in order to fill in gaps in my understanding of the history or—more significantly—to keep myself abreast of the ongoing transformations in the organization, further editions of *OBOS* in the United States, and the steady stream of new translation projects. Finally, I organized several group discussions with members of the collective concerning the history of the book's transformation within and outside the United States.[19]

The second phase of the inquiry involved an in-depth analysis of *OBOS* as a feminist epistemological project—that is, a project that is involved in generating feminist knowledge and knowledge practices. It began with a confrontation between the epistemological assumptions of *OBOS* and postmodern feminist body theory (in particular, the work of Donna Haraway, Judith Butler, Elizabeth Grosz, Joan Scott, and Susan Bordo), as well as alternative biological, phenomenological, and materialist critiques of this theory.[20] I show how *OBOS* can contribute to some of the most central discussions in feminist body theory by providing an embodied, situated, critical feminist politics of knowledge. This having been done, the stage was set for a close reading of the text itself. To this end, I drew upon the work the feminist text sociology (in particular, Dorothy Smith's work) in order to show how *OBOS* as a text could produce a specific kind of reading and a specific kind of (feminist) reader. I further developed my analysis of the production and reception of *OBOS* as a feminist text through archival research, which allowed me to show how actual readers had become feminist subjects through reading *OBOS*. At the time I did this part of my research, the BWHBC had just donated three decades' worth of papers to the Schlesinger Library—a library dedicated to women's history.[21] As I sorted through more than nine linear feet of unprocessed boxes, I discovered a wealth of minutes from meetings of the collective, describing in exquisite detail how decisions were made about what to include in the book and what to leave out, negotiations with publishers, trips abroad, and participation in various health initiatives. There were personal letters, position statements, discussion papers, newspaper clippings, and countless versions of chapters from various editions of *OBOS* in various stages of editing, along with memos from contributors and editors.[22] But perhaps the most momentous discovery of all was the hundreds of letters from readers from all over the world who wrote to the authors of *OBOS* to express appreciation, contribute their own experiences, or articulate their criticisms of the book. These letters proved to be a gold mine as they allowed me to analyze the relationship between the book and its readers through the words of the readers themselves.[23]

The third phase of this inquiry was devoted to the translations of *OBOS*. Given the diversity of languages, I was not able to read every translation. I pieced together my research on the translation projects from several sources. I went through the archives, examining the correspondence with translators and publishers, internal papers, and proposals for foundation grants for translation projects. I arranged several discussions (and many more informal conversations) with members of the BWHBC, which focused specifically on translation projects.[24] In addition to this material, I was able to interview several translators involved with the foreign editions of *OBOS* and, in other cases, was able to read what the translators had written about the translation process—often in the prefaces of the foreign editions.[25] Finally, I helped set up a dialogue among the translators in 2001. Together with the BWHBC, I organized a four-day encounter in the Netherlands where translators from different countries could compare notes and discuss the strategies they used to transform *OBOS* into a text that would be useful and oppositional within their local contexts. I used this meeting to think about the politics of translation, as well as the possibilities of transnational feminist alliances in the field of feminist health politics.[26]

The three phases of the inquiry are reflected in the organization of this book. It is divided into three parts. The first part maps the history of *OBOS* in the United States and its travels outside the United States. The second part explores *OBOS* as an epistemological project and how its knowledge practices and knowledge politics were transformed through its translations. Finally, the third part explores the implications of *OBOS* and its travels for transnational feminism in theory and practice.

The first chapter traces the history of *OBOS* within the United States from the first edition in 1970 to the latest version in 2005. Set against the shifting cultural and political landscape in the United States, it shows how the content, form, and ideology of the book changed. An explanation is provided for how a book on women's health, written by laywomen, could become a feminist "success story."

In the second chapter, the history of *OBOS* is transported beyond the borders of the United States. Beginning with the translation of *OBOS* throughout Western Europe during the 1970s, I explore how the book moved steadily farther afield, changing from a publisher-based translation to a project supported by international foundations and nongovernmental organizations (NGOs). I address the ways in which local women's groups took up *OBOS* and how they reworked and transformed it to meet their own needs. The changing relationship between the U.S. *OBOS* and its translations is examined against the backdrop of contemporary feminist debates about the dangers of U.S. feminism as cultural imperialism. I show how the international trajectory of *OBOS* provides an example of how Western feminism can become "decentered."

The third chapter takes up the history of the group that wrote *OBOS*, the Boston Women's Health Book Collective. Drawing on the stories of the founding members, I show how their collective history takes on a mythical cast, allowing the participants not only to re-member their past in a particular way but to make sense of the realities of the present. I explore the ambivalences of this myth, showing how it worked in ways that were empowering but also prevented them from coming to terms with some of the tensions and conflicts within their organization.

The fourth chapter takes up the feminist epistemological project that was represented by *OBOS*. I explore how it might contribute to several central debates within feminist body theory—conceptualizing women's bodies without falling into the trap of biological determinism, mobilizing women's experience as a critical knowledge resource without treating it as an unmediated source of the "truth," and reinstating women as epistemic agents without ignoring the structural and discursive conditions that limit their agency. By showing how *OBOS* tackles these problems, I make a case for bridging the gap that has developed between contemporary feminist body theory and feminist health activism.

The fifth chapter explores how *OBOS* accomplishes its epistemological project at the discursive level of the text. I explore the textual strategies that allow *OBOS* as a text to construct a particular kind of reading. I also draw on letters from the readers of *OBOS* in order to show how the text produces a particular kind of reader—readers who are embodied, critically reflexive, and actively engaged in taking control of their bodies. In short, *OBOS* creates feminist subjects ready to embark on a critical, collective, feminist politics of health.

The sixth chapter returns to the question of how this specific politics of knowledge could travel. Against the backdrop of critical feminist and postcolonial translation theory, I analyze two specific translation projects in more detail: the Spanish edition for Latin America and the Bulgarian translation of *OBOS*. These cases allow me to explore the issues involved in translating across cultural, regional, and national differences and to show how the politics of knowledge embodied by the U.S. *OBOS* can be transformed—and transformed in very different ways—so that it can be oppositional in specific social, cultural, and geopolitical circumstances.

The seventh chapter assesses the implications of *OBOS* and its travels. I will argue that the scope and variety of its border crossings, the diversity of its transformations, and the ways in which it has shaped encounters between feminists globally have consequences for how we think about history, the politics of knowledge, and transnational politics. On a note of measured optimism, I conclude that contemporary feminist theory may have at least as much to learn from the analysis of *OBOS* as *OBOS* has to learn from feminist theory.

Part I ✳ THE BOOK AND ITS TRAVELS

CHAPTER I

OBOS in the United States

THE ENIGMA OF A FEMINIST "SUCCESS STORY"

The scene is the summer cottage of one of the members of the Boston Women's Health Book Collective. It is a sunny day in July 2000, and three of the founders of the collective have agreed to meet with me and talk about the book that played such an important part in their lives, as well as the lives of women all over the world. There is still plenty of food on the table after our delicious lunch, and our bathing suits are hanging out to dry on the deck after our swim in the lake. But we're here to work. I am armed with my trusty tape recorder, and they immediately begin to spread out the different editions of *OBOS* on the floor.

It's an impressive display. From the early papers (typed and stapled) to the first underground publication in 1970 to the most recent *Our Bodies Ourselves for the New Century* in 1998, there are seven different editions of the book. Then there are the additional books produced by members of the collective, *Ourselves and Our Children* (BWHBC 1978), *Changing Bodies, Changing Lives* (Bell et al. [1987, 1991] 1998), *Ourselves Growing Older* (Worters and Siegal 1987, 1994), and *Sacrificing Ourselves for Love* (Wegscheider and Rome 1996). And, last but not least, there is the first self-publication in Spanish for the United States, *Nuestros Cuerpos, Nuestra Vidas* (1977), along with some of the foreign editions of the book.

Three decades of *OBOS* were before my eyes. It's clear at a glance just how much water has flowed under the bridge. The first edition looks like it should be in a sealed case in a library. The pages are yellowing and fragile newsprint with the title *Women and Their Bodies: A Course*, by the Boston Women's Health Collective, written by hand. This first edition is a booklet of less than two hundred pages, just twelve chapters with one or two authors for each, and all for the unbelievable price of seventy-five cents. The cover features a photograph of two smiling Anglo-American women, one young and one old, bearing a banner that reads "Women Unite." It's the heyday of the women's liberation movement.

In contrast, the 1998 edition is a tome of 780 pages, a glossy and somewhat intimidating reference book. It has not only grown in length, with twenty-seven chapters, but there are now three pages of contributors. The price has risen to twenty-four dollars. There are long lists of references and professional photographs. The title indicates that this is not just a course but a book for the future. The cover still has the original "Women Unite" photograph, but it has shrunk considerably and now is surrounded by many other photographs of individual women of different ages and ethnicities. One is pregnant, one has a baby at her breast, while others are gardening or engaged in sports. There are some photographs of friends together. One of the founders explains, somewhat ruefully, that the cover was supposed to project a kind of "family of man" without looking too much like "something my mother would read."

This chapter explores the trajectory that *OBOS* took from the first edition in 1970 to the latest edition in 2005.[1] I draw on interviews and group discussions with members of the Boston Women's Health Book Collective, as well as excerpts from the various editions of the book,[2] in order to show how *OBOS* changed in content, form, and political message over a period of more than three decades. Situating these changes in the shifting social, cultural, and political landscape of the book's production and reception, I address the question of how a popular book on women's health, written for and by laywomen, could become such a long-standing success within the United States.

The Early Years

"It's hard to say where the beginning starts," says Nancy Miriam Hawley, but "probably in the early spring of 1969." It was a time of activism (the civil rights movement, draft resistance, student protests) and a budding counterculture. The women's liberation movement had just begun.[3] Hawley was involved in organizing one of the first women's liberation conferences in Boston at Emmanuel College. There were workshops on different issues—everything from women and work to self defense—and her workshop was entitled Women and Their Bodies.

"It was a very exhilarating workshop," Paula Doress-Worters remembers. They talked about sexuality, abortion, birth control, and childbirth. Everyone had a "doctor story"—that is, a tale about male physicians who were sexist, paternalistic, judgmental, or simply unable to provide the information that women needed.

The group decided to continue meeting. The first plan was to assemble a list of "good doctors." However, every time someone suggested the name of a doctor, another woman would have something negative to report. The list dwindled until they finally decided that if they were not to be at the mercy of these doctors they would just have to get information about their bodies themselves.

By the fall of 1969, they were meeting regularly. The group at this point was very fluid, with women bringing their friends or sisters. Many heard about the group by word of mouth. Because, unlike today, there was so little information available on women's health, they began doing the research themselves. It was often difficult to even get into medical libraries and sometimes involved the clandestine borrowing of library cards from bona fide medical students.[4]

> We started to write little bits of experiences down, and little fragments of knowledge down, and if you were lucky or smart or something, you'd go to a library and maybe find a book on something you were writing about, but that was very rare. There wasn't that much information anywhere. Then you'd bring back whatever you could glean to the group; you'd tell people what you'd found and they'd say, "Oh, that's fine but what about this experience?" Or "This happened to me" or "This is the way my husband felt about me when I was pregnant." So you would just basically write down what everybody said. I think because a lot of us were college-trained, we ended up writing things down.[5]

They met weekly to discuss their findings, adding questions and personal experiences from women in the group. It wasn't until 1970 that they decided they were ready to offer a course on what they had discovered. The term *course* is misleading to our modern ears, suggesting a teacher imparting information to a captive audience. In contrast, these courses were more like consciousness-raising groups.[6] Women would do research on different subjects, write it up, mimeograph it, and hand it out in the group. They quickly abandoned the idea of trying to read the papers as everyone was impatient to talk. They would go around in a circle, with each woman telling her story. If the topic was menstruation, women would talk about when they first got their period, experiences with menstruation, what it was like to have terrible cramps and "have a doctor pat you on the head and say, "Just wait until you have babies; it'll be fine then." Under the motto "the personal is political," they attempted to develop a political awareness about economic and social systems that make women sick or influence the kind of health care available to them. They asked political questions about every topic: "Why hasn't anyone done research on this? Why is so much research done on men's heart problems when there is nothing on women's menstrual cramps or bladder infections?"

Wendy Sanford remembers her first experience attending one of these courses with a friend: "We drove over there together, we found the room at MIT, and we walked into this huge lounge of fifty women talking about sex. I was just flabbergasted and really shy, and they were talking about masturbation, which was a word that I never heard said out loud . . . much less the words *clitoris* and *orgasm*. I mean, those were all words that I had never heard said out loud. And it was . . . I listened. I didn't say anything. I listened."[7]

Two women who had attended the course and worked at the New England Free Press (a small movement publisher) came up with the idea of publishing the papers. The group rewrote their papers, adding the responses from women who had participated in the course, and handed them over to a small movement publisher under the title *Women and Their Bodies: A Course by and for Women*. It became an overnight sensation, selling 250,000 copies in the first year. Women were reading it as far away as Seattle and New Mexico. The New England Free Press published two editions in 1970 and 1971, the latter under the title *Our Bodies, Ourselves*.

The chapters were short, ranging from five pages on anatomy to twenty-four pages on childbirth. Other topics were sexuality, venereal disease, birth control, abortion, postpartum, myths about women, and medicine and capitalism. The book reflected the interests of the authors, who were young, white, college-educated women, many of whom were raising small children.

> It's important to remember that these first editions were not a book but course material to be used in a group for discussion. They were never considered a finished product. . . . For example, the 1971 edition begins with a note: "We want to add chapters on menopause and getting older and attitudes to children . . . would you like to make suggestions, write up your own experience, or otherwise work on the course? Please write us. The course is what all of us make of it." . . . It was very open and forward looking. There was a sense of "there's always another way to look at it." It's paradoxical that the material later became a book to be read alone by a woman in her own room.[8]

These first editions of *OBOS* were very much a product of the political climate of the late sixties. In character with the times, there was a strong emphasis on sexuality and reproduction. Abortion was still illegal; birth control was unsafe and not always available. Feminists were beginning to take a critical look at what the so-called sexual revolution meant for women. Primarily white, middle-class, college-educated women, they assumed that other women would share their experiences and interests—a stance that would come back to haunt them as differences among women became an issue of concern both within the women's movement and among feminist scholars.[9] The book was not only liberally spiced with phrases such as "we as women," but it treated issues that later would prove to be complex and contested in a deceptively matter-of-fact fashion. For example, in 1971 they wrote that "probably the most insidious mistruth about abortion is that of the so-called post-abortion guilt feelings" (BWHBC 1971, 70a), failing to anticipate the personal and normative objections that were to fuel the massive antiabortion movement just a few years later.[10] They also took a straightforwardly oppositional stance toward medicine, adopting the anticapitalist jargon of social movements of the era. The enemy was identified as the capitalist health care system, which was decried as "no more dedicated to improving the people's health than . . . General Motors [is] . . . to improving people's public transportation" (136).

Feminist Best Seller

By the fall of 1971, the group was receiving letters from women from all over the country who had things to add. The members of the group realized that they needed to update the book. At the same time, they were being wooed by commercial publishers. As one member put it, "It was a total shock, really . . . it was like 'Oh, my. What do we do now?' It was very controversial to be thinking about going with a 'capitalist pig publisher.'"[11] After "hours and hours of soul-searching discussions" about whether they would be "selling out," they decided that being able to get the book out quickly to more women in more places had priority. They finally decided to give their book to Simon and Schuster, explaining their decision to their readers in the last New England Free Press edition (accompanied by an accusing rejoinder from the New England Free Press). They consulted a lawyer, who helped them negotiate a contract that proved to be nothing short of phenomenal—even by today's standards. They had complete editorial control over the content of the book, as well as the right to veto any photographs they did not like. They insisted on a clause that allowed clinics serving women to get bulk discounts on all copies of *OBOS*. And, finally, the contract included a simultaneous Spanish translation, which would be distributed in the United States.[12] It was in the wake of negotiating this contract that the BWHBC was officially formed from the core group of twelve women, which had crystallized from the fluid membership of the first years.[13] The BWHBC became a legal corporation and did not take on any new members until the nineties.

The first commercial edition of *OBOS* appeared in 1973 and was revised and updated in 1976 and 1979. It was an immediate success, selling nearly 2.5 million copies by 1976. The increased public exposure of the book brought laudatory reviews nationwide and positive responses from readers, educators, and physicians, some of whom even suggested that it be included in the medical curriculum.[14] It appeared on the *New York Times* best seller list in 1976 and 1977. The *Chronicle of Higher Education* listed it as fifth in 1973 and fourth in 1974 on its list of best-selling books on U.S. college campuses. In 1976, it was named one of the ten all-time best books for young people by the American Library Association. Paradoxically, the popularity of the book went hand in hand with censorship attacks on the part of

New Right groups such as Phyllis Schlafly's Eagle Forum and Jerry Falwell's Moral Majority. Jerry Falwell, in particular, launched a crusade against *OBOS*, trying to have it banned in libraries on the grounds that it was obscene, antifamily, and anti-Christian.[15]

The commercial *OBOS* maintained the familiar cover with the two women, one young and one older, shown holding a "Women Unite" banner above their heads—an image that was to become the book's logo. However, any mention of the book being a "course for women" had vanished. It was typeset with professional photographs and drawings. It gained volume, increasing from 275 pages in 1973 to nearly 400 pages by 1979. Chapters were longer and ended with long lists of references, which had been missing in the early versions when information was a scarce commodity. The list of women (and some men) that helped with the book grew, and their names appeared in long lists at the beginning of each edition.

Thematically, *OBOS* continued to focus on sexuality and reproductive health. However, new issues were taken onboard. Menopause became the subject of a new chapter. Chapters on nutrition and exercise ("women in motion") were included, as were sections on common health problems. While the early editions of *OBOS* had been primarily concerned with the problem of unwanted pregnancy (birth control, abortion), they now examined the problem of "infertility." Although this was prior to the explosion of medical technologies for assisted reproduction, developments such as fetal monitoring were addressed at length. While the authors explained why and how it was used during labor, they were clearly skeptical about "doctors' eagerness to use technology before the complete range of effects is known" (BWHBC 1976, 285). They cautioned women to be wary of possible side effects and continued to warn about the dangers of medicalization. As Norma Swenson put it, the medical profession needed to be held responsible for engendering a "deep and permanent sense of doubt" in women about their ability to manage their own birth experiences or have confidence in their bodies. "We learn that our bodies are alien time bombs that can get into trouble at any moment and have to be rescued by doctors and the medical profession."[16] The authors remained committed to the "natural" birth process, focusing their attention on alternatives to hospital births and providing suggestions about how women might resist invasive procedures once in the hospital. One of the founders remembered feeling a certain "dissonance" when she had a cesarean section during the birth of her first child. "Having a cesarean section wasn't supposed to happen. . . . I was going to have a home birth, which was what people were having . . . but then I really had to have a C-section, and it was so clear to me that the health of my baby mattered over everything, and I didn't care how I had this baby at that point. . . . I didn't do it in the 'politically correct' way. . . . like 'There are more C-sections than are necessary.'"[17]

The politics of *OBOS* with regard to abortion was beginning to change as well. Abortion was still a contentious issue in the United States, but with the legalization of abortion through the Supreme Court decision of 1973 *OBOS* moved from the earlier stance that "abortion is our right—our right as women to control our bodies" (BWHBC 1973, 138) to, in 1976, "abortion as one right among many." The notion of "choice" became more central. Attention was directed to the fact that "a number of women and men believe sincerely that abortion is wrong," and the book's authors took a critical stance against the "right to life" discourse that had just begun to emerge in the United States, writing, "We defend any woman's right not to end a pregnancy if she feels abortion is wrong for her. But some who are against abortion for themselves want to restrict others' freedom. We believe they are wrong to try to impose their beliefs on us" (BWHBC 1976, 216).

The abortion chapter showed the authors grappling with a desire to respect differences in women's experience with abortion and wanting to take a clear position against the curtailing of women's reproductive rights. It was situated in the growing feminist struggle in the United States around abortion, the tactics of which were described in detail, along with equally detailed information about how to collectively combat the undermining of women's right to choose at the federal and local levels.

The authors were becoming increasingly aware of differences among women. While *OBOS* continued to be written from the perspective of "we women" (with occasional self-reflexive references to "we the collective"), there was a growing appreciation for the variety of experiences of individual women and for collective differences in the experiences of specific groups. In the context of a growing demand among lesbian women for recognition within the women's movement, the BWHBC decided to include a chapter on lesbians.[18] Under the assumption that only lesbians could do justice to the concerns of lesbians ("we were a very heterosexual group"), they handed over full editorial control to a local lesbian group, which wrote a chapter called "In Amerika They Call Us Dykes," in which lesbian sexuality—in accordance with the political discourse of the day—was framed as a "political choice." This chapter became a landmark publication on sexuality and relationships between women, providing encouragement to countless women to "come out" as women loving women. It was also far and away the most controversial chapter in *OBOS*, becoming a frequent subject of censorship both within and outside the United States. As Jane Pincus put it, "These more . . . radical women stretched our—my—ways of thinking a lot. Compared to some of them, we were pretty reactionary and bourgeois. It put things in perspective . . . [as] they were the people who reminded us that we shouldn't make compromises."[19]

By the end of the seventies, the BWHBC had become U.S. feminism's "success story." The collective was famous. The book was being used in women's studies courses and medical schools around the country. The members of the collective had regular contacts with the media, speaking engagements, and tours to promote the book. They not only had their hands full managing the growing correspondence from readers, but they had to work to keep abreast of the growing amount of information on women's health, which was needed to keep *OBOS* up to date.[20] Some of the members began a parenting group, which led to several spin-off books, *Ourselves and Our Children* (1978) and *Changing Bodies, Changing Selves* (1980) for teenagers. The book was both a catalyst and a major player in the growing women's health movement in the United States.[21] The collective members regularly attended medical conferences, lobbied for women's health issues, and participated in campaigns on women's reproductive rights. The success of *OBOS* enabled them to help other feminist groups and feminist clinics.[22] They travelled, attending international conferences on women's health, and established contact with feminist health activists interested in translating *OBOS*. As Judy Norsigian put it, "We were messianic."[23]

However, the success of *OBOS* also had its price.

Mainstreaming *OBOS*

In 1982, the BWHBC undertook a major revision of *OBOS*, which expanded the book from less than 400 pages in 1979 to almost 650 pages in 1984.[24] The need for a new book was clear. Developments in medical technology and changes in the health care system required critical assessment. Readers had been writing in with comments such as "I looked in your book for a discussion of in vitro fertilization and couldn't find it" or "This is what happened to me when I got PID [pelvic inflammatory disease]; tell other women about it so they will be forewarned and know how to get the right kind of treatment" or "Could you please say more about lesbians and medical care?" (BWHBC 1984, 13).

In the meantime, many of the founders of the BWHBC had gone on to do other things. Some had moved but stayed involved with *OBOS* from a distance. For many, doing a major update meant returning to undertake work that they considered necessary and worthwhile but was no longer as central to their lives as it had been in the seventies. Other founders remained involved on a day-to-day basis in the running of the organization that had sprung up around *OBOS* in the wake of its success. For them, working on and for *OBOS* was a way of life.

By this time, the BWHBC had, much like other activist groups involved with women's health, expanded into an organization that was run by several founders and a handful of paid staff members. While all of the founders of the BWHBC continued to author new editions of *OBOS*, many more individuals and groups contributed to making the book as coauthors of chapters, critical readers, or coeditors.[25] From the beginning, the process of making this new edition was difficult. The problem of including all the new information without turning the book into something "you needed a wheelbarrow to take from room to room" was daunting. Jane Pincus, who, along with Wendy Sanford, did the final editing, recalled the hours spent trying to streamline drafts only to find that the author of a particular chapter was furious ("All my words are ending up on the cutting room floor!"). As Pincus put it, "I went through hell. . . . It's a horrible thing to have to edit your friends."[26]

The book changed radically in terms of content, tone, and politics.

For example, sexuality lost some of its centrality, moving toward the middle of the book. In the wake of epidemic eating disorders among young women in the United States and a growing awareness of the role the media played in deploying images of female bodies, *The New Our Bodies, Ourselves* began with a chapter devoted to "body image." It was followed by a lengthy section, under the heading "Taking Care of Ourselves," that dealt with topics such as nutrition, exercise, alcohol and drugs, smoking, and alternative health practices. The themes of "environment" and "occupational health" made their appearance for the first time in response to a growing ecological awareness among social movements. "Psychotherapy" and "reproductive technologies" became the subjects of new chapters. The old section on menopause (as a medical problem) became a new and much more upbeat chapter: "Women Growing Older." This chapter was the expression of a growing constituency of militant "older women" who were organizing under such names as the Gray Panthers and were determined to address the multitude of issues facing older women (bereavement, financial hardship, sexuality, children leaving home), as well as to remind everyone that there is life after menopause.[27] For the first time, there was a chapter devoted entirely to international issues based on conversations and correspondence with women from Asia, Latin America, and Europe. It included a critique of pharmaceutical companies' practice of "dumping" drugs in Third World countries and devoted attention to an emerging international feminist movement.

Paula Doress-Worters describes the changes in the 1984 book as follows.

The conception of the book got a bit more grand. It was suddenly from birth to death. . . . When we started off, we were in our late twenties and early thirties, and we were looking at our bodies from the standpoint of reproductive health and reproductive rights. The point of it, really, from a feminist perspective, was that this would give us control over our lives, that, as women, if we didn't have control over reproduction we just had no control over our lives. So the book was very focused that way—sexuality, birth control, STDS [sexually transmitted diseases], childbirth—and, chronologically, it ended with postpartum and then it went on to some systemic critiques, etc. [Then] the book started to get really monumental. . . . It didn't look like something you would curl up with and read yourself to sleep. So I think people's relationship to the book changed."[28]

The 1984 edition of *OBOS* changed dramatically in tone as well. It became "softer," less "in your face." Terms such as *capitalism* were avoided or explained as "profit making industries" or "power dynamics between physicians and women." Some felt that the book had become less "passionate" or politically radical, reflecting some of the "fault lines" that had begun to emerge within what had previously been a fairly homogeneous group. According to one member, "Some people were still on the cutting edge politically; some people were moving in towards a more comfortable lifestyle. Some of the people who had been most radical now owned a home. There were some real differences, and they took us completely by surprise."[29]

For example, Wendy Sanford recalls some of the changes in the "In Amerika They Call us Dykes" chapter. The language felt outdated. In the interests of making it more accessible to a broader spectrum of women, the editors made a conscious decision not to produce a "cutting-edge lesbian document" but rather to focus on "consciousness raising." As Sanford put it, "It became more a chapter to educate women who picked up the book and thought that they didn't know any lesbians. And for some baby dykes who were just starting out and hadn't even breathed the word yet . . . more an educational and supportive document for women who were trying to understand a lesbian family member, trying to understand themselves, whatever. So it lost some of the luster, but I think it's been a helpful chapter to people over the years."[30]

Other members of the collective took a different view of changes in the political rhetoric of *OBOS*.[31] Norma Swenson situated these shifts in style in the Reagan era and attributed them to the backpedaling that was going on throughout U.S. society. Social movements were floundering in the face of an economic recession, the dismantling of social welfare arrangements, the rise of the religious Right, and a growing culture of individualism. The antiabortion movement was in full swing, and *OBOS* had already suffered censorship attacks from the Moral Majority because of its stance on abortion and (homo)sexuality. Thus, "We were struggling with all that. . . . There were people in the collective who were saying, 'We have to moderate our views if we're going to get our message out. If we confront people with all that stuff, we're just going to be dismissed. Nobody will read it.' . . . And the rest of us who said if ever there was a time to deal with this message it's now and through our book. So I was on that side of the street, and other people were on the other side."[32]

These changes were not specific to *OBOS* but reflected disagreements within and outside the women's movement about issues that had previously seemed straightforward. For example, the so-called sex wars in feminism had made it problematic to treat pornography as a clear case of violence against women when some lesbian feminists were arguing that women could also enjoy erotica.[33] The authors of *OBOS* grappled with how to approach the subject of pornography, ultimately admitting that they were unable to reach consensus: "We do not address the subject of pornography primarily because we disagree with one another and/or have not come to any clear positions yet. . . . We recognize that some of us will find offensive what others view as erotica, and vice versa; that not all pornography represents 'violence against women'" (BWHBC 1984, 100).

In a similar vein, they struggled with how to present new reproductive technologies such as donor insemination, surrogate motherhood, and in vitro fertilization (IVF). On the one hand, they were wary, warning their readers that "we as authors feel impelled to say that we would not advise using any of these technologies except for donor insemination" (BWHBC 1984, 323). On the other hand, they acknowledged that these technologies were complicated and some women might want to use them. Thus, they opted for the provision of the most comprehensive information possible "to help inform women considering the use of these technologies, while at the same time raising the strong doubts we hold" (318).

One of the most conflict-ridden topics in the 1984 revision proved to be the subject of psychotherapy. Until that point, the women's movement had been almost unanimously critical of psychotherapy, viewing it as a source of oppression rather than empowerment.[34] Many members of the group still felt that no self-respecting book on women's health should be promoting psychotherapy. Or, if there was a chapter on mental health, it should deal with issues such as enforced incarceration in psychiatric hospitals or abuse of tranquilizers rather than psychotherapy.

Nancy Miriam Hawley, who wrote the chapter on psychotherapy, disagreed.

I feel like psychotherapy is a really good thing for women, and women use it. Not just because I'm a professional, because it's part of my paid work. I wanted the chapter to really come from a very positive place, an empowering place, saying, yes, there are ways in which psychotherapy has been used [that have been] abusive to women and kept women in their place and stuff like that. Really, let's look at what you can do [to] . . . encourage people to look at what is available, to get help for depression. Again, it's wonderful that there is antidepressant medication. Of course, that can be used really poorly against women. People can overprescribe all the time, but if you have depression it can be a miracle drug, like penicillin was a miracle drug. So [it was] wanting to put it in a certain perspective. I think in the earlier edition there was a lot of anger about psychotherapy that got filtered into the chapter. So I didn't feel the chapter was as useful as it could be to women; it scared people off. It was very preachy. And I think we're intelligent. We can figure [it out for ourselves]. You don't need to be told what the correct party line is.[35]

The therapy chapter was included against considerable opposition from within (and outside) the collective. While the book continued to be critical of the health care system and, more generally, a profit-oriented economy that gave a low priority to the health needs of the poor, women, and ethnic minorities, it began to pay more attention to "what we women can do for ourselves and for one another" (BWHBC 1984, 13).

The 1984 edition continued to address the issue of differences among women. While introducing the perspectives of lesbians had been a central concern during the seventies, older women and women with disabilities were the focus in the eighties. However, rather than having an outside group produce its own chapter, a different strategy was developed. Individuals and community groups were asked to read many of the existing chapters through the lens of age or disability. This "intersectional" strategy not only resisted "ghettoizing" specific groups of women but allowed the reader the experience of having her eyes opened through an ongoing confrontation with the perspectives of differently embodied women.[36]

Moreover, the authors of this new edition of *OBOS* had also begun to grapple more self-consciously with the fact that the book had always been written by primarily white, middle-class, heterosexual women. "People had said we were a white, middle-class, privileged group . . . [and] there was much more a sense in feminism of needing to embrace all women. Although we thought we had been doing that initially, we had to really expand more in terms of voices and experience. It [the book] has to talk to all women."[37]

The authors wanted to respond to criticisms from readers, as well as from the feminist community more generally, about being more "inclusive." However, their desire to address differences among women was still linked to their overreaching claim that *OBOS* should be speaking to and for all women. Thus, the 1984 edition stated, "Sometimes the great differences between us—race, class, ethnicity, sexual preference, values and strategies—turn us against one another. Keeping in mind our common ground as women must be one of our main tasks. Acknowledging the past and present hurts, the inner fears of difference and the external realities which separate us can enable us to learn to hear each and every woman's voice clearly, to nurture each and every woman's life" (BWHBC 1984, 15).

This task proved more daunting as the eighties moved into the nineties and the members of the collective found themselves caught between what Sandra Morgen, in her analysis of the U.S. women's health movement (2002), refers to as "dreams of diversity" and the "dilemmas of difference" (206).[38]

Acknowledging Diversity

While there were several new editions of *OBOS* in the 1990s,[39] it wasn't until 1998 that a major revision appeared with the ambitious title *Our Bodies Ourselves for the New Century.* If at times the 1984 edition had been difficult, this new edition was "bumpy from the word go."[40] Initially conceived of as a "quick and dirty update," the BWHBC was completely unprepared for the full-scale revision that Simon and Schuster was demanding, requiring the involvement of many more people in reading, writing, and editing the chapters.

It was a time of major personal and organizational upheaval within the BWHBC. In 1995, one of the founders of the collective, Esther Rome, had died of breast cancer, leaving the collective in mourning. The husband of another founder died suddenly in that same year. The organization was in the throes of serious financial problems due to

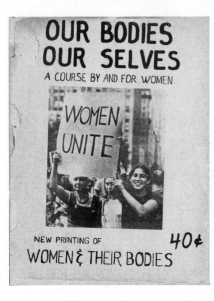

1 * 1971 edition
2 * 1976 edition
3 * 1984 edition

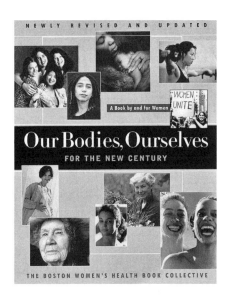

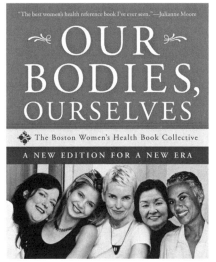

4 * 1998 edition
5 * 2005 edition

dwindling royalties and grants that had not materialized, and tensions had emerged within the organization around issues of power, decision making, and racism, all of which made the update extremely difficult to complete.[41] For the first time, the decision had been made to have the staff undertake the revision instead of having the founders come back to work on the book. A young African American woman on the staff was given the responsibility for coordinating the update, and a concentrated attempt was made by the editorial group to bring in the viewpoints of women of color at all stages of the production process (editing, reading, and contributing). While the outcome of this decision was, according to many of the members of the collective, as well as many readers, a "much better book," it was not without its price. For many of the contributors and editors, the process of bringing *OBOS* into the "new century" was alienating, upsetting, or—in some cases—just plain exhausting. Wendy Sanford remembers stepping in and "picking up the pieces" when the update process seemed doomed to fail because the coordinator "wasn't doing a very good job—or wasn't *able to* do a good job" because of the conflicts in the organization. "It was very unhealthy for me to do that," she recalled, "and yet we needed to have the book done."[42]

The cover of the 1998 *OBOS* reflected the changes in the new edition. A collage of photographic images of women underlined that the book was speaking to women of different ages, ethnicities, and sexual orientations. The original iconic "Women Unite" photograph appeared in a greatly reduced version in the upper right corner, providing a nod to the feminist movement that had given rise to the book three decades before. These "new century" women were portrayed singly, in couples, or in groups of friends but not marching down the street demanding their rights. In addition to the new look, the book had expanded in size, reaching 780 pages. It had become more like a reference book, an encyclopaedia, encompassing all the information women needed to stay healthy, while many of the "old" experiential accounts had been cut due to constraints of space.

The book opened with a section on online resources for women's health, heralding a new era in which individuals would be consumers expecting to find health information online. It acknowledged these developments, providing its readers with instructions on how to navigate the Web and evaluate the plethora of available information on women's health. The first section—called "Taking Care of Our-selves"—was expanded to include new topics: overwork (the "double burden" of paid work and domestic responsibilities), smoking as a health threat (in particular, for young women), lesbian mothers, women living with HIV, transgender issues, and the dangers of ge-netic testing and silicone breast implants. All were topics that would have been unthinkable when *OBOS* was first published. The shift in the politics of women's health had moved from criticizing doctor-patient relationships to finding ways to negotiate managed care to a stinging critique of the role of insurance companies in the health care system.

Norma Swenson, who had been unhappy with the 1984 edition be-cause it lacked political analysis and was too concerned with "soft-ening our language," was much more satisfied with this new *OBOS*, noting that, "By the time this current edition came around, the swing was back the other way, to more people feeling that we were the ones who had the true picture to begin with and we should hang onto it and make that our uniqueness because otherwise we would be indis-tinguishable from the rest of the women's health books out there."[43]

The most characteristic feature of this new edition was the criti-cal attention it gave to diversity. If *OBOS* had targeted lesbians in the seventies and older women and women with disabilities in the eighties, it now made a concerted effort to speak to younger women, women of color, and low-income women.[44] Wendy Sanford recalled with some amusement how younger women transformed the "Rela-tionships with Women" chapter.

The two women who did the lesbian chapter turned out to be post-modernist lesbians, and they took the word *lesbian* out of the whole chapter. They wanted to use the word *queer*, which would have totally offended a whole group of our readers. That's a very popular term among college lesbians and graduate school lesbians and some radi-cal lesbians. Anyway, it was great. I mean here I'd chosen these two younger women to redo the chapter, and what do they do but totally challenge how we named it! I mean it used to be called "Women Loving Women." Forget it! They just wanted to call it "Relationships with Women." Really boring. But that's what it got called. You know, *lesbian* got taken out of the title, but we put it back in here and there in the text. So we used *queer* sometimes, you know, *L/B/T* [lesbian/bisexual/transgendered] sometimes, and *lesbians* sometimes. So it was a process. It's always going to be a process when you change.[45]

Despite the polarization of the staff and the ongoing conflicts within the collective, more women of color were engaged in producing the book and critically reviewing chapters than ever before. Many of the chapters—particularly those dealing with alternative health practices, body image, mothering, HIV, and the international situation— were revised through the participation of women of color as part of the ongoing attempt to make *OBOS* more inclusive. For example, the body image chapter addressed diversity, underscoring the relationship between racism (and other "isms") and women's embodiment.

> We are wounded when a physical characteristic or set of characteristics is loaded with negative expectations. If we have black skin and African features, or light skin and Asian features, or dark curly hair and a prominent nose as do many Jews and Arabs, or if we have a visible disability, or if we are perceived as "overweight," our experiences from an early age may be marked by other people's negative reaction to our physical selves. We may come to dislike, mistrust, or even hate our bodies as a result, feeling that they, rather than the society we live in, have betrayed us. (BWHBC 1998, 34)

In a similar vein, the international perspective on health care politics, which was part of the book from 1984 on, expanded its anti-imperialist critique of the United States to a "global politics of women and health," which raised questions about feminist politics in the United States and addressed possibilities for organizing around issues of "race" and "ethnicity." Thus, the 1998 edition contained the statement, "Many North American activists have emphasized reproductive rights over other critical social and economic rights, thus failing to address adequately the needs of women, who face multiple social, economic, and health problems. The resulting tension has divided the movement worldwide along the lines of race, class, religion, and ethnicity, bringing into question the feminist slogan 'Sisterhood is Global'" (BWHBC 1998, 723–24).

The process of "making the 'we' of *OBOS* more inclusive" was also shaped by power struggles and hierarchies "on the ground"—that is, in the practical activities of producing the book (Bonilla 2005). A particularly poignant example was an episode that occurred toward the end of the 1998 revision when several founders and a staff member and junior editor—a woman of color—planned a meeting where photographs for the new edition would be selected for their capacity to represent women's "diversity." As one of the founders described the incident, "We all went around, from table to table, and we checked the photographs we thought were the best and the most powerful for just about each page of the book. It was an experience where we were all together, in person, and where we had choices we could make, where we could laugh and talk together, and it was one of those examples of really getting together and where the process of choosing had been thought out beforehand and made very easy and very accessible in spite of the number of photographs there were to consider."[46]

While she remembered the occasion as one of the only "really pleasant moments" of what had been an otherwise painful and exhausting revision process, it clearly had a very different meaning for the junior editor, who did not feel she could attend the event despite the fact that she had helped select the photographs and plan the meeting. Pincus remembered that she "was having such difficulties at the time, and I was sad because I hadn't met her yet. I never did meet her; I only talked to her on the phone. But I think she was just too hesitant to be amongst too many of the founders."[47]

These differences in perceptions of the event as inclusive or exclusive mirror the divisions that were operating within the BWHBC at this particular moment in its history. In her preface for the 1998 edition of *OBOS*, Jane Pincus tempered her hope that the political strength of feminism resided in both identifying what women had in common and respecting the special needs of groups with the recognition that "despite everyone's efforts, this unity remains fragile. Too often, differences in race, class, ethnicity, financial circumstance, sexual orientation, values, strategies, and degrees of power make it difficult to listen to one another, and these differences divide us" (Pincus 1998, 23).

Entering the Information Age

In 2005, a new edition of *OBOS* appeared with the subtitle "A New Edition for a New Era." It was in all respects a very "different book"—an assessment shared by its supporters and its critics. It was the first book to be produced "in house" (i.e., without substantial founder supervision). A young journalist with editing experience was hired to manage the update in what she described as an attempt to "pass the proverbial torch" (Stephenson 2005, 173). Together with the director of the BWHBC and two staff members, they set about making a book that would speak to a new generation of women.[48] While contributors were drawn from outside the editorial group to help revise and edit chapters, this time around there were more than four hundred people involved. Unlike the founders, who had been laywomen, these contributors were primarily professionals (health providers, journalists, and administrators). Given the scope of the project, there was less face-to-face contact between the core editorial group and the contributors, with almost all communications occurring by telephone or e-mail. While this made the production of the book more efficient, it also made it more difficult to reach a consensus on contentious topics (e.g., on elective C-sections). Decisions were made by the editorial committee, sometimes without consulting the authors of the various chapters.

The new book had a different look. The cover, which showed the faces of women of different ages and ethnicities, was clearly intended to represent the "all embracing we" of the book.[49] It was more compact and "reader friendly" with bulleted points and sidebars devoted to topics of interest or personal stories. As one editor confided, "I like to flip through a book—that's the way I would read a book, not necessarily . . . from beginning to end. . . . You see a sidebar with an interesting topic or a woman with a quote from her story, and you wonder, 'What's she talking about?' You get drawn into it."[50]

The pictures were professional—no more snapshots brought in by the authors—and an attempt was made to avoid anything that seemed "old-fashioned." "You can often date a book with pictures. It can turn potential readers off seeing people who look like they came from the Dark Ages!"[51]

The book still contained the experiential accounts that had always been the trademark of *OBOS*, but they had dwindled considerably in number. For the first time, first-person stories were not anonymous but included names and photographs. The editors adopted this idea from the media with the intention of making *OBOS* less "foreign" to readers ("They're used to seeing this kind of thing"). According to one of them, it provided a "kind of modeling effect" by letting readers know that it was "all right to speak about issues like cosmetic surgery or genital cutting or HIV."[52]

While the book remained fairly true to the 1998 edition in terms of structure and content, several chapters were reorganized to help the reader to find what she was looking for more easily. For example, the editors reasoned that not every woman would expect to find information about how to navigate the health system in the chapter on the "politics of health care," as it had been called in 1998. Topics—such as "safer sex"—that had been "buried" in earlier editions of the book were excavated and highlighted in the new edition.

In some cases, the format and content of a chapter were specifically changed in order to attract a younger audience. Writing about how she revised the "anatomy, reproduction, and menstruation" chapter, Marianne McPherson (2005) described her attempts to preserve the tradition of encouraging women to learn about their bodies firsthand, while avoiding a dry presentation or "textbook feel" (191). She transformed the old narrative of what a woman would see if she were conducting a self-exam with the help of a speculum, flashlight, and hand mirror into a "self-guided anatomy tour" reminiscent of an interactive museum exhibit, inviting the reader to pick up the tour at any point.[53] Each section begins with a boxed table (e.g., listing "common body parts"), which she can use to locate diagrams and pictures of the female body, as well as more detailed boxes containing information ranging from where body parts are located to how to do labial piercings and the advantages of pelvic floor exercises.

In a chapter that would be at home in any introductory women's studies class today, Elizabeth Sarah Lindsey (2005) deconstructed the difference between gender and sexual identity. Defining herself as "an anti-authoritarian African American high femme dyke from a working poor family," she rejected the "old" jargon of "embracing lesbianism as a political and feminist choice," noting that this stance did not resonate with the "young political queers I know" (184). She described struggling with her first impulse to discount this earlier stance as politically and socially backward, realizing that, while she lived in a different time and had a different life, she nevertheless shared with "these dyke pioneers the same desire to be heard" (185). Her first priority in the chapter, however, was to question what it "means to be a woman," raising the question of whether women are "people who are born biologically female or people who identify or live as women." She broadened the spectrum to include many genders and provided a glimpse of the diversity of struggles among queer and transgendered people. The exuberant gay parade image, "with a rainbow flag in one hand and a life partner in the other," that resonated in the earlier editions of OBOS did not fit the experiences of many queer or trans people of color, who often had to worry about losing the support of their families and communities when they came out (Lindsey 2005, 186).

While these changes reflected the interests of a new generation of readers, they remained linked to the philosophy of earlier editions of OBOS. Other changes were more dramatic. The most significant one concerned the role of information. The 2005 edition of OBOS was shaped by the information explosion about the safety and efficacy of medications, medical devices, and technologies. Since such information rapidly becomes "out-of-date," a companion Web site was developed to accompany the book. The editors left information that "remains pretty much the same" in the book while relegating information that rapidly goes out-of-date to the site. By providing the most recent information available about developments in medicine, OBOS could keep women adequately informed and ensure that the information it provided would stay relevant for a longer period of time.

In addition to the focus on keeping information up-to-date, the term *evidence-based medicine* was employed for the first time, referring to the strategy within medicine for assessing medications, devices, and procedures on the basis of research outcomes as opposed to clinical judgments. It entails providing guidelines on the basis of a consensus among experts for assessing whether sufficient testing has been done for medical findings to be considered reliable and trustworthy.[54] One editor noted that, "We have a commitment to evidence-based information, although we also recognize that [it] is not the be-all and end-all and that you have to make decisions in the absence of certainty . . . [even] when there is no clear-cut answer. . . . [We need to] do a good job of helping in the decision-making process."[55]

Despite the disclaimer that "evidence-based" is not the same as "true," this focus marked a decided shift in how knowledge and feminist knowledge politics are viewed in *OBOS*. Whereas the earlier editions adopted an explicitly antimedicalization stance, which instructed readers to approach all medical knowledge with a certain wariness, the 2005 edition is primarily concerned that women have all the "facts" so that they can make an informed "choice." It assumes that medical research, provided that it is performed under appropriate conditions, can supply women with the guidelines they need in order to make choices. In this edition, women are assumed to be, first and foremost, "informed consumers." For example, a controversial practice such as the elective C-section (a medically unnecessary cesarean section) is no longer explicitly attacked as a symptom of the overly medicalized politics of childbirth. Instead it is presented as a practice about which a woman should consider the "benefits and the risks" and make her decision "based on the best available information available" (BWHBC 2005, 469–70).[56]

For some, this shift marked the end of *OBOS* as a political, feminist book. The book had—as one founder put it—"lost its bite." For others, however, the shift involved a tempering of the "old" radical critique of medicine—a critique that could make women who use conventional medical procedures and technologies feel "bad" (i.e., guilty) instead of helping them become "informed consumers of health care" who "act to extend the frontiers of criticism and acknowledge the many individual women, advocates, and families who have learned to fight the medicalization of women's bodies from *inside* the medical establishment" (Bonilla 2005, 181, italics mine).

A Feminist Success Story

At the outset of this chapter, I raised the question of how a book initially created by a small group of laywomen could enjoy such a long and successful life in the United States. It is my contention that the answer lies in the unique conditions of its production, its ability to remain loyal to its original philosophy while responding flexibly to shifts in the U.S. social, cultural, and political landscape, and, last but not least, its capacity to address a broad spectrum of readers. It was precisely because *OBOS* was not "just another book on women's health" but rather an ongoing project, subject to constant revision and transformation, that it could remain responsive to and relevant for U.S. feminist health politics for more than three decades. While I will be exploring these issues in more detail in later chapters, let me touch briefly here on each of these features: the process of producing *OBOS*; its balancing of continuity and change in content, language, and politics; and its reception among generations of readers across the United States.

Producing *OBOS* ✳ In many ways, *OBOS* was a product of its times, and it probably could not have emerged as it did without the exuberant activism of the sixties when ordinary women felt empowered to take control of their bodies and their lives. The success of *OBOS* depended on a core group of women (the founders) with the vision, the motivation, and—not unimportantly—the time and material resources to launch and sustain such a project. The book's unprecedented and unexpected success enabled (or, some would say, compelled) them to persevere through the economic recession of the eighties, the rise of the Moral Majority, and the growing backlash against feminism. After nearly succumbing to the internal and organizational turmoil of the nineties, they made the transition from a grassroots collective to a nonprofit organization with board, director, and management structure. This shift characterized the U.S. women's health movement in general, where "different versions of the same story . . . were unfolding across the country: the ideals of the seventies and eighties were eroded and overshadowed by external assault, financial pressure, and internal division and conflict (Morgen 2002, 229).[57] What made the BWHBC different from other feminist groups that emerged in the same period was its ability to weather the storms and survive where other groups faltered. The survival of the BWHBC was not a coincidence but was contingent on a specific and unique set of circumstances.

To begin with, the very success of *OBOS* accounted for much of the group's longevity. While the group did not use profits from the book to pay the founders, the substantial royalties, particularly during the seventies, allowed it to carry on its work without the financial problems that plagued many grassroots organizations. Even when the roy-alties began to wane in the late eighties, the book's substantial repu-tation enabled the group to mobilize support from other sources, notably from foundations and individual donors.[58] Second, while the group—like others of its kind—has had its share of internal conflicts, each new edition of *OBOS* drew on a committed and seasoned group of founders who were willing, without notable reimbursement, to come back and produce the book or jump in at the last minute to do what was needed. Third, and perhaps most important, the book survived because it was never just the product of a small group of original authors. Hundreds of women (and some men) were mobi-lized to help with each new edition. Eager to contribute to a book that had been such a milestone in the United States, they brought their expertise and different political perspectives to *OBOS*—as criti-cal readers, contributors to chapters, and editors. They provided the suggestions, information, and experiential accounts that helped keep the book relevant, up-to-date, and responsive to the changing needs and interests of its readers. In short, as a project, *OBOS* was able to survive because of the group that made it *and* because it was always larger than the group that made it.

Changing Context * The popularity of *OBOS* cannot be separated from the centrality given to women's bodies, sexuality, reproduc-tion, and health within U.S. feminism. Beginning in the early sixties, the idea that the body was an important site for the construction of women's identity, as well as for the exercise of social and disciplinary practices through women's sexuality and reproduction, shaped femi-nist activism and scholarship alike (Moallem 1991). This concern was reflected in *OBOS* with its attentiveness to women's bodies, sexuality, and reproduction, as well as its critical stance toward medicine and the social inequalities that affect women's health. While its success lay in enabling a broad spectrum of women to become knowledge-able about their bodies, its longevity can be attributed in part to its ability to remain oriented to changes in the health care system, cul-tural discourses on health, and the rise of the information technolo-gies.

Initially, the cornerstone of *OBOS*'s critique of medical knowledge was the medicalization of women's bodies—that is, the social con-struction of women's bodies as deviant, ill, unruly, and requiring constant medical surveillance.[59] In accordance with much of the feminist literature of this era, encounters between male physicians and female patients were treated as the primary site for medicalization, and accordingly much attention was paid to the negligent, paternalistic, or derogatory conduct of physicians toward women. While *OBOS* never entirely abandoned its antimedicalization stance, it became less adversarial as more women entered medical schools and became physicians themselves.[60] It began looking at medicine from the inside, and, at the same time, medicine itself became more responsive to feminist concerns. The recent adoption of evidence-based medicine as an acceptable goal for a feminist book on women's health attests to this shift in stance. Medical knowledge—when based on careful and responsible research—could now be regarded as women's ally.

The book had always been critical of the U.S. health care system, where health is a consumer good and profit is more important than the equitable distribution of care. The reorganization of the medical system and the emergence of managed care and the medical insurance industry shifted the focus from the individual relationship between a woman and her doctor to helping women find their way through the complicated maze of medical services. This was undoubtedly facilitated by the growing recognition that for many women in the United States—poor women, women of color, undocumented immigrants— the private encounter between a physician and a patient plays a less significant role in women's health than the general accessibility of health care. In a context in which the U.S. health care system could not be counted on to meet even the basic health care needs of many of its citizens, *OBOS* increasingly focused on self-help and preventative or alternative forms of health care, including nutrition and exercise, as ways for women to stay healthy. Thus, the critique of medicalization was elaborated with a concern for responsible medical research, navigating the health care system, and basic health education.[61]

Since the first edition of *OBOS*, health has become increasingly commercialized, and "healthism" is nothing less than a cultural obsession (Crawford 1980). Not only has the overemphasis on "healthy lifestyles" deflected attention away from structural social inequalities as causes of ill health, but failure to "take care of oneself" has led to considerable moralistic victim blaming. With health now a "hot topic," advertising aimed at profit making targets individuals, particularly women, with messages about how they should feel and what they need to be healthy, successful, and happy. Most newspapers now feature weekly health sections, and television shows ranging from popular programs such as *The Oprah Winfrey Show* to serious documentaries devote much of their airtime to the latest health problems and medical procedures. Indeed, the concept of "women's health"— unknown prior to the publication of the first edition of *OBOS*—has since become a reputable field, requiring specific research, its own medical speciality, and its own clinics. It has generated an impressive array of popular books aimed at the female reader, which are available in grocery stores, newsstands, and bookstores throughout the United States. While the explosion of women's health books draws on a much longer populist tradition of self-improvement (Schrager 1993), *OBOS* was a forerunner and catalyst for many of these books. The proliferation of self-help books attests to the success of *OBOS* in popularizing women's health. However, it has been a mixed blessing, as *OBOS* itself has lost its uncontested position of leadership in the market. Caught between the pressure to remain commercially viable and the need to sustain its critical feminist politics, *OBOS* has had to strike a balance between being "mainstream" enough to compete with other popular books on women's health and maintaining its distinctive critical edge.[62]

When *OBOS* came of age, the "information society" was on the rise (Lash 2002). Whereas the early editions were produced in an era when there was very little available information on women's health, the later editions were produced in an era when information was everywhere. In the United States, individuals are bombarded with facts and figures about new medications and procedures. Given the dizzying expansion of medical technology in the past three decades, it has become increasingly difficult just to keep abreast of the latest developments. Moreover, medical information has a short shelf life, requiring constant vigilance by anyone who wants to remain au courant. Advertisements for antidepressants, tranquillizers, and cosmetic surgery are ubiquitous on TV and in popular magazines. With the arrival of the Internet and the rapid dissemination of communications technologies to a broad public, information about nearly any health issues is readily available to anyone with access to a computer. These changes had enormous consequences for *OBOS*. In addition to having to instruct its readers in how to navigate the Internet for relevant information on women's health, it increasingly came under pressure to deliver comprehensive information in a context in which information is quickly out-of-date. The emphasis on informed medical consumerism and the importance of women being able to make choices were inevitable in the era of information technology, but it also created tensions with the earlier commitments of *OBOS*—most notably, the commitment to women's experiential knowledge as a resource for engaging with medical knowledge and the authors' conviction that medical knowledge is never straightforwardly factual but full of uncertainties and biases, which require critical scrutiny.[63] The result was a complicated balancing act, which often generated critiques among disappointed readers who found the book alternately too commercial or too political. However, without this balancing act it is unlikely that *OBOS* would have survived into the twenty-first century.

Different Readers, Different Readings * From the beginning, the authors of *OBOS* wanted to speak to a broad spectrum of women. They believed that by providing experientially based, critical knowledge they were opening up individual and collective avenues of empowerment to *all* women. The book's emphasis on personal experiences and its direct, engaging, and accessible presentation of medical and other information were intended to draw in as many differently embodied and differently situated readers as possible. However, the project of encompassing all women was not without its problems. While the authors of *OBOS* initially addressed their readers in an unreflective way as "we women," as conflicts around racism, class privilege, and homophobia arose within the feminist movement, they became more sensitive to the additional work that needed to be done in order to make *OBOS* inclusive of a greater diversity of women. Their initial strategy was to hand over chapters to women who could write from firsthand experience. In subsequent editions, a more intersectional strategy was followed whereby specific readers were enlisted to read chapters through the lens of difference (able-bodiedness, age, race or ethnicity, and class) in order to maximize the critical potential of different perspectives. It was, ultimately, however, their strategy of mobilizing hundreds of readers from different groups to help read, criticize, and (re)write *OBOS* that made it, literally, a more collaborative, and therefore more inclusive, feminist enterprise.

Obviously, no book can appeal to everyone. The rise of neoconservatism, the religious Right, a vibrant pro-life movement supported primarily by women, and a virulent backlash against feminism in the media have made many U.S. women unreceptive to feminism in general and probably less likely to read an explicitly feminist book like *OBOS*. Moreover, *OBOS* has been less successful in directly addressing low-income readers. It is often viewed as a book that primarily targets "white middle-class women who grew up reading [it] and their teenage daughters" (Lindsey 2005, 184). Less affluent or educated women would be unable to afford it, let alone have the time and opportunity to read it.[64] Nevertheless, at least part of the reason why *OBOS* has been able to speak to as many women as it has lies in the authors' sensitivity to "missing readerships" and their determination to find ways to bring these readerships "into the fold."

In conclusion, the secret of *OBOS*'s success has been its capacity to remain a living document. Never the final word on women's health, it has always represented itself as a temporary outcome of an ongoing process of collaboration among authors, contributors, and readers. If a particular edition was thought to be inadequate or disappointing, the reader could take comfort in knowing that the book would be transformed "next time around." It is this—I would argue—more than whether the book fulfilled all of its promises—that accounts for its remarkable and unique success and its longevity in the United States.

But *OBOS* is, by no means, confined to the United States. It was, from the beginning, a world traveler. And it is here that we may find an additional—and perhaps more significant—insight into the enigma of its success.

CHAPTER 2

OBOS Abroad

FROM "CENTER" TO "PERIPHERY" AND BACK

In the winter of 2000, a Dutch health activist and photographer, Marlies Bosch, attended a conference for Buddhist women organized in Ladakh in northern India. She had been invited to photograph the event, but, since she was there anyway, she offered to conduct a workshop on women's health for the conference participants. To her great surprise, she found her workshop overflowing with more than three hundred young Tibetan nuns, all anxious to learn about their health. Within minutes, the room was buzzing. "It was completely new to them—they knew absolutely nothing about their bodies," Bosch recalled.[1] She continued the conversation in a smaller group of nuns, sitting on the floor in a circle and talking about "where the blood came from," "why you have pain before the blood comes," and whether their "channels are locked because they are nuns and don't have babies." The young nuns were entranced and wanted more, begging the activist to return and conduct another workshop. Fearing—as she put it—a "new kind of colonialism in gift wrapping," she agreed to another workshop, this time, however, for a small group of nuns who would educate their "sisters" in neighboring nunneries. She developed a course, using *OBOS* as a basis, and returned to Ladakh in the summer. Nuns came from far and wide, often making the arduous journey over mountain paths to attend the course. The course was such a success that they decided to translate *OBOS* (at least those parts of it that would make sense for young nuns) into Tibetan. Together with Bosch and a local traditional healer, the nuns contacted the BWHBC, which wrote a letter in support of project funding, and the "snowball started rolling."[2]

This story may seem exotic, but it is not an exception. Since its

6 ✳ Tibetan nuns talking to the Dutch health activist Marlies Bosch. (Photograph courtesy of Marlies Bosch.)

inception, *OBOS* has not remained within the borders of the United States. It has "traveled," that is, been taken up, translated, adapted, and disseminated by local women's groups across the globe. As of 2006, there were twenty foreign-language editions of *OBOS*, as well as seven books in other languages that were "inspired" by it. In addition, ten translations or adaptations are nearly completed or awaiting funding for distribution. And, finally, many more groups have indicated that they would like to do a translation and are in the process of getting started.[3] In short, the end is nowhere in sight.

The international success of *OBOS* raises several interesting questions. The first concerns how a distinctively U.S. book could become so popular with women's groups outside the United States. What was its appeal and how could it travel to so many different locations? The second question concerns what happened to the book in the course of its travels. What kinds of changes needed to be made to address the concerns of women outside the United States? The third question concerns the political significance of the travels of *OBOS*. To what extent does its global dissemination, particularly in what has been called the Third World, make it just like other Western products (such as Nestlé's milk or Coca-Cola) that have inundated less affluent nations, undermining indigenous people's struggles to improve their circumstances?[4] In other words, is the global circulation of *OBOS* just another example of "cultural imperialism," this time dressed up in feminist robes?[5]

In this chapter, I will be using *OBOS* as a case study through which to explore these questions. Taking its international trajectory as a starting point, I show how feminist knowledge and body/politics that are produced in the United States circulate and what happens when they are taken up and transformed by local women's groups outside the United States. The contradictory and often surprising encounters that emerge across national, cultural, and geopolitical borders provide the material for a grounded assessment of *OBOS* in terms of both its "imperialistic" tendencies and its potential for generating transnational feminist alliances.

OBOS Abroad

Initially, the authors of *OBOS*, the members of Boston Women's Health Book Collective, did not anticipate that their book would become such an international success. Nor did they imagine all the work that this success would entail. Norma Swenson, one of the collective's founders, remembered thinking how "utterly absurd" it was when one of the members of the collective joked that someday *OBOS* would sell a million copies and be translated into Chinese. "We all had this romantic attachment to Chinese women back then," she recalled.[6] None of the original members of the collective took this prediction seriously. However, by the late nineties *OBOS* had not only sold more than four million copies, but it had been translated into multiple languages, including Chinese.

The global dissemination of *OBOS* falls roughly into three stages: from the U.S. edition to publisher-based translations in Western Europe in the seventies, to "inspired" adaptations in Asia, Africa, and the Middle East throughout the eighties and early nineties; and to the more recent collaborative, foundation-sponsored projects in nations of the so-called Third World and Eastern Europe.[7]

The first translations of *OBOS* began to appear in Western European countries. By the early eighties, it had been translated or adapted and had inspired similar books in Italy (1974), Denmark (1975), France (1977), the United Kingdom (1978), Germany (1980), Sweden

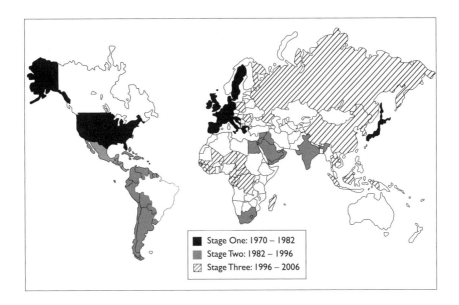

Dissemination of *Our Bodies, Ourselves*, 1970 to 2006

(1980), Greece (1981), the Netherlands (1981), and Spain (1982). Many of these books were revised after the major update of the *New Our Bodies, Ourselves* appeared in 1984.[8] A Japanese *OBOS* was published in 1975 and revised in 1988, and a "pirated" version of the book appeared in Taiwan in 1976.

By the middle of the eighties, *OBOS* had embarked on its second stage of border crossing, "escaping to the East and the South," as one founder put it, "often in someone's backpack."[9]

Stories abound about how dog-eared copies of *OBOS* were taken along on trips to South America, Africa, or Asia and left behind for local women to use. Many members of the BWHBC recalled hearing about how the book had turned up in strange places: a small village in Mexico or a clinic in rural Senegal. Translations or adaptations began to be published outside Europe: a Hebrew version for Israel appeared in 1982.

Several books on women's health that were not direct translations acknowledged that they had been inspired by *OBOS*, including an Arabic *The Life of a Woman and Her Health* (1991) for Egypt; *A Hundred Thousand Questions about Women's Health* in Telugu (1991), which, after becoming a landmark success and going through many printings, was adapted, revised, and published in English for an

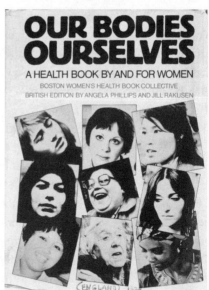

7 * 1974 Italian edition
8 * 1975 Danish edition
9 * 1977 French edition
10 * 1978 United Kingdom edition

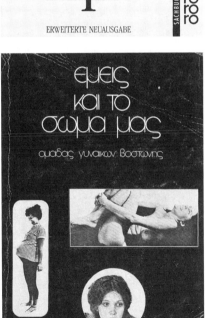

11 * 1980 German edition
12 * 1980 Swedish edition
13 * 1981 Greek edition
14 * 1981 Dutch edition

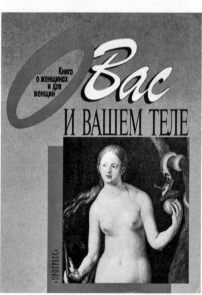

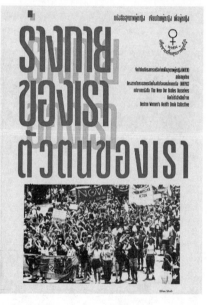

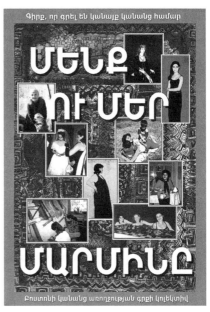

19 * 1998 Mandarin Chinese edition
20 * 2001 Armenian edition
21 * 2001 Bulgarian edition
22 * 2001 Serbo-Croatian edition

Indian audience in 2004 under the title *Taking Charge of Our Bodies: A Health Handbook for Women*; and *The South African Women's Health Book*, which was published in English in 1996. A new Spanish adaptation of *Nuestros Cuerpos, Nuestras Vidas* for the United States and Latin America was published in 2000.[10]

By the nineties, the third phase was well under way, with *OBOS* making major inroads in the less affluent nations of Central and Southeast Asia and Africa—or what might be called the Third World—as well as in much of postcommunist Eastern Europe. It was translated into Russian in 1995,[11] into Thai in 1996, and into Mandarin Chinese in 1998. In China, it went through several printings and is currently in the process of being adapted. The Korean *OBOS* appeared in 2005, as did the Tibetan *Healthy Body, Healthy Mind*. An Indonesian edition is completed but awaiting funds for distribution. New projects for translating and adapting *OBOS* have been started in Vietnam and in Nepal. In 2004, a new French *Notre Corps, Notre Santé* for francophone Africa appeared in Senegal, and a Nigerian women's group is currently looking for funding for a series of pamphlets, loosely based on *OBOS*, to be translated simultaneously in Hausa, Yoruba, Igbo, Shante, Fante, Egun, "pidgin English," and English. In 2001, an Armenian *Menk ou Mer Mamine* appeared, and a Turkish translation is being organized by a coalition of women in Istanbul.[12] Several Eastern European countries have their own *Our Bodies, Ourselves*: Bulgaria (in Bulgarian, 2001),[13] Serbia (in Serbo-Croatian, 2001), Moldova (in Romanian, 2002), and Poland (in Polish, 2004).[14]

I will now take a closer look at how *OBOS* traveled, addressing some of the reasons for the particular shape of its international trajectory.

Global Trajectories

When the first translation of *OBOS* appeared, the U.S. women's movement was in full swing and there was a growing demand for translations of U.S. feminist work throughout Europe. This flurry included *OBOS*, as feminist groups and individual women interested in translating the book sought contact with the BWHBC. European publishing houses were only too happy to take on what had already been a best seller in the United States.

The initial response of the BWHBC to this interest was a combination of astonishment and a sense of being overwhelmed. However, as information began to reach the members about the exploitative conditions under which some of the translations were being undertaken, they began to take a more active stance. For example, in France the translators not only adapted the book on an unpaid basis, but they were not even paid for their photographs. Anxious that women translating *OBOS* should be reimbursed for their work, two members of the BWHBC traveled to Europe in 1976, establishing contacts with the translators and talking to publishers. In addition to their concerns about the welfare of the translators, the members of the BWHBC were not always happy about what was happening to *OBOS*. They discovered, after the fact, that the publisher of the pirated Taiwanese edition of 1976 had used a cover showing a beautiful woman with long, flowing hair and "Westernized" features, eyes cast down while her scantily clad body was made available to the viewer.

In Italy, the publisher also initially put a beautiful, leggy model on the cover of *Noi e il Nostro Corpo*, and the Dutch version, *Je Lichaam Je Leven* featured a "lurid cartoon" (One of the members of the BWHBC recalled, "We made them tear it off, cover by cover, and replace it with a plain red cover with black lettering.")[15]

Based on these encounters, the BWHBC began to negotiate contracts for foreign editions, which stipulated that only local feminist groups could translate *OBOS*. All foreign-earned book royalties were to return to these groups to be used as they saw fit for women's health projects. The main concern of the BWHBC at this point was to ensure that local feminists would have editorial control over the translation and would be able to adapt the book to fit their own social, political, and cultural context. Mindful of its own experiences with censorship in the United States, the BWHBC was also concerned that the "problem" chapters on controversial subjects such as abortion, lesbian relationships, or masturbation would not be deleted by conservative, male-dominated publishing houses. To this end, it began to establish guidelines, which stated that no foreign adaptation could use the *OBOS* title if it did not include at least some part of every chapter of the original book.

Many of the translators corresponded with the BWHBC members, informing them of difficulties or asking for help. Some sent detailed accounts of proposed changes or came to Boston to visit the collective. Advice came in the form of practical suggestions: how to organize a translation collective, how to include as many women's voices as possible, and how to promote the book once it was finished. They were also cautioned, "Always go to interviews in twos and never engage in a debate in which your opponent is a physician!" While the BWHBC was supportive of the groups working on the book, it respected their autonomy. For example, following her trip to Europe in 1976, one of the members of the collective wrote a position paper in which she warned the other members to be prepared for differences in the French edition of *OBOS* given the "strange picture" she had received of the "dominance of psychoanalysis over current French feminism."[16] She went on to argue for carefully distinguishing between what "might really represent a disagreement with our basic philosophy" and decisions made by the translators, which should be supported and even defended by the BWHBC.

By the late seventies, *OBOS* had moved beyond Western Europe. Women's health had become the focus of an international women's movement.[17] International conferences were held in Mexico City in 1975, Rome in 1977, Copenhagen in 1980, Nairobi in 1985, San Jose in Costa Rica in 1987, and Cairo in 1994, with workshops devoted to women's health as a standard part of the program. Members from the BWHBC attended these conferences and met with activists from other countries. They began traveling, before and after these conferences, paying visits to groups interested in translating *OBOS*.[18]

From the outset, the BWHBC had used the royalties from *OBOS* to distribute copies of the book to women's groups and clinics. They began to distribute health packets containing the latest information on birth control, drug experimentation, the controversial promotion of Nestlé's milk, and the dumping of dangerous contraceptive devices in Third World countries. For many women's groups throughout Africa, Asia, and the Middle East, these packets were their first introduction to *OBOS*, and they served to kindle their desire to translate the book into their own languages.

While *OBOS* was speaking to a broad international audience, interest in the book began to wane in Western Europe. In part, this was due to the fact that the U.S. book had been substantially revised in 1984 and, in the process, had nearly doubled in size. Foreign publishers were increasingly reluctant to take on the translation of such an opus. Moreover, fewer European feminist groups were willing to embark on a revision of *OBOS*, regarding it as a relic of seventies feminism. Subsequently, most of the early Western European editions went out of print.

In contrast to the waning interest in *OBOS* in Western Europe, translations were in great demand in Eastern Europe, Asia, and Africa. This development was directly related to the emergence of nongovernmental organizations (NGOs) interested in women's issues and the involvement of outside funding agencies, which were eager, or at least willing, to finance "women's projects" in "developing countries."[19]

Following the demise of the Soviet Union, U.S.-based philanthropic foundations such as Soros Open Society began to support projects aimed at promoting feminism in Eastern European countries. U.S. feminists would recommend literature while local women's groups throughout Eastern Europe made lists of books they would like to translate. Invariably *OBOS* was at the top of these lists. Once Soros had agreed to fund the translations, local women's groups (e.g., a network working against sexual violence in Belgrade or a gender studies center in Gdansk) undertook the translation.

The Ford Foundation also provided funds for translations. For example, it subsidized the translation of *OBOS* into Chinese. The official version, from which government censors had deleted chapters on lesbian sexuality, masturbation, and pornography, was published in 1998 with considerable official fanfare.[20] The first fifteen thousand copies of the translation sold out before the book left Beijing. However, this was only the beginning. The Women's Health Network in Beijing began the arduous process of producing an unofficial version, this time including the sections that had been deleted, and adapting the translation to meet the specific concerns of Chinese women. Similar processes, whereby an "official" (i.e., censored) translation was made and subsequently adapted by women's groups working under their own steam, occurred in Thailand and Indonesia.

These later translation projects invariably involved collaboration between local women's groups (composed of feminist activists, health providers, and women's studies scholars) and the BWHBC, which provided information, advice on translation, publishing, and distribution, as well as practical support in the daunting business of getting funding. While the BWHBC could not subsidize the translations itself, it drew on its own network to, for example, find individual donors in the United States who were willing to support a specific project.[21] It mobilized its own international contacts to facilitate translation projects,[22] set up meetings for translators at international health conferences, and organized an online discussion group so translators could compare notes.

However, even with this support and external funding, the latter-day translation projects often encountered insurmountable obstacles. These ranged from power outages and shortages of paper, computers, and printers to insufficient travel funds and even—more dramatically—publishing houses going bankrupt (Russia), earthquakes (Armenia), general economic crises (Indonesia), and conflict situations (the women in Serbia worked on their translation, literally, with "bombs falling on their heads" during the U.S. attack on Belgrade).

In conclusion, three decades after *OBOS* first appeared in the United States, it had become a transnational phenomenon. After taking Western Europe by storm, it had crossed into the Middle East, South America, Asia, and Africa, where it continued to gain in popularity. The relationships between the U.S. collective and the translation projects involved a complicated and ambivalent mixture of noninterventionism and interventionism. The publisher-based European translations had been fairly autonomous—and, indeed, were able to be so due to the contracts negotiated by the BWHBC, which have given translation projects full editorial control and access to all foreign royalties. The BWHBC jumped in when necessary, however, to do battle against exploitative publishers or to save contentious topics such as lesbian sexuality or abortion from state censorship. In the later translation projects, ideologically charged issues often presented insurmountable problems for local women's groups, which had to worry about censorship of the entire book if controversial passages were included. While the BWHBC became increasingly *less* interventionist concerning the content of the translations, it found itself becoming *more* interventionist in helping projects get started; locating funding for translating, printing, and distributing the book; and, more generally, providing support to sustain projects under difficult circumstances. As Sally Whelan, who coordinated the translations from the U.S. office, noted (with just a trace of weariness in her voice), "We were just glad when the book could get out at all, and we did what we could to help."[23]

I will now turn to the second question I raised at the outset of this chapter, namely, how *OBOS*—a "typically U.S. American book"—was translated to address the specific concerns of women living outside the United States. From the beginning, it was clear that *OBOS* could not simply be translated but invariably required some adapting in order to address the needs and experiences of women in different contexts.[24] The BWHBC had always believed that, ideally, women's groups in different locations would use *OBOS* as a source of inspiration and write their own book. While some groups did just that, others engaged in a combined strategy of translating and adapting *OBOS*, which can be categorized according to the degree to which the foreign edition resembled the original book.

Direct Translations ＊ Strictly speaking, very few of the foreign editions could even be considered direct translations—that is, verbatim renditions of the original in another language. Even the early books initiated by foreign publishing houses tended to delete or "sanitize" parts of the original book (usually the controversial chapters on lesbian sexuality, masturbation, and abortion). For example, the Taiwan edition (1973) not only omitted the entire chapter on lesbian sexuality and relationships but also toned down all references to homosexuality in other chapters.[25]

In mainland China, publishers were concerned about topics such as prostitution and safe sex, which they considered obscene under Chinese law. Moreover, they found it difficult to square China's "one child policy" with the women's rights orientation of *OBOS*—a critique that the translators strategically countered with the argument that the book was not *against* family planning but rather *for* a more "patient-centered" policy that was "compatible with women's needs."[26]

In Japan, customs officials seized copies of the U.S. *OBOS* as "pornography" (representations of genitalia and pubic hair were cited as particularly offensive), sparking a lively debate in the local newspapers about "Western-style feminism."[27] The dismissal of feminism as a "foreign export" is a familiar strategy, enabling the portrayal of unwelcome changes as unforgivable betrayals of deep-rooted customs and values in non-Western contexts. As Uma Narayan (1997) has noted, the condemnation of feminism as "Westernization" rests on a spurious belief "that there is a pristine and unchanging continuity in their 'traditions and way of life,' until we feminist daughters provided the first rude interruption" (23). In contrast, most feminist groups in Japan regard feminism as the outcome of their own experiences and construct their own agendas, often noting that their movement began at the same time as feminism in the United States.[28] The feminist translators of *OBOS* in Japan publicly rejected censorship strategies and did not hesitate to include photographs of local women giving birth—ironically, something that did not raise the ire of the government censors who had banned the U.S. text. They acknowledged that, while "some will inevitably be bothered by the explicitness of many of the photographs," it is important to educate Japanese women about their bodies and enable them to "express their own experience of their bodies, free of any social or cultural taboos."[29]

Direct translations were usually produced in cases in which resources were too limited to do a full-fledged adaptation. For several projects, a direct translation was a matter of expedience, often the only way to get funding from foundations that were reluctant to subsidize the more intensive process of adapting the book. The translation became a "dummy copy," which was subsequently passed on to local women's groups. These groups subsequently embarked on a process of adapting the translation over a period of many years, often without funding and at great personal cost. In Thailand, where anything related to sex or sexuality was "taboo" ("Women are supposed to stay mute when the topic is brought up"[30]) and subject to censorship, the sexuality chapters in *OBOS* were translated by determined activists and academics in the early 1980s. However, it took many more years for the entire book to be translated, let alone adapted.

The fate of the Spanish translation of *OBOS* is a particularly dramatic one. This was the only "homegrown" translation—that is, the original contract with Simon and Schuster included a provision that the book would be simultaneously translated into Spanish and disseminated in the Latina community in the United States. A group of Latinas—Amigas Latinas en Accion Pro-Salud (ALAS) worked together with and under the auspices of the BWHBC with one of its members, Elizabeth MacMahon-Herrera later being included in the founder group of the BWHBC. The first Spanish *OBOS* appeared in

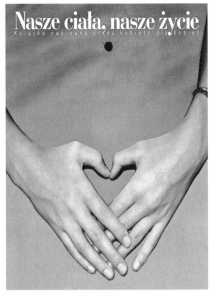

23 * 2002 Romanian edition
24 * 2004 Polish edition
25 * 1976 pirated Taiwanese edition
26 * 1988 Japanese edition

1977, but the poor quality of the translation was a bone of contention for many years. There was already an enormous demand for the book in Latin America, where any translation of *OBOS*—even a bad one— was treated as better than nothing. However, by the early eighties members of ALAS were protesting that a bad translation was "insulting to Latina American women."[31] In their view, the original text had been written too much from "a white woman's dominant worldview" and had little more than "window dressing" (e.g., photographs of Latina women) to offer its Latina readers in the United States and Latin America. These discussions were part of a more general concern, particularly among U.S. feminists of color and Third World feminists, that U.S. feminism reflected the experiences, needs, and interests of white, middle-class, heterosexual women while erroneously assuming that women share a "common world as women"—an "already constituted, coherent group with identical interest and desires, regardless of class, ethnic or racial location, or contradictions" (Mohanty 2003, 21).

By neglecting the important work of developing a culturally sensitive text that would reflect the experiences of Latinas in both the United States and Latin America, *OBOS* ran the risk of arrogantly imposing its own brand of feminism on women in the South and refusing to acknowledge class, ethnic, and racialized divisions among women within the United States. According to ALAS, "for the book to be done well and really reflect the experiences of Latinas, it had to be done by Latinas."[32] The struggles of the Latinas to transform *OBOS* into a text that would reflect their experiences and help them in their specific struggles for empowerment became an ambitious and arduous project that ultimately took more than fifteen years to complete.[33]

Translations and Adaptations * In contrast to direct translations, the majority of the foreign editions fell under the category translations and adaptations. The original *OBOS* was reworked and contextualized in accordance with the translators' notions of what was appropriate, useful, or necessary in their particular situation. Throughout the seventies and eighties, changes in *OBOS* were fairly minimal, reflecting a similarity in feminist issues between the United States and Western Europe. For example, the Swedish translators felt that *OBOS* placed too much emphasis on sexuality. "We had a ten-year advantage over the United States where the sexuality debate only began in the late sixties."[34] The Dutch translators rejected the division between lesbian and heterosexual relationships as too "strict." It did not fit the Dutch context, nor did it correspond with their own feeling that homosexuality and heterosexuality are a "continuum with lots of feelings in between."[35] The Dutch edition also included lengthy passages on feminist therapy—a subject that was considered to be of particular relevance in the Netherlands. The German adaptation, *Unser Körper, Unser Leben*, was the subject of considerable dispute among local feminist groups, which felt that the book was not radical enough and was much too fixated on childbearing and breast-feeding. As one translator provocatively noted in a letter to the BWHBC, "we prefer to influence debates in the direction of HOW we have our children and IF we choose to have any. But this is not the only destiny for us. Don't you agree?"[36]

The foreign versions invariably had to take differences in abortion laws and histories of feminist struggle around reproductive health issues into account. In some countries, abortion was still illegal or controversial for religious reasons. The context not only affected how information was presented but which issues needed to be emphasized. For example, the Japanese translators were especially concerned with increases in gynecological surgery due to a spate of unnecessary cesarean sections and ovariotomies, which had recently been performed in one of their local hospitals. A long tradition of pronatalist policies made infertility an important concern for the Romanian adaptation, while the declining birth rate and economic hardships that caused dramatic emigration, not to mention the strong historical memory of the 1915 genocide, made contraception a contentious issue for the Armenian *OBOS*.[37]

The chapter in the U.S. *OBOS* on the health care system always had to be rewritten, or at least substantially reworked, in the foreign editions. While most translators adopted *OBOS*'s antimedicalization approach and agreed that medical expertise needed to be debunked, differences in European welfare systems often shaped their critiques. In countries with national health systems and guaranteed medical insurance, criticisms tended to be more muted and directed at improving existing facilities rather than mobilizing autonomous consumer networks. The editors of the British *OBOS* noted that physicians in the United Kingdom were less likely to prescribe hormone replacement therapy for menopausal women or perform radical procedures for breast cancer than were their North American counterparts. In general, they seemed less concerned about how to force doctors to be more responsive to women's needs than about how to preserve a National Health Service that was constantly threatened with extinction.[38]

However, for most of the translations and adaptations, the structure, content, and "spirit" of the original *OBOS* were maintained.[39] Changes minimally entailed deleting an occasional paragraph or section. For example, the Serbian translators deleted the chapter on nutrition because—as they put it—"it seemed terrible to speak of food when people were starving."[40] Most adaptations added explanatory footnotes to contextualize the text for local readers, as well as practical information about local health care services and feminist organizations. The Latin American translation and adaptation eliminated the entire chapter on the medical system, reasoning that in a context in which medical care can address only about 10 percent of people's health concerns it made no sense to devote a whole chapter to institutionalized medical care. Instead the translators wrote a chapter on how to make connections with community groups and feminist organizations.[41] In nearly every translation or adaptation, the U.S. photographs were replaced with photographs of local women and the covers were designed to appeal to local readers.[42] When it was not possible to include the experiences of local women due to time and financial constraints, the translations or adaptations adopted creative solutions such as providing vignettes (Latin America), developing interactive Web sites that encouraged women to talk about their experiences (Poland), or, as was the case with the Serbian *OBOS*, leaving enough space in the margins of the printed page for women to write in their own experiences. As one Serbian translator noted, "These books will have many owners."[43]

"Inspired" Versions * In some cases, the decision was made not to translate and adapt *OBOS* but rather to use it as a source of inspiration and write a new book using the same process as the original. For example, in Denmark a group of feminists was so enthusiastic about the original book that it couldn't resist writing its own. These feminists set up a collective along the same lines as the BWHBC and proceeded to talk about their bodily experiences and put together position papers on various health issues to be discussed in the group. The book was published in 1975 under the title *Kvinde Kend din Krop* and went through four revisions, all under the auspices of the original Danish collective.[44]

In a similar vein, in India the Hyderabad Women's Health Group decided at the end of the eighties to produce a handbook on women's health in Telugu (the second most widely spoken language in India). It was to be similar to *OBOS* but grounded in Indian women's experiences and concerns. Under the title *A Hundred Thousand Doubts about Women's Health* (1991), the book began with the premise that a woman's health was as much the state of her body as the context in which she lived—a context that included "a woman's family, caste, her community, the medical profession and her access to medical facilities, the state and even the World Bank and the conditions it made for extending loans to India."[45] This "inspired version" of *OBOS* sold several hundred thousand copies, becoming a "landmark in the history of feminist publication in India."[46] After being widely used among feminist groups and NGOs in India, a new edition was published in English under the title *Taking Charge of Our Bodies* in 2004. The editors, several of whom had been involved in the earlier version, described this new edition as a "continuation" that incorporated suggestions and stories, as well as topics that had been considered "too hot to handle" the first time around.

Several years after the Telugu version appeared in India, other inspired books began to appear in Africa. A U.S. expatriate living in Johannesburg who knew about *OBOS* decided she wanted to create a similar health book "by and for South African women." She helped set up the Women's Health Project with other feminist activists and health workers, and together they wrote *The South African Women's Health Book*, which was published in 1996. While the content and organization of the book differed from its U.S. counterpart, the process was similar. Written in a highly racialized context, attention was given to including the "voices" of different women. The book was read by special interest groups for "tone" and tested in focus groups, which were organized throughout South Africa. The result was a fairly weighty tome, criticized by some for being "such a thick book" in a country where many South African women would never be able to read it. The editors, however, countered this criticism with a reminder that the book was meant to be read aloud and discussed, noting, "We carry the Bible all the time. So it doesn't matter if it's a thick book, if it's helpful."[47] Nevertheless, as one editor acknowledged later, in order to reach "the woman on the street," a short pamphlet would probably have gone down much better.[48]

When feminists from Dakar, Senegal, decided to create a book for francophone Africa, they wanted to do "an original work," a book inspired by but not identical to the U.S. *OBOS*. In collaboration with a research initiative funded by the Population Council, they produced *Notre Corps, Notre Santé: La Santé et la Sexualité des Femmes en Afrique Subsaharienne* (Our Body, Our Health: Sub-Saharan Women's Health and Sexuality), which was, after many delays and obstacles, published in 2004. The collaboration was not without its difficulties, involving population specialists with little affinity with feminism, as well as participants from widely disparate regions. It was written in French (the working language of West and Central Africa), but the authors were mindful that the majority of local women were illiterate and did not speak French as their first language. They therefore wrote the book primarily for health care providers, paralegals, and members of grassroots associations, who would be able to use it to educate women about their bodies and health. While the book encompassed many of the topics that are standard fare in most adaptations of *OBOS* (body image, sexuality, menstruation, pregnancy, family planning, and menopause), it also dealt with issues of specific interest to sub-Saharan women—for example, the pernicious legacy of colonialism and the horrific effects of the World Bank's structural adjustment policies, which have left women with little or no access to health care, land, jobs, or schooling. The book also grappled with cultural and religious ideologies that impinged on women's rights and bodily integrity (e.g., the myth that a man infected with AIDS needs to have sex with a virgin "to purify himself"). Other topics included female circumcision, skin bleaching, and the tendency among women to eat high-fat foods and avoid exercising because, in contrast to the United States, in Africa thinness is often associated with poverty and AIDS).[49] While the result was a very different book than the U.S. *OBOS*, the authors collaborated with the BWHBC throughout the process of making it, getting it published, and distributing it—a collaboration that has continued with an eye to future revisions and common projects.

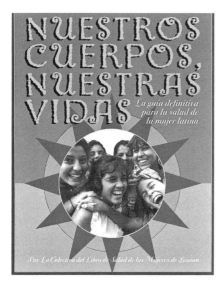

Like the projects mentioned above, members of the Egyptian group that took on the project of producing a book on women's health in Arabic acknowledged that they had "borrowed" much of the philosophy of *OBOS* for their book. They even made frequent references to their "Boston sisters" (Hill 1994, 18). However, they insisted that the U.S. *OBOS* was "couched in a cultural context alien to most Egyptian and Arab women" and reflected the "priorities of American women" (Farah 1991, 16). They wanted to produce their own book, which would take the Egyptian and Arab cultural context into account and emphasize the problems facing women in the Arab world. Inspired by *OBOS*, *Hayāt al-mar'a wa'sihatuhā (The Life of a Woman and Her Health)* was published in Egypt by the Cairo Women's Health Book Collective in 1991. It is worth looking at this book in detail in part because the authors wrote eloquently about what made their book different from the U.S. *OBOS* and can therefore help us understand some of the problems and pitfalls of transferring a U.S. cultural product to another, very different, cultural context (Farah 1991; Ibrahim and Farah 1992; see also Hill 1994). There are, however, additional reasons for taking a closer look at this particular adaptation of *OBOS*. Women in non-Western contexts are often represented as the oppressed victims of a despotic patriarchy in need of support and salvation by their more emancipated sisters in the West. The notion of Western superiority produces a set of images of Third World women—images such as those of "the veiled woman, the powerful mother, the chaste virgin, the obedient wife, [which] . . . exist in universal, a-historical splendor, setting in motion a colonialist discourse that exercises a very specific power in defining, coding, and maintaining existing First/Third World connections" (Mohanty 2003, 41).

This kind of dualistic thinking not only obscures the disempowering conditions under which many women in the so-called center live, but it fails to do justice to the struggles of women in other parts of the world who grapple daily, and with considerable creative agency, with the oppressive contingencies of their lives. The Egyptian case provides an illustration of how non-Western feminists, drawing on a critique of Western modernity and traditions of opposition in their own context, adapted and transformed, but also distanced themselves from, Western feminist ideas and practices that do not reflect the realities of their lives.

The Cairo Women's Health Book Collective, a group of feminist activists, academics, and health care providers, assumed that Egyptian women, in particular, and Arab women, in general, had their own specific health problems. They also realized that since feminist movements have their own histories of struggle and their own battles to fight both the issues and the rhetoric in which they are framed would be different from one context to another. In contrast to U.S. feminism, they did not define their struggle against patriarchy or oppressive husbands but against the Egyptian government, Western cultural and economic domination, and global forces that impose harsh economic policies and alien lifestyles (El Dawla et al. 1998, 103). Starting from a reproductive rights perspective, they wanted to borrow insights and information from the U.S. women's health movement. They were, however, also influenced by the prevailing sentiment of anti-imperialism and anti-Americanism endemic to many contemporary political movements in Egypt (Al-Ali 2000). Although the group was secular in orientation, its members were also part of a culture in which the Islamist movement enjoys considerable popularity. Most women in Egypt, whether Muslim or Copt, are religious, and cultural tradition is considered to be the locus of the most salient norms by which women are judged (El Dawla et al. 1998, 75).

In this context, the adaptation of a U.S. book was bound to be controversial. Considerable juggling would be required if the women were to produce a book that would be acceptable to Arab women and culturally sensitive to the Egyptian context. They had to avoid offending the religious feelings of their local readers while sustaining a strong commitment to women's reproductive and social rights (Ibrahim and Farah 1992, 7). The result was a delicate balancing act whereby contradictory messages were presented, often side by side. The flexible strategy adopted by the Cairo group in deciding whether or not to include certain issues and how to address them is illustrated by the following three examples.

The first concerns the Cairo group's stance toward medicine. Like the original *OBOS*, the Egyptian book was critical of medical knowledge and practice, which was explicitly depicted as "Western." While the authors supported women's right to have access to all available medical knowledge about their bodies and health (the cover of the

30 * 2004 edition for
    francophone Africa

31 * 1991 Arabic edition

book shows a young woman with bare arms, Western attire, and flowing hair peering intently through a microscope), they also accused Western medicine of being authoritarian and disrespectful of women's needs. Underprivileged women often experienced demeaning treatment when they entered a modern clinic in Egypt, where male physicians trained in Western medicine were contemptuous of Islamic codes of modesty. Many Egyptian women were, therefore, reluctant to be examined by male doctors for fear that they would discount the importance of virginity for unmarried women and that their hymens would break during gynecological exams (Hill 1994, 4–5). Taking a balanced stance, the authors urged their Egyptian readers to critically question both medical and cultural diagnoses, emphasizing women's right to seek further information.

The second example is the book's treatment of sexuality. While the explicit mention of sexuality, including lesbian sexuality, and the celebration of sexual enjoyment were revolutionary eye-openers for the U.S. readers of *OBOS*, sexuality was not a particularly controversial subject in Egypt, where women's sexual pleasure was taken for granted and women's networks had always allowed extensive talk about the details of sex. *Hayāt al-mar'a wa'sihatuhā* encouraged sexuality as a "healthful and fully acceptable practice." Women's pleasures were emphasized, even including detailed instructions designed to clear up any confusion about where the man should "insert" his penis during sexual intercourse (Hill 1994, 10). However, sexuality was not discussed in its own chapter—as was the case in the U.S. *OBOS*—but instead placed in a chapter on "marriage," indicating that sexuality outside marriage, as well as between women, was strictly off limits. Although the Cairo authors did take up the issue of lesbian sexuality and discussed it at length within their group (since—as they put it—it was so clearly "regarded as a path toward liberation by many women in the West"), they pragmatically decided not to include it in their book, as it would have invoked certain censure from religious authorities for something that—in their view—was not a "viable life style" in Egypt (Farah 1991, 17). Another "hot item"—masturbation—was treated in a similarly ambivalent way. On the one hand, Egyptian readers were reassured that it was "natural" for their children to masturbate. On the other hand, mothers were encouraged to tell their children to go out and play ("do something worthwhile") rather than masturbate. Rape was more controversial. Some group members felt that women brought rape on themselves through immodest clothing, while others did not like the idea of framing rape in a chapter on violence against women by men. They argued that violence is also perpetrated by women against women (daughter-in-law abuse, female circumcision). Ultimately, rape was included as a topic, but it was embedded in a chapter that included violence against women by men and women.

The third example concerns female genital circumcision and, more generally, the issue of how to deal with "cultural traditions." The issue of female genital excision has stirred up considerable debate both within and outside of Egypt.[50] Western feminists have paid considerable attention to female circumcision in connection with Muslim women, often to the extent of reducing the entire issue of Muslim women's health to it. The Cairo authors agonized about how to take a stand against the practice without alienating their readers, who had an understandable aversion to the myopic and paternalistic interventions of Western feminists. After many discussions, they decided to take a multilayered approach to the issue. They described the differences in kinds of female circumcision, provided information on the psychological and social damage which the practice often entails, and explained the cultural factors that allowed for the continuation of the practice among Egyptian women.[51] As the book was being tested on different groups of Egyptian women, the authors routinely took along a friendly imam who, in the course of the discussion, would stand up and announce that there was nothing in the Q'uran that required female genital excision, thereby lending the book legitimacy among religious women.

Hayāt al-mar'a wa'sihatuhā marked the beginning of a new approach to feminist health politics. It demonstrated that women's bodies and health concerns cannot be separated from the social, cultural, and political contexts in which they are located. The Cairo Women's Health Book Collective borrowed the collective process of critical knowledge making that had been the trademark of the U.S. *OBOS*, yet they dramatically altered its content. They situated themselves as part of an "imagined feminist community,"[52] but they used their points of difference with their Boston sisters as an opportunity for discussion and disagreement. These discussions also helped them to determine their standpoint on issues that were controversial in their own cultural and political context.

The Egyptian case was instrumental in helping members of the U.S. collective understand that Western views are culturally specific and cannot provide solutions to the ailments of women in other cultures. Their ability to entrust "their" text to the Egyptian collective for use as it saw fit attested to this new awareness. The Egyptian example also served as an inspiration for women in other cultures to engage in similar translation and adaptation processes. The story of *Hayāt al-mar'a wa'sihatuhā* is routinely circulated to new translation and adaptation projects as part of the guidelines provided by the BWHBC, and many of the later projects have openly acknowledged their debt to their Egyptian "sisters."[53] In this sense, it is not simply the U.S. *OBOS* that has traveled; its translations (and translation stories) have traveled as well.

Decentering *OBOS*

The most salient feature of the global dissemination—or, more accurately, the global localization—of *OBOS* is the unpredictability of the way the book moved, appearing unexpectedly and often inexplicably in strange places and subsequently taking on a life of its own.[54] As one collective member put it, "You have the *book*, and then there is the *life* of the book."[55] Although its travels began, somewhat as might be expected, with *OBOS* moving from the "West to the rest" (Hall 1992), its trajectory quickly became more complicated, bearing little resemblance to a uniform and unidirectional route by which a Western cultural product suddenly appears in non-Western contexts, displacing or homogenizing local cultures. The global dissemination of *OBOS* can best be described as a set of uneven, contradictory, and incomplete processes whereby the book appeared (and reappeared) in new contexts, both carrying its original meanings and acquiring new ones as it was taken up and adapted.

Nowhere is this better illustrated than by the most recent manifestations of the book's trajectory whereby the translations of *OBOS* have themselves begun to circulate. In some cases, they have returned to the United States where they are being distributed in refugee and cultural centers serving immigrant communities. For example, *Nuestros Cuerpos, Nuestras Vidas* is currently being used and adapted for Latina communities throughout the United States, the Bulgarian translation has made its way to a Chicago center catering to a large Bulgarian community, and the African francophone book has been taken up by a community center in Montreal for use with Haitian immigrant women. This flow of knowledge "back to the origin" is still in its early stages, and it, too, has been anything but straightforward. Community organizations invariably attempt to balance their need for "culturally specific" versions of *OBOS* with the requirements of immigrant women for practical information and advice on how to negotiate the complexities of the U.S. medical system. However, this trajectory illustrates the necessity of viewing the global dissemination of *OBOS* less as the imposition of Western feminism on the rest of the world, a kind of cultural imperialism, than as a "continuous process of re-articulation and re-contextualization," which—according to Stuart Hall—is exactly what the "global circulation of cultural texts is all about."[56]

In contrast to globally exported commercial products such as Nestlé's milk or Coca-Cola, *OBOS* was never simply "consumed" by women in different parts of the world. It underwent continuous and often dramatic revisions in the process of being translated and adapted. Translators not only went to considerable lengths to make *OBOS* culturally and politically appropriate to their local circumstances, but they did not hesitate to take a critical stance against the "Americanness" of the book. Translators were openly critical of the United States's history of imperialism and its policies of structural adjustment, which were damaging to women's health in "developing" countries. They often took issue with the modernist notions of individualism embedded in the U.S. book, as well as with its consumerist approach to medicine and its Western notions of sexual freedom. They had few qualms about abandoning the original text altogether if the discrepancies between the U.S. context and their own circumstances proved too great. The translations, indeed, provide ample testimony to the creative agency of local women's groups in developing flexible and effective strategies for making their versions of *OBOS* sensitive to their local political and cultural climates, as well as to differences and schisms within their own feminist movements. The diversity in the ways the book was adapted and disseminated demonstrates that U.S. feminism was not simply imposed on women outside the United States. Nor did it displace or homogenize indigenous knowledge and knowledge practices. The translation processes involved an ongoing and open process of confrontation, negotiation, and transformation whereby the meanings of the "original" were irrevocably changed through their rearticulation in another language and another context.

One of the most important features of the global localization of *OBOS* was what traveled and what did not. The global appeal of the book did not reside in its content, its form, or even its feminist ideology. What traveled was *how* the U.S. collective had created the book in the first place. The image of a small group of laywomen talking about their embodied experiences and critically assembling useful information about their health needs fired the imaginations of women in different parts of the world and served as an invitation for them to do the same. It was the collective process of making and disseminating critical knowledge about women's bodies, sexuality, and health that ultimately proved translatable and amenable to adaptation by women living in very different times and under different conditions than the original U.S. group. In contexts in which the combination of poverty, illiteracy, and at times multiple dialects made *OBOS* less important as a book to be read privately by an individual woman, it became more important as an educational tool for helping women talk about their bodies and health issues. In this sense, the translations remained more loyal than the original to the spirit of the earliest rendition of *OBOS* when it was intended as a course for women to be used by women collectively to discuss their own and each other's bodily experiences. Thus, it could be argued that, through the translations, *OBOS* as a global feminist project of knowledge has come full circle.

The global localization of *OBOS* initiated a process of decentering whereby the translations became the U.S. book's raison d'être while the bwhbc gradually moved from the undisputed "center" of the project to a more peripheral position as facilitator of its life outside the United States. As *OBOS* moved farther afield, it became clear that ideologically charged issues could present insurmountable problems for local women's groups, which had to worry about censorship of the entire book if controversial passages were included. Increasingly, decisions about the content of the book were left to the translators. Ironically, while the U.S. collective became *less* interventionist concerning the content and form of the translations, it became *more* interventionist in helping women's groups from less affluent countries get the book published and distributed. In part, this reflected the U.S. collective's acknowledgment of their position of relative power vis-à-vis the translation projects, as well as their willingness to devote time, energy, and material resources to helping with other feminist projects. However, it also reflected the dwindling impact of *OBOS* within the United States, as well as conflicts on the home front, which made the translation projects seem like the most vibrant and viable feature of their feminist agenda. In this sense, the translations were mutually beneficial, thereby illustrating the interdependency between U.S. and other feminisms. Collaborations across borders were shaped by the local and global constraints under which women's groups invariably operate.

In addition to decentering the collective, the U.S. text changed radically as a result of the translations. The most immediate effect was increased attention to global health issues. Beginning with the 1984 edition, "developing international awareness" became a topic, and the authors announced that their commitment to "feminism as a political perspective must look across national boundaries to address all the issues that affect women's lives." They then proceeded to explain why U.S. women needed to become informed about women in other parts of the world and to take responsibility for the ways U.S. policies affect the lives of women elsewhere.[57] As they put it, "Opening our eyes to common issues and being aware and respectful of our different realities, women around the world can better understand and help one another" (BWHBC 1984, 611). In addition to situating women's health as a global issue, part of an international feminist health politics, each new edition of the U.S. *OBOS* was produced so that it could be literally "passed on." This involved a series of interventions, including making every aspect of the book available electronically; negotiating global rights for photographs and printed material; providing guidelines on how to produce, distribute, or update the book; and sustaining an interactive Web site and a discussion list for "global conversations."

In conclusion, the global process of translating and disseminating *OBOS* has brought the U.S. collective and the translators together in a common project, compelling both to acknowledge and confront their cultural and social divisions as well as their interdependency. In this respect, the history of *OBOS* and its translation resonates with Sara Ahmed's (2000) analysis of transnational feminist alliances as "strange encounters" between women who are *both* radically different *and* already linked through the ubiquitous and contradictory processes of globalization. The differences between differently located women, together with the opportunity of meeting, necessitate a dialogue. It is a dialogue that must take place precisely *because* we don't speak the same language. It is through these strange encounters that transnational feminist communities may be formed—communities that are shored up by the possibility of "remaking what it is that we may yet have in common" (180).

Part II ✳ FEMINIST POLITICS OF KNOWLEDGE

CHAPTER 3

Between Empowerment and Bewitchment

THE MYTH OF THE BOSTON WOMEN'S HEALTH

BOOK COLLECTIVE

One of my first and favorite experiences with the present inquiry involved attending a meeting of women's studies scholars at Columbia University. I had just arrived from Europe for a six-month fellowship to do a collective history of the BWHBC based on interviews with its founders. I remember sitting at the table, still suffering from the last vestiges of jet lag, and being asked to introduce myself. As I described my plans, the women in the room—most of whom were feminist academics of my generation—began nodding and smiling. It was clear that this particular feminist collective had struck a chord—at least among women of a certain age, class, and ethnic and educational background. When I finished, much to my surprise, they began clapping. As one member of the audience later confided: "What a great project! It's about time that someone is finally going to write this history."[1]

I remember this not only because it was such an extraordinarily warm welcome to New York, signalling an auspicious beginning for a brand new research project. It also struck me, as I listened to their applause, that this would not be a straightforward history of a well-known U.S. feminist collective. It would be a history that U.S. feminists wanted to hear and, indeed, as I later discovered, "loved to tell."[2]

This chapter tells the story of the BWHBC. I explore how the founding members of the collective make sense of their history and, in so doing, produce and reproduce it as a feminist myth. This myth includes an origin story about how a group of ordinary women, sitting around each others' kitchen tables and talking about their bodily experiences, could become agents of historical change. It has the ingredients of a heroic tale with plucky female protagonists who bravely take on a series of powerful adversaries (the medical establishment, the pharmaceutical industry, the religious Right, and the patriarchal, class-based, racist, social order) and come out victorious. And it is a family saga about a group of women who created an enduring personal bond that enabled their political project to survive and thrive for more than three decades. In analyzing these mythical aspects of the collective history, I will show how the founders used this myth in making sense of their history and constructing a history that made sense in different and sometimes contradictory ways.[3] The myth not only enabled them to understand their individual and collective experiences at different periods, but it provided the motor for the group's activism. The myth also generated a powerful symbolic imagery, which influenced the impact they were able to have on women across the globe. However, the same myth had a shadow side. It allowed the members of the group to deny or gloss over events in the present that did not fit their collective sense of who they were or what their project was about. It then became an impediment to a more historically informed and self-reflexive understanding of themselves and their project, leading ultimately to the dissolution of the collective and a somewhat tarnished political vision in need of repair.

Before I take a look at the narratives of the founders, a few words are in order concerning the circumstances in which I conducted the interviews—circumstances that ultimately gave the stories I was told their characteristic shape and style.

Background

When I began interviewing the founders of the BWHBC in the fall of 1998, the collective was in a state of disarray. It had recently gone through a period of personal and organizational upheaval, and it was unclear whether the collective would continue to exist let alone whether there would ever be another edition of *OBOS*. Like many grassroots feminist groups, the BWHBC had expanded into a nonprofit organization since its beginnings in the early seventies.[4] The collective began hiring staff in the late seventies to help manage some of the work generated by the book's success (correspondence, gathering information, publicity). While most of the founders were white, middle-class, college-educated women who became feminists in the early seventies, the staff included women from different generations and different socioeconomic and ethnic backgrounds. Throughout the eighties, the BWHBC became increasingly bifurcated into a staff responsible for the daily running of the organization and a close-knit group of founders who were the public face of *OBOS*. When the collective began to have serious financial problems in the wake of dwindling book sales, hiring conflicts, and contentious discussions about how to restructure the organization to address issues of recognition, decision making, and accountability, outside consultants were brought in to advise about changes in the organizational structure and to help address the issue of racism at all levels within the organization. These efforts were not entirely successful. In 1995 the staff announced that it was bringing in a union. After a tumultuous period of negotiations, a major financial crisis necessitated "voluntary" layoffs. The staff lost all confidence in the organization and resigned en masse in 1997, publicly accusing the BWHBC of racism and, more generally, "unsisterly" behavior.[5] Several staff members also filed a complaint of discrimination against the BWHBC—a complaint that, nearly five years later at the time of this writing, is still pending. Thus, when I began my inquiry, I found the BWHBC in shambles and its future uncertain.

Given these recent events, I expected a somewhat wary reception on the part of the founders. I imagined that they would be reluctant to speak to an outsider about events that had probably been painful and conflictual and were still largely unresolved. As the founders of one of feminism's most popular and well-known projects, I suspected that they would be worried about damaging or discrediting a project that had been, for many, their life's work. And, on a more mundane level, I wondered whether they might not simply be weary of having to repeat a story that each of them had told so many times before.[6] To my surprise, however, most of the founders were not only willing but often eager to speak with me about their collective history. Not everyone, of course, was equally forthcoming about the recent troubles. Several founders who had been intimately involved in the most recent history, as well as actively involved in the current organization, tended to be circumspect and avoided giving me information that might incriminate the group, preferring instead a more "canned" version of the collective history.[7] However, for others the interview seemed to provide an opportunity to set the record straight or—as one founder put it—to help get rid of the "cloud hanging over the collective." The interview offered an opportunity to talk about events that had been confusing, painful, or upsetting. Thus, from my perspective as a researcher, this particular cloud had a silver lining as it enabled me to obtain much more complex and interesting oral histories than would have been possible under more felicitous circumstances. Had I conducted the interviews ten years earlier (or even ten years later), I might have received a simple rendition of the myth ("the story we love to tell"). What I got instead, were interviews that showed how the founders of the BWHBC struggled to reconcile the cherished image of their collective history with the more contradictory and problematic events of the recent past.

However, the events also made my work more difficult. The recent conflicts made it clear that there were going to be many different sides to this particular story. While the founders were willing to tell "their" side, the staff members were often reluctant to meet with me. In fact, I was only able to find one former staff member who would agree to an interview and only on the condition that we would steer clear of the recent conflicts in the group. The archives were similarly disappointing. The minutes of meetings held during the period of unionization and leading up to the exodus of the staff were not open to public view and to this day remain sealed in the archives under the heading "sensitive material." To make matters worse, the United States was in the throes of the Clinton-Lewinsky affair, and many of my colleagues at the Oral History Research Office warned me that my research notes could be subpoenaed (shades of Linda Tripp). One colleague, somewhat jokingly, suggested that I might be wise to avoid the "problem" altogether and end my history of the BWHBC in 1995!

Thus, I was faced at the outset with the problem of how to present what had clearly been a highly conflictual period in the history of the BWHBC and, in particular, how to address the important and complex issue of racism in feminist organizations. While I assumed that the women of color on the staff would have had plenty to say about this, I had no direct access to their versions of what had happened. I also struggled with the problem of my complicity as a white woman interviewing other white women about racism. I did not want to position myself as one of the "worthy white few"—a term used by Simonds (1996, 190) in her research on racism in a feminist health clinic—who, in contrast to the white founders, had the "correct" take on racism. This seemed not only arrogant in view of the long-standing ideological and practical struggles that had been waged within the BWHBC around the issue of power and racism but also analytically less productive. I decided instead to use the interviews I had conducted with the founders as a resource for exploring how white, middle-class feminists grapple with—and, in some cases, avoid grappling with—the painful issues of racism and inequalities of power in feminist organizations.[8]

Origin Stories

In the 1973 edition of *OBOS*, members of the BWHBC wrote about their own history, calling it "A Good Story." This story was retold in slightly different variations in later editions, allowing the group to document and circulate its own history to millions of readers. Endlessly recycled in the popular press and scholarly articles and anthologies, it took on the status of a foundational myth for U.S. feminism (Morgen 2002, 21). In the 1973 edition of *OBOS*, it read, "It began at a small discussion group on 'women and their bodies' which was part of a women's conference held in Boston in the spring of 1969. These were the early days of the women's movement, one of the first gatherings of women meeting specifically to talk with other women. For many of us it was the very first time we got together with other women to talk and think about our lives and what we could do about them" (BWHBC 1973, 1).

What started out as a small workshop at a local conference became a watershed moment in feminist history. While the time and location of this particular event are clear, the specific details have become veiled in the mists of time. For example, I was told over and over again about one woman who got up and wrote the word *clitoris* on the blackboard—at that time, nothing short of a revolutionary act. This incident was sometimes reworked to express the shock of hearing words like "orgasm" or "masturbation" spoken out loud to someone explaining how to masturbate, using a drawing of a woman's genitals on the blackboard.[9] While the details of the story vary, everyone uses some version of the origin story to commemorate the moment of awakening.

"I can sit back and think about the awesomeness of the fact that we were sitting around talking about our sexuality. Now today, in 1999, we don't think twice about it. But this was thirty years ago."[10] This meeting not only marked the beginning of the group. It was the moment when individual women became involved in making history, of being involved in "something much bigger than ourselves." As one founder recalled, "It was very exciting to be part of this kind of a story. It was a very good story. It had all these elements that were kind of personally and politically satisfying. You always want to do something in your life that contributes to the greater society, and this really did. We could feel it."[11]

Another founder remembered this period as the only moment in her life when it was possible to experience "a feeling . . . that you could make a difference and change structures that had been in place for centuries, that anything was possible . . . It was a wonderful time."[12]

Like many activists in social movements in the late sixties, the founders of the BWHBC saw themselves as rebelling against an old order, rejecting all that was patriarchal, authoritarian, or traditional. They believed that they were part of a turning point in history, a brand new phase in which all the old oppositions between men and women, old and young, black and white, poor and wealthy, could be transformed, once and for all. Passerini (1990) refers, somewhat skeptically, to this conception of historical origins as the myth of the *puer aeternus*, the eternal child. The "new at all costs" is celebrated, and a sense of "from this point on nothing will ever be the same again" is established (55–56). One founder remembers going to a meeting following that famous Emmanuel College workshop. At the time, a young college graduate, married and the mother of a baby, she was suffering from postpartum depression. She found herself suddenly talking about her loneliness and depression and realized—lo and behold—that she'd been blaming herself for something that was not her fault. "It was like a light bulb went off in my head," she recalled. "I still feel tears when I think about that moment."[13]

From a historical perspective, the origin story of the BWHBC makes little sense. The conference in the spring of 1969 can hardly be regarded as the beginning of the U.S. women's movement, which was already well under way by then. However, as a representation of the past it provided an ideal founding myth because it replicated what many women at that particular historical moment were experiencing: being in a room full of women for the first time, having one's eyes opened, the "aha" experience, which was the bread and butter of consciousness-raising. The origin story was so powerful precisely because it could stand in for similar epiphanies that were occurring across the United States. It allowed women who were not there at the very beginning to participate in a shared history. It became an exemplary and infinitely repeatable story of how women became feminists. Nowhere is this more clearly expressed than in the words of Helene Rodriquez-Trias, a pediatrician and well-known health care activist, who wrote in the preface of the 1996 edition about her own initial encounter with *OBOS*, "In 1970 . . . I was forty-one and just beginning to heal from a traumatic few years of a disastrous marriage. I had just arrived from Puerto Rico and was struggling to find my identity as a Puerto Rican professional and a single mother in New York City. When I read that first edition, titled *Women and Their Bodies*, I felt a surge of joy. The authors spoke to me as if I had been part of their discussion group" (BWHBC 1998, 9).

This quality of transferability did not, however, preclude discussions about who was "*really* there at the very beginning," indicating that the origin story was also about demarcating lines of belonging. One of the recurrent features of my interviews with the founders was that each would begin her recollections with a somewhat rueful "You know, I wasn't there at the *very* beginning" and subsequently provide a more accurate location of herself as a player in the group's history ("I came in much later, after the MIT meetings"). Ironically, it wasn't until my very last interview that I discovered the founder who was undisputedly there from the start, and even she began the interview by stating, "I wasn't there at the very beginning. . . . It all started much earlier with the emergence of second-wave feminism in the U.S."[14]

But if not every founder was there at the beginning who did belong to the BWHBC? The "we" that is so confidently displayed in each rendition of the group's history was in actuality a changing and fluid entity. During the early years, it involved a large group of women coming to meetings and participating in the course that resulted in the first underground edition *Women and Their Bodies* (1970). The

BWHBC didn't emerge as an entity until 1972 when a core group of women signed a contract with Simon and Schuster and decided to close its doors to new members.[15] By the eighties, an organization had grown up around the book, and in 1983 two staff members, Sally Whelan and Pamela Morgan, who had been working since 1979 and 1980 as librarian and coordinator, respectively, were officially invited to become members of the BWHBC. Elizabeth MacMahon-Herrera, who had initiated Amigas Latinas en Accion Por Salud and worked within the BWHBC as a liaison with the Latina community, was the first woman of color to become an official founder of the BWHBC in 1996. While the term *founder* suggests an original group, it was not, in fact, part of the vocabulary of the BWHBC until a retreat in 1996, when Elizabeth MacMahon-Herrera, along with Sally Whelan and Pamela Morgan, was officially recognized as a founding member of the BWHBC. This new language for distinguishing between the "old group" and the newer staff and board members cannot be separated from the conflicts that were occurring at that particular moment within the organization—something to which I will return later in this chapter.

Although the trajectories by which individual women became founders of the BWHBC differed, the notion of an original group remained symbolically linked to the mythical story of the organization's history. As one of the later founders noted, somewhat dryly, "This original group stuff is important to people. . . . It's like when a crystal is formed or something; it doesn't change. Once that structure is set, it's set, and I suppose it may grow different arms but that original piece is there and very firmly in place. . . . It . . . just goes on and on and on and lives on in the imagination of everyone."[16]

Nowhere is this more clearly illustrated than in two popular representations of the BWHBC. The first is a 1993 film called *Shaking the Tree*, which celebrated the history of the collective.[17] The film opens with one of the best-known early photographs of the group.[18]

The photo, reproduced in figure 32, shows a group of eleven young, white women, with long hair and seventies-style clothing, smiling, sitting, or standing around a tree on a summer day. The film documents more than two decades of political activities around women's health that had been undertaken by the BWHBC. The founders were clearly not the only ones engaged in these activities, and the film makes a point of including women of color in its representation of

32 ✳ The Boston Women's Health Book Collective in the early 1970s. *Front, left to right*: Norma Swenson, Pamela Berger, Ruth Bell, Nancy Hawley, Judy Norsigian. *Standing, right to left*: Wendy Sanford, Paula Doress, Esther Rome, Joan Ditzion, Wilma (Vilunya) Diskin, Jane Pincus. (Photo courtesy of Phyllis Ewen.)

the history of the BWHBC. However, as the film comes to a close, we are not shown an image of the current organization with its diversity of members, who were responsible for so much of this work. Instead, the closing shot returns to that early photograph, implying continuity with the original group, a continuity more imaginary than actual.

This same imaginary continuity is suggested in another iconic photograph, reproduced in figure 33, which was reprinted in later editions of *OBOS*, as well as in many of its translations and adaptations. This time the photograph shows the expanded group of founders sitting in a living room.[19] Crowded together, smiling at the photographer, one of the founders is shown holding the photograph of a recently deceased member of the group, Esther Rome. This photograph in a photograph is slightly illuminated, forming a focal point in the image and, symbolically, a center that holds the group together. It

33 * The founders of the BWHBC in 1996. *Front, left to right*: Pamela Berger, Vilunya Diskin (holding photograph of Esther Rome), Sally Whelan, Pamela Morgan. *Second row, right to left*: Paula Doress-Worters, Nancy Miriam Hawley, Elizabeth MacMahon-Herrera, Jane Pincus, Joan Ditzion, Ruth Bell Alexander, Judy Norsigian. *Back, left to right*: Norma Swenson, Wendy Sanford. (Photo courtesy of Judith Lennett.)

suggests a continuity with the initial group, which—despite the historical events of the past decades—has not, and, indeed, cannot, be disrupted, not even by death.

Ordinary Heroines

"You may want to know who we are," the authors of *OBOS* write in the preface to the 1973 edition. "Our ages range from twenty-five to forty-one, most of us are from middle-class backgrounds and have had at least some college education, and some of us have professional degrees. Some of us are married, some of us are separated, and some of us are single. Some of us have children of our own, some of us like spending time with children, and others of us are not sure we want to be with children. In short, we are both a very ordinary and a very special group, as women are everywhere" (BWHBC 1973, 2–3).

In this first version of "A Good Story," the authors present themselves as "ordinary women" who met informally at each others' homes, in living rooms, or at kitchen tables to talk about their bodies, their sexualities, and their health. It is precisely the mundane quality of these meetings that enables their story to become one with which women in and outside the United States can identify. While they indicate their age, class, and marital status, there is—in this first story—no mention of race. The "whiteness" of the group is constructed as an unmarked norm, conflating the ordinariness of the group with being white. As Ruth Frankenberg (2001) has noted, the "invisibility of whiteness" allows whiteness to "assume its own normativity," allowing us to think that "everyone is the same as me" (81). Many of the founders were mothers, and by situating themselves as mothers they indirectly distanced themselves from some of the more radical branches of the early U.S. feminist movement, which problematized motherhood and, more generally, heterosexuality. For example, one founder remembers attending a women's liberation meeting in Boston during the early seventies where a member of Cell 16, a militant local group of radical feminists, began shouting, "Down with the nuclear family." She laughed, recalling, "And here we were, holding our babies to our bosoms. Protectively."[20]

While not all of the founders were mothers at that time, their positive stance toward motherhood allowed them to appeal to women who were put off by the antifamily sentiments in the early U.S. women's movement.[21] As one founder put it, "We were almost alone among feminist groups and health groups in wanting to try to treat these issues evenhandedly. . . . There was some kind of phobia that was set up in feminist consciousness . . . about birth. [This was] partly because becoming a mother had become so normative in the fifties. . . . You had to become a mother. . . . Part of what second-wave feminism was about was challenging that and saying, 'We have a right to have identities as women without becoming mothers and certainly without being married.'"[22]

The founders were anything but representative of most women in the United States, even by the standards of second-wave feminism. They were not only college educated, but many had husbands who supported them, enabling them to volunteer enormous amounts of time and energy to producing *OBOS*. During the eighties, this situation changed as most of the founders were no longer able to engage in unpaid political activism on a full-time basis. Many embarked on careers in other areas—as academics, public health educators, social workers, artists, or even a college chaplain. The few who continued working as full-time health activists did so for the typically low wages that go hand in hand with jobs in nonprofit organizations.[23] Whatever their position within the organization, none of the founders was, of course, ordinary in the sense that they all possessed considerable social and cultural capital in the form of education, experience, and skills (Bourdieu 1986). This is certainly part of the explanation for the extraordinary job they did in making *OBOS* a national and international success. However, in constructing themselves as ordinary women, they downplayed the ways in which they were exceptional—something that was to come back and haunt them when they brought women into their organization from less privileged backgrounds, women who did not have the same education, experience, and skills. Thus, the myth of ordinariness worked to minimize the ways in which they were privileged by focusing on those aspects of their lives that made them "like women everywhere."[24] "We were ordinary women," one founder recalled. "We weren't highly trained professionals. And how it worked was we realized that we had problems we wanted to solve, and we didn't want to solve them by ourselves. We couldn't solve them by ourselves, alone. But we could solve them, perhaps, together, and this is what we tried to do. Sometimes it worked, and sometimes it didn't. But the method is there, and I think people relate to that. And because we weren't high-powered professionals I think we weren't intimidating, so people could identify with us."[25]

The ordinariness of the founders took on a heroic character as they told how they—as laywomen—went to battle against the medical profession, the pharmaceutical industry, and U.S. capitalism. In this rendition of their history, they emerge as resourceful heroines who surreptitiously entered medical libraries to look for information and refused to be intimidated by medical texts. They often stressed how little they knew about health matters in the beginning. "All we knew is that we weren't getting adequate treatment." Their story took an exciting turn, however, when they discovered that "these stupid professionals didn't know what they were talking about even in terms of their own literature. They weren't reading it, they weren't applying it, there was no science under it."[26]

The appeal of this story resides in the fact that they, as ordinary women—that is, women without medical training—were able to see through the discourse of one of the most powerful institutions in the United States and unmask it as "unscientific." This was more than a simple questioning of the authority of medical knowledge. It paved the way for *any* woman to believe that she, too, could criticize dominant forms of knowledge.

Many of the founders told stories about their struggles to put medical knowledge in an accessible form that women could use to empower themselves. However, few had had any experience with writing beyond the occasional term paper in college. As one founder put it, "I had been an art major. I'm not a literary person. . . . And here we were, publishing this book! My God! . . . [And now it's] passed out in college dormitories, all over the U.S."[27]

After their book became a best seller, the founders looked for ways to talk about their success without undermining the notion that they were still ordinary women. One observed, "We thought that doctors would be furious with us, that we would be pariahs or something. [But the] doctors loved it, took it up, and were giving it to their patients. . . . All of a sudden we went from being this sort of marginal, underground group to being the darlings of the press and the medical establishment. We were getting invitations to speak at medical conferences."[28]

The story took on a "rags to riches" quality as the founders described their inexperience with public speaking and how they helped each other learn how to present their arguments convincingly by role-playing together ("You'd call in media training nowadays"). They recalled going in pairs to speaking engagements ("much more fun") and how they learned through trial and error to deal with the media. Through these stories, they demonstrated that, even after they had become successful, they were still ordinary women who helped one another under the motto "Together we are strong."

But perhaps what made the success of *OBOS* a truly heroic tale was its unexpectedness. The founders remembered joking with one another in the early seventies that their book was going to "sell a million copies someday." But they never expected their joke would become a reality. One recalled, "We were all very surprised at the real success of this book, . . . that is, surprised in the sense that—especially [for] those of us on the Left—we've always worked for causes, and we've always been marginal. But we plug along because we believe in it. We think it's right, and we think it's the only way to live. But it's not like we've had huge successes, and this was a huge success."[29]

As one founder put it, the book had become "much, much bigger than ourselves." Years later, many of them were still trying to come to terms with the unprecedented success of the book and, along with it, their own fame. According to one, "When my daughter comes home and says, 'Mom, you're in my history book,' it's really quite extraordinary. It makes me realize everybody is part of history, that's what history is: just people like us coming together for a variety of reasons to accomplish something that turned out to be important. But while they were doing it they didn't realize just how important it was going to be."[30]

Taken together, the image of the group as just ordinary women helped construct a heroic tale in which any woman could go beyond the confines of her everyday life and become a player on the field of history. She could accomplish something for other women—something that she could never have imagined. By downplaying the conditions that made their group extraordinary, they could send the message "If we can do it, so can you." In this way, the story of how they took on the medical establishment could become a source of inspiration for women living under different conditions of disempowerment, allowing them to imagine how they, too, might embark on a heroic struggle of their own.

Like any myth, however, this one had a shadow side. By ignoring the role class and racial privilege played in how the group emerged and the success it was able to have, it contributed to the illusion of a level playing field in which any woman, regardless of her circumstances, can do the same. While this was inspiring for many women, it also, at times, stood in the way of a more realistic assessment of differences among women and, in particular, the difference that privilege made in how differently located women could work together in feminist projects.

Family Bonds

Since its inception, each new edition of *OBOS* has provided an update on the lives of the founders. In the seventies, the founders described themselves as young mothers, while in the later versions they had become grandmothers whose "dramatic affairs" had been replaced by "hot flashes." The reader was kept up-to-date on their lives with photographs of the collective's members growing older. The photographs not only showed the founders but also their children and partners, creating an image of an extended family. As one of them put it, "We've seen each other's children grow up. We've seen each other through marriages and divorces and deaths of parents and now deaths of partners and a death of one of our members. So it's sort of like we've been through the whole life cycle together."[31]

While the members were not bound by actual ties of kinship, this image of family is frequently reproduced, albeit in different versions.[32] One of my favorites is a vision of the group's future that includes "sitting around in rocking chairs in our eighties or nineties going around the circle and talking about our lives." This mythical tale would pop up in prefaces to *OBOS*, in histories that various members of the group wrote about themselves, and in media accounts.[33] I heard many renditions of this rocking chair myth during interviews with the founders. For example, one founder invoked the story to remember the founder who had died, noting how she (Esther) had always said that her husband, who was a carpenter, would make the rocking chairs for them: "I have this image of us all sitting on this porch, each one in a rocking chair, and we're going to be rocking there. And in some transcendent way, that's going to happen."[34]

This image of the group as a family allows the expression of a powerful and lasting connection among its members. As trope, it provides a seductive image of women loving and sharing an intimacy with one another, while at the same time avoiding any suggestion of homosexuality. In this image, male partners await (supportively) with the children on the sidelines ready to return at a moment's notice.

As an illustration of how "very personal and very connected" the group was, several members told me the following story. It describes an incident that occurred when one of the founders was going through a divorce and they were all sitting in someone's living room.

> She was talking. She was sitting right there, and she was talking about the divorce and she was feeling—you know how one would feel. We had yarn in our hands, and we passed it from one to the other, then passed it from one to the other, just talking quietly and passing yarn, and we had made around her a kind of web of yarn. . . . By the time she

was finished, she was all enclosed within us, this web of women, who had just spontaneously created that. And we clipped off our [strands of yarn], and she took it home.[35]

Other founders described playing baroque music (calling them-selves the Slow Movers because they only played the slow second movements), celebrating seders, or having meals together where everyone contributed her favorite recipe. They also embroidered a wedding canopy on which each member contributed her own bird or tree, "And whoever gets married in the group now can use the wedding canopy . . . can stick it in a tree in the garden when she gets married. Those kinds of things just happened for us."[36]

The stories about these kinds of rituals were frequently told as part of the collective historical narrative. They reproduced a family image, which underscored the timelessness and enduring quality of the col-lective bond. It was this characteristic interplay of family and collec-tive work that became a part of the mythical narrative of the group. As one recalled, "We took care of each other. . . . We shared every-thing together. . . . We were really, really important to each other in ways that went beyond the workings of writing the book."[37]

This image of family, however, was not simply a way to construct the connection between the members of the group. It was also used to explain some of the difficulties in the group. For example, one founder remembered her struggles in trying to write chapters for the book and having the group "tear her chapter to bits." She would spend weeks going through it, agonizing that her writing had been too superficial. She recalled, "They would just make me feel like a fool. But even that, however harsh it seemed at the time, was done with the underlying sense that 'We're all equal here. Everything you say is important.' It was really like the best family experience a person could have. Almost unconditional love, I would say, was the under-lying message. Some people were better writers than others. Some people had clearer ideas than others did. Some people were more academic than others. Yet everyone's work was honored."[38]

The image of a loving family suggests that differences in ability among the members of the collective did not influence their overall worth. "We're all equal here" resonated with the family adage "We love you just the way you are." (Obviously, the family trope would have been less practical in an organization in which members were expected to perform their tasks efficiently and effectively.) The myth of family was also used to account for moments in the collective's history when relationships were less than harmonious. Members of the group often "rubbed one another the wrong way," had disagreements or misunderstandings, and even became estranged for long periods of time. However, despite these conflicts, they continued to view one another as the "people you go to." Thus, the myth of family—which, after all, routinely has its conflicts—prevailed, even though individual members sometimes admitted feeling "stuck" with one another. According to one, "So I really basically consider this my family, and even though I'm closer to some people and more distant from others, when there is some crisis, these are the people I go to and who come to me, regardless of the closeness of the personal relationships at this point in time. . . . I do think that [it was] based on shared work, shared passion. Because I think otherwise some of the folks I wouldn't have picked as friends, and they probably wouldn't have picked me as a friend."[39]

For the founders who joined the collective later, it was often difficult to come to terms with the notion of a "ready-made family." One newcomer remembered her feelings of discomfort at being confronted with "this group of people who had been intimately involved with each other's personal lives and work lives for fifteen years." She described attending meetings where everyone was sitting around someone's living room: "People tried to make us feel welcome in the sense that, okay, we're going around the circle for anyone to share, you know, what they're going through and what's happening. But to me . . . it was like the expectation of instant intimacy where it just didn't fit, you know. . . . So we often skipped our turn. You know, we'd say 'I pass.'"[40] She never doubted the well-intentioned desire of the others to include newcomers in the group, but, as she put it, "there was no way to catch up." Laughing, she remembered how one of the older founders referred to the newcomers in the collective as "the cousins"—those "strange cousins who usually aren't at the reunions and then suddenly they show up."[41]

While bringing new members into the "inner circle" proved more difficult than anyone had anticipated (a point to which I will return), the tendency to think of the collective as a family was marked, even among those who, from time to time, suffered the consequences. One member recalled, "As people I love them dearly. We've lived and worked together. We're like family. It took me a long time to even say that because I felt very different. But I can say that because of the work and because of the sharing and the fighting and everything else."[42]

The "family saga" not only allowed the collective's members to present themselves as engaged in a common cause, but it imbued their relationships with a personal commitment. Their work and their lives became inextricably intertwined. It allowed them to frame their conflicts as family problems, problems that could, for the most part, be taken in stride without damaging their relationships. While not all of the founders spent time together or even stayed in touch over the years, a sense of eternal connection ("through thick and thin") echoes through the family stories that were told about their history.

The family trope is not without its problems, however, and has been the subject of considerable critique on the part of feminist scholars, in particular with respect to the use of "sisterhood" as a metaphor for political alliances among feminists.[43] Jane Gallop (1994) has criticized what she calls the unmitigated heterosexism inherent in the notion of a feminist family. It relies on "good daughters" who are loyal to the nurturing tradition of their mothers and sets up an adversarial opposition with "bad daughters" that paralyzes the creative energies of individual women. It also obstructs alliances among women who, by virtue of their multiple belongings with respect to sexuality, class, or race, cannot view themselves unproblematically as family members.

Negotiating Myth and Historical Realities

In 1979, one of the founders, Wendy Sanford, wrote a history of the first decade of the BWHBC under the title "Working Together, Growing Together." Often cited and reprinted, it is an upbeat tale of the first ten years of the collective, full of excitement and energy and written in a personal style with anecdotes and self-reflection. Her narrative looked back on that first decade from the vantage point of the present—and in 1979 this was the heyday of *OBOS* in the United States. Drawing upon the mythical narrative of the group, she linked the strong personal relationships among its members to their unique style of working, stating that the collective's combination of connection, commitment, and consensus was "why we've survived and still love each other" (Sanford 1979, 86). The myth enabled her to conclude this history on a hopeful note, expressing confidence that the collective would be able to meet any challenge the next decades had to offer. It also provided a seductive model for other feminist groups that might be striving to survive their own internal conflicts and the external constraints of the Reagan era.

Twenty years later a very different history of the BWHBC appeared (Norsigian et al. 1999). Written by six members of the collective, it could not have been more different from the story of "working together, growing together." In this history, the mythical narrative ("A Good Story") was reduced to a mere sentence: "In the '70's we worked together in 'cottage industry' mode at home . . . often meeting together around our kitchen tables" (35). The new history was considerably less personal and more distanced. It was no longer the story they "liked to tell" but rather a history of ups and downs. It was a history that required reflection—and, in some cases, justification. The discord that had plagued the group throughout the nineties was duly reported, with the founders acknowledging that they had not been entirely successful in "finding common ground and ways to bridge racial, ethnic, and class differences." They recognized that one of the "great challenges we face" was the "importance of supporting the leadership of women of color and low-income women within our own organization" (36). This history, too, ended on a positive note and drew on those aspects of their political work that had been successful: the "building of broad alliances" within a global women's health movement. Thus, the reasons for their optimism had shifted from the survival of their own group in the United States to the possibility of alliances with women outside the United States.

These two histories, written twenty years apart, show how much water had flowed under this particular bridge—from a mythical history of a unique group to a demythologized narrative full of self-criticism and a realistic assessment of the group's successes as well as its failures. How did this transformation take place?

Becoming a Collective

During the first decade, the eleven women who made up the collective were meeting weekly, often at each others' homes. They spent nearly as much time talking about their lives as they did talking about "business." While making *OBOS* was what had initially brought them together, the balance between the desire to talk about themselves and the increasing demands of the book was sometimes a source of contention.

Like most feminist groups of that era, the collective eschewed formal structures, assigned roles, and hierarchies of any kind. Unsurprisingly, some members found themselves carrying a disproportionate part of the collective workload. One remembered, "People were so close, very close, as friends, not just as coworkers. It was hard to demand accountability and to say, 'You're not doing a good job.' I think it was really hard. Plus we were a collective; we weren't working for many years with a hierarchy, where somebody had authority over somebody else."[44]

From the beginning, decisions were made by consensus—a feature that made the BWHBC distinctive. In practice, this meant that a decision might be made one week, only to be altered several weeks later when one of the members had a strong objection. It was often frustrating, as one founder noted, "Because you couldn't always get consensus. Very often someone chose not to obstruct a vote: 'Okay, I don't agree, but I won't veto it.' And that was frequently done by people who didn't want to stop the process. They needed to voice the fact that they were sort of 'odd woman out.'"[45]

The discussions were considered at least as important as the actual decision, and each member of the group was given a chance to express her opinion. Disagreements were discussed until a course of action could be found that everyone could live with. As one member put it, "For the most part people did have a voice, but there were times when we had to create mechanisms whereby people could be heard so it wouldn't be just a matter of who was the loudest, who spoke the most."[46]

As Sanford (1979) noted, this method of working was the "very core of how and why we continue to exist" (86). Nowhere was the style of these early meetings more clearly reflected than in their minutes. They provided a blow-by-blow account of each member's contribution, sometimes verbatim ("Then Norma said . . ."), showing how intimately the personal was intertwined with the "book work." For example, in a 1979 meeting on "individual and group goals," the contribution of each member was recorded in detail, including items such as having "personal discussions like we used to" or discussing "what we are going to do with our money." But they would also contain personal information such as "I'm going to school at Tufts." The minutes were often full of humorous asides ("Would somebody like some cold duck?" accompanied by a cartoon drawing of a duck going "quack, quack") or—after a very long meeting—a drawing of a woman, sitting with her head wearily propped up on her hands, saying, "One more hour. . . ."[47] One of the more artistic founders often illustrated her minutes with drawings of members of the collective— recognizable even today.[48]

While the collective's consensual approach to decision making was lauded both within and outside the United States, it was the members' attention to dealing with personal conflicts in a supportive and honest way that captured the imaginations of many feminists of the era. Sanford (1979) offered a particularly candid account of how the group coped with the individual members' feelings of being neglected, excluded, or unappreciated. For example, when one member of the collective became increasingly dominant, they discussed how she could develop so much influence that she could sway people's decisions in ways that other members could not. Tensions were inevitable and intense conflicts arose around issues of power, but the collective treated power as a problem for the whole group, not just for a particular individual. Sanford noted that the "more timid of us" were able to explore why "we gave her more power than she perhaps even wanted," while the individual was able to confront her own ambivalence about being put in "the big sister role" whenever things got rough. In Sanford's words, "Gradually, a strong sense of self-respect and equality has developed among us, and we find ourselves with a changed notion of what power means for our group. . . . One of the things we wrestled with . . . was our expectation that one member's influence necessarily diminished the others. As we emerged from that struggle with our group intact and our friendships deepened, we realized that there can be power without dominance, that power can be sharing, or 'power with'" (1979, 87).

Turning Point

The turning point for the collective came in 1983 when the original group opened its doors to two new members, Sally Whelan and Pamela Morgan. Since the mid-1970s, they had been hiring staff to manage some of the work that had emerged around the book, and these two individuals had been working for the collective since 1979 and 1980, respectively. However, it proved a "traumatic" event—"ridiculously so, in retrospect." According to one of them, "Until five years ago I don't think I . . . really understood the depth of it and why it was so hard for some people to move out of that. That what it had meant to their lives was so monumental and so profound. . . . There wasn't a conscious ethos of hanging onto it and yet, in practicality, I think there was."[49]

One of the founders remembers initially having mixed feelings when she heard that these relative newcomers to the organization felt that they deserved to be considered part of the original group. For her, the issue was not whether they had contributed to the organization but that the collective wasn't something you could "join." As she put it, "It seemed ridiculous to me because how could you want to be part of the original group when you weren't part of the original group? I didn't get it. So at that session two years ago they explained their position, and it was wonderful to hear what they had to say. And, of course, they were right. They were part of the founding of the book, as it took the next step, and that was legitimate as far as I was concerned. I think everybody felt that."[50]

This comment illustrates how some of the founders grappled with their desire to be inclusive and their desire to hold on to the origin myth—a shared history that was unique. It wasn't until much later—at the retreat in 1996 when several members were given the official title *founder*—that her eyes were opened to the fact of the "book having a life of its own." She realized that there were differences in "who *we* are in relation to the book." This realization was exhilarating. "It was a true love fest," she told me. "If you could have been a fly on the wall. . . . It was unbelievable."[51]

Other founders were less positive about the nostalgia of some of the collective members for the old days.[52] Remembering the arrival of new members who "hadn't shared endlessly the last decade of history with us and didn't care what our grandparents were doing," one founder remarked, "There was quite a culture shift that I think certain of the earlier founders had a hard time with and didn't do very graciously—or gracefully—that shift. I think for a long time it was pretty difficult . . . because there was this incredible nostalgia for the early days which, I think has actually crippled our work at different points. I think it has been very counterproductive."[53]

For her, the whole notion of an original group was an obstacle that stood in the way of the future of the organization by producing a legacy of nostalgia and resistance to change. However, after reflecting on the problems that had emerged over taking in new members, she realized she had been focusing too much on the problematic aspects of this nostalgia. It was also necessary for the founders to acknowledge how positive the past had been before they "could let it go."[54] Her remark is perceptive and expresses how deeply equivocal nostalgia can be, both within feminist organizations and as a more general cultural phenomenon. On the one hand, it is a response to a felt disenchantment with the present, offering consolation by "re-enchanting" the present with fond memories of a golden past. On the other hand, it creates an emotional gulf between those with first-hand experiences and those without—a division that intersects and reinforces other divisions (Gabriel 1993, 137).

Unsurprisingly, the newcomers to the collective were most distant from the "myth of the BWHBC" and were therefore able to speak about it critically. For example, one of the newcomers, who had arrived in 1979 to organize the documentation for *OBOS*, described working for the organization long after many of the original members of the collective had moved away or gotten jobs and were less involved in the day-to-day running of the organization. However, when the BWHBC celebrated its twenty-fifth anniversary in 1996 (by that time she had been in the organization for seventeen years!), she recalled her chagrin when the media only seemed interested in interviewing the original group and were constantly expressing amazement that "you've all stayed together and you've carried on this work for this long." Shaking her head, this "newcomer" explained, "It's a lovely myth, but it really *is* a myth."

I don't want to belittle the founders who stayed on to carry out the daily work . . . but it was really [new people coming in to help] for the book and, when there wasn't a book, carrying on the life of the organization. . . . The book itself brought in founders once again, like whenever there was an edition founders would come back in to work on the book, right up until this last one. And it couldn't happen without them. But then there's this whole other life because the book and its reputation generated such an enormous demand for the resources of the collective, both for information, for speakers, for networking, for international work, for the adaptations, for all kinds of things, that there had to grow up an institution that was different from the informal working group and collective that met weekly at the beginning.[55]

Interestingly, according to her the 1996 retreat mentioned above was much less of a "love fest" than an attempt to "educate and raise the consciousness of the founders." As she put it, they "just didn't get it," didn't understand that an institution had grown up around the book and people who were involved with this institution needed to be credited "because we had really been founders even if we weren't there from day one, even if we weren't founding authors of *OBOS*."[56] Rather than recycling the myth of the BWHBC, she emphasized the need to "look back and correct history a little bit. . . . It's still a wonderful history, [and] we don't have to belittle the history by debunking the myth a little bit and just setting the record straight, you know."[57]

Turbulent Years

By the 1990s, the BWHBC bore little resemblance to the group of women that had met in each others' homes to talk about themselves and work on the book. While the original founders continued to meet, they were largely absent from the day-to-day life of the organization, which had become largely staff run. Several members of the founder group were also part of this staff, giving them a very powerful position within the organization. A board of directors composed of the founders and women from the community existed, but—as one founder put it—"it was a board that was asleep at the wheel."[58]

The rest of the staff consisted of a fluctuating group of women who differed from the founders in several important ways. They were often younger, having come to the women's movement later than most of the founders. While they were committed to the work they were doing, it was also for them a paid job rather than a way of life (as it had been for the founders in the early years of the collective). Unlike the founders, these staff members expected to be paid for their work and were less inclined—or able—to donate untold hours of unpaid labor to the organization. They were also less involved with the book itself than with the "results of the book" (correspondence, telephone calls, documentation, and so on). As one founder, who had also worked as a staff member for many years, put it, the staff wasn't doing the "shiny, fun stuff" that the founders got to do (giving lectures, working on the book); the staff did the "scut work." She remembered coming in every day but feeling invisible, just not "part of the *family* business [italics mine]."[59]

The gap between the founders and the staff was exacerbated as the BWHBC began to "diversify." Like many feminist groups that emerged in the late sixties and early seventies, the BWHBC was becoming increasingly aware that as a predominantly white, middle-class, and college educated collective, it needed to include more women of color and women from different ethnic and class backgrounds. As one founder put it, "If you're going to be taken as a group that speaks for all women, you've got to be much more 'all women' than we were."[60]

The founders were aware—at least in principle—that a serious commitment to diversity would involve change at both the individual and the institutional levels, requiring a major overhaul of their hiring practices and processes of decision making. They began by inviting women from the Latina and African American communities to serve on the board, by strengthening their outreach activities to these communities, and by making the hiring of women of color as staff members a priority.

Despite these efforts, however, by the late nineties tensions were running high. A racialized structure of privilege and power was built into the organization with a white, founder-dominated board making the decisions and representing the public face of the BWHBC, on the one hand, and staff members, several of whom were women of color, doing the daily work of running the organization without getting recognition for it on the other. It was inevitable that conflicts between the white women who occupied positions of power and authority and the women of color who did not would be played out as a race issue. These conflicts were not specific to the BWHBC and were, in fact, similar to what was happening in many other feminist grassroots groups across the United States that had been founded by predominantly white, middle-class women.[61] Sandra Morgen (2002) provides an excellent analysis of the context in which the BWHBC and other feminist grassroots collectives attempted to negotiate their vision of a multiracial feminism with the hard realities of giving up class- and race-based privilege and forging workable alliances across lines of race and class in the workplace, where "dreams of diversity often collided . . . with dilemmas of difference" (207). The story of the BWHBC does not stand alone but is part of a larger story of the politics of race and class in U.S. social movements. Like many other groups, the BWHBC responded to internal conflicts by conducting antiracism workshops and working to develop a more equitable organizational structure. When these measures failed, the founders hired consultants and the staff brought in a union. As one founder put it, "It's just classic, I guess. . . . Everyone says, you know, that the founder generation is the innovative, creative generation, and then they're really not. . . . They're not as good at the organization building and that aspect of the work. Or they're not interested in it or whatever."[62]

Looking back on what happened, another founder noted, "We were trying to do something very hard and were not doing it. . . . We weren't prepared for it. You don't hire women of color unless you have people who can mentor, and you don't hire women of color or different class backgrounds unless you have policies and procedures all in place."[63]

Many of the founders were retrospectively critical of the policy of hiring women of color and women from less privileged class backgrounds under the motto "We're all equal" or "Everyone can do everything." While this might have been a successful strategy in an organization of women with similar class and educational backgrounds, in this case it assumed a level playing field that obfuscated differences in educational and class privilege and ignored the experience and social capital that the founders had accrued from years of experience working on *OBOS*. The invisibility of privilege is almost synonymous with what "being white" means in the United States. Eliminating such systemic forms of privilege necessitates considerably more than some additional mentoring of newcomers. It would have, at the very least, involved a sustained and ongoing analysis of how white privilege intersects with power at all levels of the organization (Frankenberg 2001; Zajicek 2002). While many of the founders were ideologically committed to this kind of analysis, in practice it did not happen often enough, and when it did it was often too little too late.

In the summer of 1995, in the midst of what seemed to be interminable discussions about how to restructure the organization, the staff decided that it needed to bring in a union. The founders reacted with confusion and disbelief. Still working through many unresolved power issues within their own group and mourning the loss of one of the members to breast cancer, they had to face the fact not only that their organization was deeply polarized but that the staff did not have confidence that the problems could be resolved without the help of a union. While most of the founders were quick to acknowledge that in a racially divided society like that of the United States racism would hardly come to a halt at their own front door, as tensions mounted around issues of race and racism they increasingly reacted evasively or defensively. Whereas the women of color in the organization saw covert racism and subtle exclusion at all levels of the organization, the white women in the BWHBC became less able—or less willing—to reflect on white privilege and more concerned with protecting their vision of the organization from a critique that was simply too unpalatable to bear. Their narratives were characterized by avoidance of the "R word," and explanations for the present state of affairs downplayed or reframed the significance of race rather than confronting it directly. As one founder put it,

> A lot of the conflict that happened around race I feel happened because there weren't uniformly agreed-on standards of evaluation and accountability. And so the rules weren't all evenly applied, and certain founders felt like they didn't have to obey certain rules, like to get there on time. And so if you try to get other people to get there on time it feels unfair to the newer staff to be held to an accountability that the founders aren't. Because they're used the going and coming. They've been here twenty-five years. So a lot of the staff conflicts, I think, could have been helped by having a really clear, good, universally agreed upon personnel policy.[64]

While this attempt to explain the problem in terms of inadequate organizational rules or accountability captured one level of the conflicts occurring in the organization, it left unexplored both the racialized structures of privilege within the organization and the resentment that such differential treatment is likely to evoke in the context of a racialized society like that of the United States. Other founders focused on their own powerlessness in the face of the seemingly intractable conflicts within the organization. The political paralysis resulted in an oscillation between feeling guilty and blaming others. Brown (2001) has called this a form of "Left melancholia" whereby the loss of a sense of progress in history propels former activists into a state of mourning as they discover their inability to effectively combat the sources of racism, poverty, violence against women and so on. According to one of the founders, "It always seemed to me that things we had done so naturally, at the very beginning got turned into kind of 'hokey.' Eventually, we always had to have facilitators . . . to help us analyze what was wrong with us, to help us try and get along and understand each other in the enlarging group we were becoming. [But] when we started in the seventies we did it all ourselves because we could do it ourselves. That was part of it, taking that power."[65]

Others took refuge in feelings of betrayal. As one founder notes, it was hard to see the actions of staff members as being in "good faith" after they had all spent "hours and hours" meeting together, trying to create an "organization that makes sense." She continued,

> I mean, I'm not anti-union . . . [but] the whole thought was that we could really communicate and work out whatever it was, blocks or whatever, and . . . no, they were going to unionize and it was the only way. They felt that since things were so unclear about the founders and privilege . . . that that was the only thing they could do. It was beyond discussion. It became totally irrational, I think. . . . The other thing that made it even more complicated is that everything was also being discussed in racist terms, which is also crazy. So it was like people who knew the collective said, "Oh, it's so frustrating and sad." . . . But that was what was going on.[66]

In this narrative, the lines have already been clearly demarcated between the "we" (the founders and board) and the "them" (the staff). Although she still struggles to remain aligned to the staff ("I'm not anti-union, but. . . .") and acknowledges that there were grounds for complaint ("founders and privilege"), the staff's side of the story is not only left out or kept vague ("things were so unclear"), but their responses are portrayed as "irrational" and unconstructive ("beyond discussion"). According to Zajicek (2002), one of the dominant repertoires among white feminists for talking about "race" is to engage in a kind of "power reversal," whereby white feminists emphasize their powerlessness and victimization, while the reactions of members of minority groups characterized as angry, exclusionary, or divisive even to the extent of using racism to exercise power illegitimately, sometimes referred to as "playing the race-card" (165–167).

Reflecting on those turbulent years, one of the founders who had joined to collective later provided an assessment of the BWHBC as a group caught between its own myth and the realities of its present situation: "This is a group that will really try to honor its word and really try to live by its ideals and is certainly fallible and human. There's a real pattern in the collective of making big boo-boos, both . . . interpersonally and . . . organizationally, just striving to be creative and striving to be accountable and striving to apologize."[67]

The Myth of the BWHBC:
Idol of Bewitchment or Symbol of Empowerment?

In 1997, four former staff members wrote a letter to the well-known feminist journal *Sojourner* accusing the BWHBC of racism. "It is difficult to convey the sadness and disappointment we feel regarding the recent turn of events in an organization that we once lovingly deemed as ours. . . . Our sadness and pain on a personal level are a reflection of a much deeper sense of betrayal. We expected and deserved better!" (Bonilla et al. 1997, 4). Their explanation and assessment of the events obviously differed from those of the founders, who also wrote a letter explaining their "side" in which they emphasized the transitions the organization had been going through and their commitment to providing a more equitable working environment for all staff ("Needless to say, there is a lot to learn, and we are committed to learning it") (Bell Alexander et al. 1997, 5). What is remarkable, however, is how far away from the myth of the BWHBC the founders appear to be in their matter-of-fact portrayal of organizational transition, while the staff expresses a commitment to the myth of a loving family that has been "betrayed" by recent events. This same commitment is reflected in the way *Sojourner*, speaking in the name of the broader feminist community, expresses undisguised dismay at the conflicts. Under the dramatic headline "It Happened Here, Too!" the reader is informed that he or she may "find it painful to reconcile these images of the organization" because *OBOS* has been such an "intimate part of many women's lives" (Mains 1997, 10–11). The implication is two-fold. On the one hand, there is a recognition that the BWHBC was hardly the only feminist organization to encounter these problems and many feminist collectives in the United States that had emerged during the seventies had undergone similar conflictual trajectories as the predominantly white, middle-class founders had to make way for a new generation that was differently located in terms of class and race. On the other hand, the BWHBC is treated as an exception, the last place anyone would have expected to find racialized power inequalities. There is a refusal to believe that U.S. feminism's favorite project—a project that had provided one of the foundation myths of U.S. feminism (Morgen 2002)—could be unsuccessful in fighting racism in its own organization.

In order to understand these contradictory responses, it is necessary to return to the mythical narrative of the BWHBC and explore how it could—in the words of Kearney (2002, 90)—generate both "symbols of empowerment" and "idols of bewitchment."

I have shown how the story of the BWHBC provided a mythical narrative that allowed a sense of shared history and shared identity for the members of the collective. It also allowed many women from different generations and walks of life to vicariously participate in this history and identity. However, as we have seen, this same mythical narrative made it increasingly difficult for the members of the BWHBC to come to terms with the historical realities of exclusion and power inequalities that were occurring in their midst. The seeds of this complicated mix of empowerment and bewitchment can be found, however, in the mythical narrative as origin story, heroic tale, and family saga.

As an *origin story*, the myth provided a moment of awakening, after which the world never looked the same again. It allowed countless women, both within and outside the United States, who had not been present at the beginning to recognize their own experiences as part of a larger historical movement, thereby stimulating their politicization as feminists. While the myth created an empowering symbol that drew women from different locations and generations into a kind of imagined community, it proved to be considerably less empowering for women on the home front. There it became an exclusionary story, dividing old-timers from newcomers, founders from staff, and, more generally, women from one another along the lines of class, race, and sexuality. As Lisa Adkins (2004) has convincingly argued, when feminist consciousness becomes a legacy—a torch to be passed from one generation to the next or from one group of women to another—the present and future become positioned as being in constant debt to the past. The meeting at Emmanuel College—an event that itself took place under specific historical circumstances—became just such a torch. It took on the static character of familial property, providing the only conceivable model for becoming a feminist. It is one of the ironies that, while the BWHBC founders were proficient in developing a critical and reflexive approach to passing on their book, they encountered many difficulties in passing on their organization in a way that would allow new members to reinvent it. The myth of the origin of the BWHBC worked to obstruct rather than open up the possibility that the group might become something completely different.[68]

As a *heroic tale*, the myth provided a feminist David and Goliath story about a group of ordinary women who resourcefully and successfully took on some of the most powerful institutions in the United States—the medical establishment, the pharmaceutical industry, and patriarchy—and beat them at their own game. It allowed a broad range of women without notable material or professional resources to imagine that they, too, might become "heroes in their own lives" (Gordon 1988). By showing how women could become empowered by working together, it provided a powerful catalyst for an international women's health movement.

This same heroic tale, however, became an obstacle when the enemy was no longer firmly located outside the collective but could also be found within. The notion that heroes could also be powerful managers or that even ordinary women could have privileges at their disposal complicated the heroic tale. As myth, it offered little discursive space for critical reflection concerning the ways class, race, or sexuality invariably shape interactions among women in a racially divided society like that of the United States. It provided little help in understanding how interactions among differently located women might evolve in less than heroic ways. In the wake of painful and intractable conflicts around power inequalities and racism, the heroic tale stood in the way of the critical and reflexive analysis of how the legacies of racism and the injuries of class haunt the present. Ultimately, it prevented the collective from finding new ways to think about the future without resorting to powerlessness and political despair (Brown 2001).

As a *family saga*, the myth of the BWHBC provided a seductive image of how women can develop a bond strong enough to survive personal conflicts and collective crises, allowing them to grow old together "still talking about our bodies and ourselves after all these years." The image of family resonated with the already familiar feminist discourse of sisterhood but elaborated it into a powerful image of feminist community that inspired other feminist groups both inside and outside the United States that were struggling to reconcile their desire for personal connection with their political activities and commitments. However, the family saga, already showing signs of wear and tear within the collective, became a barrier to change as the organization expanded and took on new members. Organizational conflicts were couched in the exclusionary language of family, with the increasingly frequent use of a dichotomizing "we" and "them." The inability of the collective to absorb newcomers into the family not only evoked disappointment and resentment among those on the "outside," but it induced unproductive reactions of guilt and defensiveness among those on the "inside." The family myth allowed legitimate grievances on the part of the staff to be personalized or treated as a problem of loyalty (betrayal) rather than power. It stood in the way of the necessary interrogation of the ways institutionalized, heterosexist, and racialized structures of power operate at all levels of society, including within feminist organizations committed to gender equality, struggles against racism, and social justice.

The mythical narratives accounted for the longevity of the collective—and no founder, however disillusioned or disheartened with the present state of affairs, expressed any doubts about that. However, the recent conflicts within the organization necessitated a painful renegotiation of these narratives, resulting, ultimately, in a transformation of the organization. My interviews attested to how the founders of the BWHBC grappled with the painful realities of the present against the backdrop of their mythical past. They had different strategies for dealing with discrepancies between myth and reality. Some looked back on the "good old days" with undisguised nostalgia, expressing confusion and bewilderment about the present state of affairs. Others tried to place recent events in a structural analysis of racialized conflicts in grassroots organizations in general, thereby trying to understand the present without diminishing the past. Still others used the present to take a critical look at the past, rearticulating the myth into a more realistic appraisal of their history. And, finally, some did what overburdened activists often do— they soldiered on, perhaps sadder but wiser but primarily concerned about the work that needed to be done in order to get the book out one more time."[69]

Today the BWHBC is a completely different organization. Most of the founders have left and are, at most, tangentially involved with it. Many seem to be watching from a distance, somewhat reticent in their assessment of its present activities. The organization itself has been completely reorganized. It now functions as a small nonprofit organization that brings out revised editions of the book, does outreach work in the Latina community, and, last but not least, facilitates the translation and adaptation of *OBOS*. The present organization bears no resemblance to a collective let alone a family. In order to avoid associations with its former collective past, the organization has also recently changed its name to simply Our Bodies, Ourselves. It is now "just a nonprofit organization," and no one seems to want it to be anything else. The BWHBC ultimately abandoned the myth that had sustained it for more than thirty years to begin anew, this time on a more realistic, or at least more pragmatic, basis. While the new organization continues to struggle with the legacy of the past, it has demythologized itself, at least in its everyday incarnation.

Outside the United States, however, the myth of the BWHBC continues to live on, appearing scarcely the worse for wear in the preface of each new translation of *OBOS*. Again and again, local women's groups situate their adaptations of *OBOS* in a history that begins with that famous meeting in Boston in 1969 and ends somewhere completely different—in Serbia or India or Senegal.

This immediately raises the question of how the myth continues to be mobilized, particularly in the light of the history of the U.S. collective. Have the translators been misled concerning the history of the BWHBC? Do they actually believe that this is "how it all happened?" Do they see the myth is an accurate representation of U.S. feminism?

It seems to me that it is safe to assume that feminist activists in other parts of the world are not likely to subscribe to fairy tales and that they will—like the BWHBC—have their own problems to contend with in their own organizations and social movements. It is, in fact, most likely that they will be less concerned with the past history of the group, or even the past life of *OBOS*, than with the future—what the book can mean in the context in which they live and work.

But the myth does allow them to reinvent a history that can include themselves and—more generally—the women they wish to reach through the dissemination of *OBOS*. It is useful precisely because it does not provide an accurate representation of one feminist group specifically located in time and space. On the contrary, as myth, the story of the BWHBC offers an "exemplary and infinitely repeatable paradigm," which allows a "remaking of the world" in light of its "potential truths" (Kearney 2002, 131). When the translators "borrow" the myth of the BWHBC, they do so, first and foremost, in order to legitimate their own projects. It allows them to construct a shared history, a history that does not belong to the BWHBC alone, or even to U.S. feminism, but potentially to all women across the globe. The story of how ordinary women in the United States were able to learn about their bodies, sexuality, reproduction, and health can be mobilized by other ordinary women to make a case for doing something similar—but also different—in their own local contexts. At their best, myths create a shared "community of memory" (Ricoeur 1978). By transcending the localness of actual events and organizations, they can allow political activists to situate their activities in a broader national—and even a global—story. It is in this sense that the myth of the BWHBC opens up "a space where women can triumph together" (Morgen 2002, 22), providing a powerful symbolic imagery for a transnational feminist politics of the body.

However, myths do not always provide social imaginaries that can open up genuinely shared horizons. Depending on how they are interpreted, they can also be mobilized in the name of repression, bigotry, racism, or nationalism. In social movements, myths have from time to time obscured the historical character of events, allowing activists to remain identified with a utopian vision in the face of contradictions within their own organizations. In this sense, they can constitute a "refusal of history," becoming, ultimately, the source of a movement's dissolution and downfall (Portelli 1990; Passerini

1990, 1996). This does not mean that myths are unimportant. On the contrary, activists cannot do without myths as "symbols of empowerment," enabling them to "transcend" the present and imagine what a better world might be. However, if their myths are not to become "idols of bewitchment" (Kearney 2002, 88–90) political activists need to remain in an ongoing dialogue with history. Myths require an ongoing confrontation with the realities of the past as well as the present. In short, they need—from time to time—to be demythologized.

CHAPTER 4

Reclaiming Women's Bodies

COLONIALIST TROPE OR CRITICAL EPISTEMOLOGY?

In 1996, *Contemporary Sociology* celebrated its silver anniversary by devoting a special issue to "the ten most influential books of the past 25 years." One of these books was *Our Bodies, Ourselves*. Lest the reader wonder what a popular feminist book on women's health was doing among such lofty scholarly masterpieces as Michel Foucault's (1977) *Discipline and Punish*, Edward Said's (1978) *Orientalism*, and Immanuel Wallerstein's (1974) *The Modern World System*, the authors reviewing it noted that *OBOS* exemplified the transformative influence of feminism on *both* popular and academic knowledge.[1] They pointed out that a one-sided emphasis on "scholarly books" would have relegated social theory to individual—usually male— "theory stars." "*Our Bodies, Ourselves*" they stated, "reminds us that knowledge is produced not solely in the academy and that some of the most productive new veins of research and analysis arise from radical movements" (Gordon and Thorne 1996, 324–25).

Interestingly, just as social theory has begun to acknowledge its debt to *OBOS*, feminist theory has been almost universally silent on the subject. While the historical significance of *OBOS* as a catalyst for feminist health activism and its role in inspiring research on women's health are recognized by feminist scholars (Clarke and Olesen 1999a, 14), it is rarely viewed as having anything of relevance to offer feminist theory. This is especially surprising given the amount of attention that the topic of the body has received within contemporary feminist theory. With the plethora of recent publications devoted to feminist theoretical perspectives on the body, not a single one does more than mention *OBOS* in passing and none of the anthologies concerned with women's bodies and embodiment has included a chapter or even an excerpt from it.² Thus, it is safe to conclude that while *OBOS* has played a formative role in feminist (health) politics it has had little effect on the direction taken by current feminist body theory.

In a recent article, Kuhlmann and Babitsch (2002) have explored the reasons for what they call the "dissociation process" between contemporary feminist body theory and research and activism on women's health. In their view, postmodern feminist theory is the culprit. Its concepts and theories have become so esoteric, so ethereal, so divorced from women's everyday experiences with their bodies that they have been of little use to feminist health activists. This kind of abstract theorizing has not only prevented feminist health activists from profiting from the insights of feminist body theory, but it also signals an even more fundamental problem in the theory itself—specifically, a neglect of the materiality of the (sexed) body and the concrete processes of health and illness (433).

In order to better understand this dissociation process, let us take a brief look at an example in the form of a well-known and oft-cited essay by Donna Haraway called "The Virtual Speculum in the New World Order" (1999). Haraway is one of the most important contemporary feminist theorists on the body and, more generally, on the feminist politics of knowledge. She is generally given credit for raising—and, indeed, even answering—the questions that are most crucial for a feminist understanding of the body in the context of proliferating information and biotechnologies and the relationship of the body to the issues of women's subjectivity and agency. In this particular essay, which has been lauded as no less than an attempt to bring feminist theory into the new millennium by "opening up the New World Order for our collective examination and consideration" (Clarke and Olesen 1999, 25), Haraway addresses the politics of the women's health movement and takes a critical look at the role *OBOS* has played in shaping the direction these politics have taken.

Haraway provocatively couples *OBOS* (the book and the slogan) to feminist self-help, which was popular in the U.S. women's health movement in the early seventies. Initially developed by primarily white, middle-class, U.S. women, feminist self-help involved women meeting in small groups, sharing information and stories, educating themselves about their bodies and the medical establishment, and looking for remedies to minor bodily problems. It incorporated practices ranging from self-exams (breast, cervical, vaginal, and vulvar) to alternative therapies (home treatments for vaginal infections, nutritional changes, herbal remedies, and menstrual extraction) to support groups around issues such as cancer, menopause, weight management, AIDS, incest, or substance abuse.

Although *OBOS* and self-help were never identical,[3] *OBOS* did draw on many of the insights of self-help. For example, it encouraged its readers to explore their own bodies—sometimes with mirror in hand—a strategy that I will discuss in more detail in the next chapter. However, it is the emphasis of *OBOS* on women "discovering" their bodies and "recovering" ownership of their sexuality and reproduction through knowledge of their bodies that is the particular object of Haraway's critique.

> Armed with a gynecological speculum, a mirror, a flashlight, and—most of all—each other in a consciousness-raising group, women ritually opened their bodies to their own literal view. The speculum had become the symbol of the displacement of the female midwife by the specialist male physician and gynecologist. The mirror was the symbol forced on women as a signifier of our own bodies as spectacle-for-another in the guise of our own supposed narcissism. Vision itself seemed to be the empowering act of conquerors. More than a little amnesiac about how colonial travel narratives work, we peered inside our vaginas toward the distant cervix and said something like, "Land ho!" We have discovered ourselves and claim the new territory for women. In the context of the history of Western sexual politics—that is, in the context of the whole orthodox history of Western philosophy and technology—visually self-possessed sexual and generative organs made potent tropes for the reclaimed feminist self. We thought we had our eyes on the prize. I am caricaturing, of course, but with a purpose. *Our Bodies, Ourselves* was both a popular slogan and the title of a landmark publication in women's health movements. (Haraway 1999, 67)

According to Haraway, when women look at their bodies through a speculum they unwittingly adopt the same objectifying medical "gaze" that historically has been central to the medical appropriation of women's bodies. By separating the feminist subject (who can "discover" and "recover") and the female body (as passive object), feminist health activists are merely reproducing medical discourse, thereby imitating masculinist dualisms about women's embodiment. Tongue in cheek, Haraway compares such activism to a well-known 1973 feminist cartoon of Wonder Woman, dressed in steel bracelets and stiletto high heels, who seized a speculum from a stethoscope-wearing doctor in white, while announcing: "With my speculum, I am strong! I can fight!" (68). For Haraway, the belief that women's privileged access to their bodies provides them with authentic knowledge beyond the purview of science and culture is mistaken. Feminist knowledge cannot exist outside dominant forms of knowledge. In Haraway's view, these would-be feminist "explorers" are no different than the male doctors they are attacking, and, indeed, they may even be considerably worse. Haraway employs the trope of "colonial travel" to compare feminist health activists to white European male colonizers who were also engaged in a discovery project—this time the project of conquering indigenous peoples in faraway places. The implication is that the "speculum" employed by white, well-educated, feminist health activists in the seventies represents a practice that is just as power laden as the colonial project and is, therefore, just as likely to be disempowering for nonwhite, non-Western women because it obscures dramatic differences in morbidity, mortality, and access in health care among U.S. women (72).

Haraway admits, of course, that she is providing something of a "caricature" by comparing feminist self-help to the "whole orthodox history of Western philosophy and technology," not to mention the nefarious masculinist colonial project of conquering land (nature) and peoples (natives). However, she defends her strategy as an important, and indeed necessary, intervention in U.S. feminist health politics. Her concern is the development of a critical and reflexive politics of knowledge—what she calls "the right speculum for the job" which will acknowledge differences in women's health and create structures of accountability between differently located women within the United States and worldwide. As Haraway puts it, it is only then that a "truly comprehensive" feminist politics of health can emerge (84).

While I believe that Haraway's claims are both important and in need of some critical attention,[4] it is not my intention here to criticize this particular essay. I have referred to Haraway's essay at some length because it is exemplary of a much broader and far-reaching phenomenon with feminist body theory—namely, the tendency to treat health activism as theoretically naive and methodologically flawed—and therefore has little of relevance to offer feminist body theory.

In this chapter, I will provide a more careful (and less caricatural) consideration of *OBOS* and, by implication, feminist health activism. To this end, I will not be treating *OBOS* as "just" a popular book on women's health but rather as an epistemological project.

OBOS as Epistemological Project

By epistemological project, I mean any project that centers on knowledge and knowledge practices. Traditionally, epistemology has dealt with questions such as the nature of knowledge, justification, objectivity, and epistemic agency. Feminist epistemologists have dealt with these questions and introduced new problems, including the politics of knowledge and the impact of the social position and the sexed body of the knower on the production and reception of knowledge (Alcoff and Potter 1993, 1–2). By these standards, *OBOS* is an epistemological project par excellence because it focuses on knowledge about the female body, on what counts as authoritative knowledge, on how this knowledge is justified, and on women's status as epistemic agents.[5]

As an epistemological project, *OBOS* has taken the female body as a starting point for understanding the condition of being a woman in a social order hierarchically organized by gender and other intersecting categories of inequality. The female body in *OBOS* is a complex, dynamic, multilayered entity, however. It is an *anatomical* body with breasts, clitoris, vagina, and uterus. It is also a *physiological* body, which may menstruate and have the capacity to become pregnant and which may or may not bear children.[6] It may become ill or disabled, will inevitably grow older, and will eventually die. It is an *experiential* body, which is lived and given meaning by the subject as she moves about in the world around her. And, finally, it is a body that is embedded in a *culture* that, to a greater or lesser degree, devalues femininity. In this culture, women's bodies are stereotyped, subjected to violence, exploited in the workplace, marginalized or excluded from the public domain, and subjected to the insults of racism and class inequities. Thus, in *OBOS* the female body in all its complexity is presented as the site from which women engage with the world, making it a potential locus for resistance and political action.

Second, *OBOS* has attributed authority to women's embodied experiences. Women are encouraged to take their bodily experiences seriously as a valuable source of knowledge. These experiences cover a broad spectrum, from sexuality and relationships, raising children, health problems, and finding one's way through the health care system to living in a society structured by poverty, racism, and gender inequalities. Women are invited to use these experiences to think critically about medical procedures and remedies and to develop strategies for staying healthy. Experiences are also treated as a necessary resource for interrogating cultural understandings that deny, distort, or misrepresent women's bodies and the circumstances and conditions of their embodied lives. Knowledge without experience is cast as the dividing line between the powerful and the marginalized whereby experiential knowledge provides women with the critical tools necessary for their survival.[7]

Third, *OBOS* treats women as active knowers rather than passive objects of the knowledge practices of others. By gaining knowledge about their bodies, it shows how women can gain control over their lives. This notion of agency is not the same as the "Just do it!" philosophy that pervades contemporary Western culture and is popular within self-help culture (Bordo 1997). In *OBOS*, the act of becoming knowledgeable, of understanding one's own experiences and using them to engage critically with dominant forms of knowledge, is treated as both individually and collectively empowering for women. By sharing the process of producing and disseminating alternative forms of knowledge about women's bodies and by finding ways to form coalitions with differently situated women across multiple locations, *OBOS* offers a vision of a collective feminist politics of knowledge that has shaped contemporary feminist health activism (Murphy 2004, 141–42).

Despite its far-reaching influence within the women's health movement as an epistemological project, *OBOS* has drawn little attention from feminist body theory. In my view, this is unfortunate because it is precisely through its epistemology that *OBOS* has the most to offer. In order to pave the way for a more productive and mutually beneficial exchange between feminist body theory and feminist health activism, I will now turn to three highly publicized debates within contemporary feminist body theory. The first debate concerns the female body and the uses (and abuses) of biology in justifying gendered inequalities as "natural." The second debate concerns the validity of women's experiential knowledge as an arbiter of the "truth." And, finally, the third debate concerns how to conceptualize women's agency with regard to the production of subversive or empowering forms of knowledge. I will show how the confrontation with *OBOS* as an epistemological project can contribute to these debates, thereby making feminist body theory more amenable to the concerns of feminist health activism.

The Biological Body

Beginning with Simone de Beauvoir's (1953) famous adage that "a woman is not born, but rather becomes a woman," feminist theory in the West has been preoccupied with shifting attention away from biology as an explanation for inequalities between the sexes to the social and cultural conditions that produce femininity and masculinity. One of the central tasks of feminist body theory has been, then, to avoid biological determinism by finding ways to conceptualize the body without reducing gendered inequalities to biologically based differences between women and men.

This has been a long-standing theoretical project with a wide diversity of perspectives and strategies. It began with the conceptual distinction between sex and gender, which became the cornerstone of modernist feminist body theory (Fraser and Greco 2005). The concept of sex was relegated to the realm of biology, implicitly specified in terms of anatomy, chromosomes, and hormones, while gender, in contrast, was used to refer to "all other socially constructed characteristics attributed to women and men" (Oudshoorn 1994, 2). Distinguishing between sex and gender got rid of the problem of biological determinism—at least for the time being. However, it did not resolve the problem of essentialism—that is, the assumption of an a priori, ontological, or biological "essence" for sexual difference. Under the influence of postmodernism, it became clear that the separation of biological sex from cultural gender was no longer regarded as an adequate solution to the problem of essentialism as it left the biological body as a kind of implicit "coat rack" for gender (Nicholson 1994).

Feminist body theory, therefore, began to look for ways to theorize the body that would avoid biological determinism without running the risk of essentialism. For many, the solution to this problem seemed to reside in treating the body as a "text" on which culture inscribes its meanings (Bordo 1993) or as an "imaginary" site, an effect not of genetics but of relations of power. In this way, the entire notion of an anatomical or biological body could be viewed as little more than a discourse produced by a specific culture. As Gatens (1999) put it, while Western culture chooses to represent bodies anatomically, making the anatomical body the touchstone for culture, "another culture might take the clan totem as the essence or truth of particular bodies" (230). Judith Butler (1989, 1993) took an even more radical approach to the problem of essentialism by questioning the entire distinction between biological sex and cultural gender. She rejected any notion of a physical substrate or even a surface on which culture imposes its meanings, arguing instead that bodies are best viewed as "performances" whereby sex—analogous to gender—is a contingent, fluctuating series of performative constructions. Although Butler claimed that her conception allowed space for the "materiality" of the body, it was a relentlessly discursive materiality, divorced from women's flesh and blood bodies.

Another strategy for avoiding both biological determinism and essentialism entailed dismantling the dualisms in Western thought that associated women with their bodies to begin with while allowing men the masculinist fantasy that they could transcend their bodies as "disembodied minds" (Bordo 1987). These dualisms trap women in the constraints of the flesh, making them prisoners of their bodies, while men are presumably able to "leap out of the marked body into a conquering gaze from nowhere" (Haraway 1991b, 188). Women are not alone in being reduced to their bodies. People of color, the elderly, the homosexual, the fat, and the disabled are also defined through their bodes as the "other" to white, Western, bourgeois men (Young 1990a).[8] Feminist body theorists such as Bordo, Haraway, and many others have devoted considerable attention to exposing the gendered character of Western dualistic thinking, showing how binaries, which hierarchically privilege mind over body, rationality over emotions, culture over nature, and human over animal, are implicated in hierarchical relations of power. As a theoretical solution to the problem of dualistic conceptions of the body, Haraway

(1991) introduced the metaphor of the cyborg, which imaginatively disrupted all conventional attempts to classify bodies in terms of conventional binaries. This metaphor enabled a conceptualization of the body as an endless process of morphing into new and uncategorizable forms (part human, part animal, part machine, both masculine and feminine, etc.). While the cyborg body seemed particularly suited to a postmodern information society, with its "codes, dispersal, and networks" (211), it was a decidedly ethereal body, farther removed from the material body than even Butler's conception. In an attempt to "bring the body back in," Elizabeth Grosz (1994) provided a different, though equally nondichotomous, conception of the body, which could also "destabilize" oppositional categories, "upset" binaries, and install "indeterminacy" as the primary concerns of feminist body theory without losing sight of the body itself. Her version of "corporeal feminism" focused on the fluidity of the body, that is, a "volatile body" that is able to "transform or rewrite its environment, to continually augment its powers and capacities" (188). She did not abandon the "organic body," as some of her predecessors had done, but her focus was on how it was constantly being supplemented and transformed through the incorporation of external "objects" into its own internal spaces.[9] She concentrated on how material bodies were imbricated in a constant process of transformation, of becoming. By stressing the fluidity of bodily boundaries and the dynamic interaction between the internal and the external, between the body and its surroundings, Grosz attempted to salvage the flesh and blood body while countering any suggestion that biology was destiny.

Notwithstanding the differences between these perspectives and strategies, they share a common concern with deterministic, essentialist, dualistic, and static ways of thinking about women's bodies. Each theorist in her own particular way has been successful in pulling the rug out from under biological determinism and, more generally, criticizing the role that biology has played in justifying inequalities between the sexes as "natural." While theoretically this has been extremely important, as a focus for feminist body theory it is not without its drawbacks. As Kuhlman and Babitsch (2002) have noted, "We must face the question of what price we are willing to pay in exchange for the delimitation of naturalized categories" (436). By making the body central to the theoretical projects of dismantling biological determinism and essentialism, deconstructing dualisms, and emphasizing fluidity and transformation, the price may be—ironically—a disembodied body. As Spelman (1988) puts it, feminist body theory seems to have fallen prey to a kind of "somatophobia" whereby women's flesh and blood bodies have vanished from sight and we are left with the body as a mere metaphor for other, more pressing philosophical concerns. Even theorists who explicitly attend to the "materiality" of the body (like Butler) or want to "bring bodies back in" (like Grosz), hardly pay any attention to the sensual physicality of the body. Feminist body theory seems to specialize in the surface of the body, a "body without organs" (Braidotti 1999) or, for that matter, bones, muscles, glands, or capillaries. The fragmented, fluid, and performed body that appears in feminist body theory bears little resemblance to the bodies that most women would be able to recognize as their own. Moreover, feminist body theory implies a transformability that belies the bodily constraints with which most women must live at different periods in their lives. While theoretical constructions such as the cyborg are useful for imagining the body in new ways in an increasingly technologized world, it has little to offer when it comes to understanding the vulnerabilities and limitations of the body that accompany illness, disease, disability, or the vicissitudes of growing older. The ubiquitous feminist theoretical rebuttal of biological determinism and essentialism has led to theories that deny the entire realm of the biological as having significance for feminist body theory. As the feminist biologist, Linda Birke (1999) warns, this failure to engage with biology—except to criticize it—"serves us ill, not least, because it is through the biological body that we live in and engage with the world at all" (175).

In contrast to feminist body theory, which has tended to subordinate the flesh and blood body to its theoretical projects, *OBOS* places the physical body on center stage. It offers a way of thinking about the anatomy, physiology, and organicity of women's bodies while avoiding the pitfalls of biological determinism, essentialism, and dualistic thinking. At the same time, *OBOS* seriously takes up the feminist critique of biological determinism, dualistic thinking, and essentialism but without completely rejecting biology. Highly critical of masculinist medicine's obsession with "wombs on legs" (Birke 1999, 12), *OBOS* questions any discourse that reduces women to their biology. However, biology is also regarded as a potential helpmeet when it comes to providing a complex and multilayered conception of the body as essential to a feminist epistemological project. As *OBOS* demonstrates, knowledge about women's biological bodies and how they work can be an integral part of a feminist body theory.

While *OBOS* rests on the assumption that most women have a body that is coded female, it firmly rejects any notion of an "essentially female" body by problematizing the automatic connection between the biological female body and gender identity. The subject of variations in gender identity was taken up in *OBOS* and the assumption that gender identity requires a specific kind of sexed body was problematized. *OBOS* focused on the varieties of gender identity, including transgender, transsexuality, and other "gender outlaws." Thus, while *OBOS* attends to anatomical specificities and physiological processes that are shared by many women, it also emphasizes the diversity and variety in women's (material, anatomical, and physiological) bodies.

Like feminist body theory, *OBOS* does not treat bodies as static entities, hermetically sealed off from the world. However, unlike feminist body theory, it adopts a holistic perspective toward the body whereby bodies are viewed as self-organizing, dynamic systems. Thus, *OBOS* both takes up and expands the notion of the body as "cultural text" (Bordo), as an assemblage of "performances" (Butler), and as "imaginary" (Grosz, Gatens) by including a body that is more than "skin deep." It shows that understanding women's bodies requires engaging with what goes on "under the surface" of the body, as well as with how the "inside" of the body interacts with and shapes women's interactions as embodied subjects with the world "outside" their bodies. This perspective treats bodies as both capable of change in interaction with the life circumstances of individual women and the cultural conditions under which they live and yet are also endowed with an organismic integrity that provides each body with its own idiosyncratic developmental history.[10] Rather than subordinating the body to a theoretical project, *OBOS* takes the body as a starting point for exploring how women actually negotiate deterministic or essentialist understandings of women's bodies or exploit dualisms in the context of their everyday lives.[11] While feminist body theory seems to prefer a discourse of fluidity, fracturing, and lack of fixed boundaries in order to show how the body's capacities can be enhanced through technology, *OBOS* reminds us that it is ultimately the physical body that calls a halt to the endless manipulation of the body through technological intervention.[12]

Finally, while feminist body theory, with its predilection for metaphors of fluidity and change, has failed to provide concepts that are salient for understanding the everyday realities of living in, with, and through a body with limitations. By exploring the vulnerabilities of women's bodies (how bodies age, suffer injury or illness, and become disabled or infirm), *OBOS* provides a conceptualization of the body as not so much "without boundaries" as "temporarily able-bodied." It elaborates the consequences of the body's vulnerabilities for how our social environment should be organized in order to take differences in embodiment into account.[13]

Experiential Knowledge

Feminist theory has always entailed a critical engagement with science and, in particular, with its spurious claims to objectivity and value neutrality. Initially, women's experience was taken as an essential ingredient of this critical endeavor. Theorists such as Dorothy Smith (1990a, 1990b, 1987), Lorraine Code (1991), Sandra Harding (1991, 1986), Liz Stanley and Sue Wise (1993), Patricia Hill Collins (2000), and many others put forth women's experiential knowledge as an important epistemological resource for unmasking the objective and value-neutral pretensions of masculinist science. They argued that experience provided a basis for an alternative, critical feminist epistemology grounded in the material, social, and cultural realities of women's lives.[14]

The ascendancy of postmodernism made this project considerably more complicated, however. In a seminal essay with the telling title "Experience" (1992), Joan Scott challenged the appeal to women's authentic experience as a basis for feminist epistemology. She argued that the general assumption that experience could provide an "originary point of explanation," let alone "incontestable evidence," rested on theoretical quicksand (24). In her view, experience was strictly a "linguistic event," which had no independent existence outside the language and discourses that constructed it (34). Scott's use of the "linguistic turn" to critically interrogate the centrality of experience for feminist epistemology has been highly influential. It has been taken up by many contemporary feminist theorists as a call to uncover the cultural biases and ideological commitments that inevitably mediate the experiences of individual women. As a result, feminist projects dedicated to recovering women's authentic experiences (or "voices") came to be viewed as hopelessly naive and ill-conceived.

Donna Haraway (1991b) elaborated this theoretical critique of experience by arguing that feminist theory itself could not aspire to a more "truthful" view of the world by drawing on women's experiences. In her view, all knowledge—including feminist knowledge—remained partial and would always be dependent on the social, cultural, and geopolitical location of the knower. Haraway's concept of "situated knowledges" provided a more sophisticated way of conceptually linking experience to the knower's location. Theoretically, it also offered a theoretical (and methodological) model for feminist inquiry into women's experiences, which would be both critical and self-reflexive. Unfortunately, however, Haraway's notion of "situated knowledges" stayed within the confines of her theoretical project of deconstructing the modernist discourses of science. This project, like Scott's, took precedence over, and at times—as we have seen—got in the way of, exploring women's experiences as situated knowledge and of assessing the possibilities this particular form of situated knowledge might have for feminist epistemology.

Without a doubt, Scott, Haraway, and many others have issued an important warning against treating "experience" as self-explanatory. Their reminder that experience is always ideologically mediated by cultural discourses and institutional arrangements is well taken. They have made a strong case for developing a feminist epistemology that can account for how all domains of knowledge, including feminist knowledge, are ideologically constituted and, therefore, cannot be drawn on as an unproblematic source of the "truth."

However, as many feminist scholars have already noted with growing concern, discrediting women's experiences altogether may risk "throwing the baby out with the bathwater" (Varikas 1995, 99). It leaves feminist theorists empty-handed when it comes to understanding how individual women give meaning to their lived experiences and, in particular, how they negotiate the tensions between these experiences and the cultural and institutionalized discourses in which they are embedded. It ignores how women's subjective accounts of their experiences can provide starting points for the critical interrogation of the social, cultural, and political contexts in which these accounts are embedded and from which they derive their meaning (Mediatore 2003). When women's experiences are placed in scare quotes, as just one discourse among many, the possibility that they may not simply reproduce but also disrupt powerful institutionalized discourses is overlooked.[15] In short, postmodern feminist theory produces more problems than it resolves when it discredits women's experiences as an important source of knowledge.

The very notion that feminist scholars should have to choose between treating experience unreflectively as an authentic source of knowledge or rejecting it as ideologically contaminated is itself a "false dilemma" (Alcoff 2000, 45). There is no reason why the postmodern claim that experience is "never epistemologically self-sufficient" cannot be reconciled with a stance that regards experience as "epistemologically indispensable" for feminist theory (45).[16] Feminist theorists don't have to draw on women's experiences in a naively empiricist way, that is, in order to "pin down the truth." Instead they can treat these experiences as an object for further analysis, thereby showing how women in their everyday lives "endure as well as react against discursive practices on multiple bodily, emotional and intellectual levels" (Mediatore 2003, 120). Taking issue with what she calls the "high altitude thinking" of postmodern feminist critiques of experience, Kruks (2001) has argued that it is time to move away from "endless theorizing about theory" and begin the more important task of "retrieving" women's experiences for a more "grounded" theoretical analysis. Individual women's subjective accounts of their experiences and how they affect their everyday practices need to be linked to a critical interrogation of the cultural discourses, institutional arrangements, and geopolitical contexts in which these accounts are invariably embedded and which give meaning to them. In other words, rather than discarding experience as a "suspect" concept, feminist scholars should be devoting their energies to finding ways to *theorize* it (131).

As an epistemological project, *OBOS* resonates with these critiques. It amply demonstrates how women's experiences can be retrieved as a form of sentient, situated knowledge and can be used as a resource for feminist critiques of science and medicine. This knowledge is produced when individual women connect the physical, cognitive, and cultural dimensions of their embodied lives at the site of their bodies.

First, by showing what it feels like to have a particular bodily sensation (from menstrual cramps to labor pains) or to experience specific embodied events (childbirth, breast cancer, or bereavement), *OBOS* constructs women's experiential accounts as sentient knowledge. It draws on the experiences of differently embodied women in order to elaborate what it might be like to live in a specific kind of body—a disabled body, a lesbian body, the body of a woman of color. It does not treat this sentient knowledge as an unproblematic source of the "truth" about all women or even all women in a particular group. Instead women's perceptions, feelings, and understandings are validated as a useful resource in the ongoing, contradictory, and open-ended process of becoming knowledgeable about their bodies. The epistemological use of sentient knowledge produces a kind of "theory in the flesh" (Moya 1997), a theory that explores the physical realities of women's lives, including "our skin color, the land we grew up in, our sexual longings" (135). As theory in the flesh, *OBOS* helps to explain how these physical realities produce the conditions under which women can become knowledgeable and profoundly inform the contours their knowledge can take.

Second, by assembling the experiences of differently located women, *OBOS* explores the material effects of class, "race," and sexuality on women's embodied experiences. These different experiences are contextualized, enabling them to become a situated knowledge about how women's embodied lives are shaped by their living in a specific place at a particular moment in history.[17] While *OBOS* does not deny that women's experiences are shaped by cultural discourses and institutional structures, it does not treat these experiences as merely "discursive constructions" but rather as creative, multilayered, socially situated responses that are only partly ideologically constituted" (Mediatore 2003, 123). Thus, *OBOS* does not take women's experiences at face value, as—in Scott's terms—"revealing" the truth about women's lives but rather makes them discursively available. In this way, women's experiences can become accessible for further interpretation and debate.

Third, *OBOS* employs accounts of women's embodied and embedded experiences more specifically as an essential resource for developing a critical response to the discourses and practices of medicine. By juxtaposing women's experiences with medical knowledge, *OBOS* provides an occasion for a critical encounter between medicine and the embodied particulars of women's lives. It allows women to use their experiences to critically access and, when necessary, question the validity of medical knowledge for their particular health needs and within the specific circumstances of their lives. It counteracts the exclusion of women in the production of knowledge and produces alternative, and often oppositional, interpretations of women's health and health care needs. By drawing attention to the ways in which medicine historically has marginalized, distorted, or pathologized women's bodies, *OBOS* attempts to make it plausible that the use of women's sentient, situated knowledge can help make medicine more reliable, more responsible, and ultimately more responsive to women's health needs.

Women as Epistemic Agents

Contemporary feminist theory has struggled with the problem of how to theorize the relation between power and knowledge and, more specifically, the issue of women's agency. Many feminist theorists have drawn on the work of Michel Foucault, whose conception of power lends itself to exploring how cultural discourses construct femininity, shaping women's identities and embodied experiences, as well as their bodily practices (McNay 1992). Within this perspective, agency is brought about through the interplay between multiple and contradictory discursive systems. This notion of discursive agency has been taken up by feminist body theory to show how gender is continually "performed" through the body (Butler 1989) or to delineate the active participation of women in oppressive regimes of body surveillance and maintenance such as dieting, exercise, or cosmetic surgery (Bartky 1990; Bordo 1993; Davis 1995).

While Foucauldian feminist perspectives acknowledge that women's agency is integral to how discursive power works, they rest on a somewhat uneasy footing when it comes to women's epistemic agency—that is, the actions of embodied subjects capable of rational reflection and able to make experientially based evaluations of existing discourses. For example, Susan Bordo (1993), one of the leading feminist theorists of the body, explains the phenomenon of women's eating disorders as the outcome of a collision between contradictory cultural discourses available to women in Western culture, that is, discourses about femininity, beauty, and possibilities for protest or rebellion. She situates women's agency primarily in their active participation in disciplinary cultural discourses and body practices. From this perspective, women's agency is not necessarily empowering and subversive; it can also be disempowering and compliant. Even when women believe that they are exercising their individual freedoms—for example, when they refuse to eat or "choose" to embark on rigorous regimes of body maintenance—their agency is, in actual fact, merely a discursive by-product of the pernicious discourses of choice that pervade Western culture and channel women's energies into the hopeless quest for the perfect body.

While this strand of feminist theory has been influential in deconstructing the notion of an autonomous female subject, as well as severing the automatic link between women's agency and their empowerment, it is not without its problems.[18] Feminist scholars such as Smith (1990a, 1990b, 1999), Kruks (2001), Mohanty (2003), and others have argued that the focus on agency as an artifact of discourse can obstruct our ability to understand how women actively gain, evaluate, and critically interpret knowledge about themselves, their lives, and the world around them. By exaggerating the pervasive power of cultural discourses to shape women's bodily experiences and body practices, the notion of a female epistemic agent—that is, an agent capable of reflection and intentionality and able to envision a course of action that could (conceivably) empower her—is discredited. The conflation of agency with choice as a cultural discourse allows its dismissal as an erroneous belief in absolute freedom or the ability to act completely in accordance with one's personal wishes. It discounts the messy, ambivalent choices that individuals make in their everyday lives—choices that are neither free nor entirely in accordance with their wishes (Davis 2003). This strand of feminist theory fails to imagine how women might ever mobilize knowledge, embedded as it is in oppressive cultural discourses and institutional arrangements, for their personal empowerment let alone for collective feminist projects aimed at the empowerment of women more generally.

It is here that *OBOS* can be useful for bringing into relief what is missing in postmodern feminist body theory: a conception of epistemic agency that links women's knowledge practices to their possibilities and opportunities for individual and collective empowerment. First, instead of relegating women's agency to a discursive effect, *OBOS* conceives of agency as the outcome of the practical and—to some extent—intentional activities of situated knowers, who continually perceive, interpret, reflect on, and rework their experiences. This conception of agency assumes that women are "practical subjects" who are engaged in projects that "transform something into a further possibility" (Kruks 2001, 120). Women's experiences are not only the product of discourses converging at the site of the female body, but they are also integral to women's practical projects of empowerment. These projects can be anything from becoming more informed to getting support from friends to finding the right kind of professional help. They may also involve accepting the limitations of one's body or acknowledging the limits of medical knowledge. In this way, *OBOS* celebrates the subtle and variegated ways that women act, not in the sense of making clear-cut choices between an array of desirable and less than desirable options but in the sense of how women routinely engage in small acts of resistance and subversion in the context of their "trying to survive" (Lugones 2003).

Second, while *OBOS* proposes a notion of epistemic agency that invariably involves some degree of intentionality, it does not ignore the socially structured relations of power under which women's actions take place. In other words, it does not adopt what Maria Lugones (2003) has criticized as the "highly attenuated understandings of agency in late modernity," which abound in much of contemporary feminist body theory (6). Rather, *OBOS* clearly shows how poverty, poor housing, unemployment, and racism constrain women's possibilities for staying healthy or taking care of themselves and their families. While considerable attention is paid to the ideological effects of cultural discourses—for example, by representing women's bodies as inferior or blaming women for their own health problems rather than, say, environmental pollution or poor nutrition—women are not treated as "cultural dopes" who have had the ideological wool pulled over their eyes.[19] The book draws on a more sociological understanding of agency whereby the individual women are regarded as competent actors with a wide-ranging, intimate, and subtle knowledge of the circumstances in which they live (McNay 2000; Davis 2003, 1988). More specifically, *OBOS* explores the conditions of constraint and enablement under which women can become critical feminist subjects capable of drawing on their sentient, situated knowledge as a resource for generating empowering courses of action with regard to their lives, bodies, and health.

Third, *OBOS* provides a glimpse of how epistemic agency might be linked to resistance and empowerment—a problem that has been the source of some concern among feminist theorists. It shows that resistance to hegemonic discourses and the development of subversive alternatives requires more than a "recycling of existing metaphors and rhetorical strategies" (Mediatore 1998, 121). It requires an ongoing process involving interpretation and critical reflection, as well as the rearticulation of available cultural discourses into alternative forms of knowledge. By delineating the process by which differently situated women come to favor specific concepts or strategies over others and how these decisions are shaped by situational, biographical, and sociopolitical circumstances, *OBOS* contributes to a more comprehensive understanding of the relation between power, knowledge, and agency.[20] It demonstrates that even those who have been marginalized in the production of knowledge can be situated as epistemic agents capable of generating alternative and even oppositional forms of knowledge.

While *OBOS* treats epistemic agency as the sine qua non for the empowerment of women individually and collectively, it is not simply aimed at empowering individual women to become more knowledgeable about their own health. It also allows them an imaginative entry into the experiences of different women and, along with it, the understanding that each woman has her own specific project, depending on the circumstances of her embodiment and the social, cultural, and political context in which she lives. The recognition that others—however differently located—are also involved in intentional projects is what ultimately allows for reciprocity and the possibility of collective action (Kruks 2001, 124–25).[21]

In conclusion, while postmodern feminist theory has focused on the power of discourse to shape women's practices, it has tended to adopt a discursive concept of agency. Viewing agency as a discursive effect, however, makes it difficult to account for how individual women might resist dominant forms of knowledge or produce alternative, oppositional knowledge. In contrast, *OBOS* demonstrates that the recognition of the power of discourse does not automatically have to result in the abandonment of women's epistemic agency. It shows that women are capable of deliberately and strategically interpreting their lives and actively pursuing potentially empowering courses of action. And it provides ample proof of how women can become epistemic agents who are able to critically and reflexively think about medical discourses. Its approach toward agency is not abstract but based on the practical activities of differently located women. As such, it can offer contemporary feminist body theory valuable insights into how, why, and under what circumstances women might actively employ knowledge in the pursuit of an oppositional feminist politics of health.

Bridging the Gap

This chapter opened with a discussion of the dissociation between contemporary feminist body theory and feminist health activism. As case in point, I drew on an essay from a well-known feminist body theorist, Donna Haraway, in which she provides an ironic critique of *OBOS* and, by implication, U.S. feminist health activism. I have taken issue with Haraway's critique not only because it does not do justice to the politics of knowledge that *OBOS* represents but, more important, because it represents a tendency to exacerbate the gap between feminist body theory and feminist health activism. Like Haraway, many postmodern feminist theorists have equated *OBOS* with U.S. feminist health activism, treating it as a political project rather than an epistemological project that is relevant to feminist body theory.[22] The result is a missed opportunity for a potentially more productive mutual exploration of areas of intersection between feminist body theory and feminist health activism and a chance for both to learn from one another about the production and reception of feminist knowledge and knowledge practices.

Contemporary feminist body theory has been primarily engaged in the theoretical project of criticizing essentialist and deterministic notions about the female body, uncovering the discursive underpinnings of women's experiences, and delineating the ways in which women's agency is culturally and socially constructed. While this theoretical project has been important—and of potential value to health activists—it has also distanced itself from the embodied experiences and practices of women in the concrete contexts of their everyday lives. By treating OBOS as nothing more than a "popular book on women's health," feminist theory has ignored the possibility that the situated knowledge practices of feminist activists might have theoretical relevance not only for thinking about the production and reception of feminist knowledge "on the ground" but also for addressing some of the theoretical problems that have plagued feminist body theory since its inception.

By considering *OBOS* as an epistemological project, I have shown how it might contribute to some of the theoretical problems that have concerned feminist body theorists, especially the problems of how to conceptualize the biological female body, women's embodied experience, and women's epistemic agency. While *OBOS* obviously does not completely resolve these problems, it does provide useful ways of thinking about them. It can help "ground" feminist theoretical discussions more firmly in women's sentient and situated knowledge. More specifically, it provides avenues for the development of feminist body theories that are *less* disembodied, less disembedded, and *more* relevant to women's health concerns (Kuhlmann and Babitsch 2002, 433). By joining forces, feminist body theory and feminist health activism could develop a more effective critique of medicine and cultural discourses about women's bodies, as well as a more reflexive and potentially subversive feminist politics of health.

In this chapter, I have focused on the contribution *OBOS* as an epistemological project might make toward bridging the gap between feminist body theory and feminist health activism. However, there are other reasons for taking a closer look at its politics of knowledge. One of the most exciting aspects of *OBOS* as an epistemological project is its capacity to travel across borders of class, race, and sexuality, as well as national and cultural borders. It has invited differently embodied women across the globe to use their specific experiences to engage critically with the authoritative voice of medicine and situate their health concerns in the broader social, cultural, and political context of their lives. It has not only been more than a popular book on women's health; it has also been more than a typically U.S. feminist epistemological project. In the course of being taken up and adapted by different women's groups across the globe, *OBOS* has proved to be a "traveling theory" (Said 1983)—that is, a theory that, through its circulation across borders within and outside the United States, has been able to shape and transform knowledge about women's bodies and health in many other parts of the world. For feminist theorists who have been concerned about the hegemony of First World feminist scholarship, it may well be time to stop focusing on those theories that are most firmly embedded in the context being criticized (Western philosophy, modern medicine, the U.S. academy) and begin considering theories that have demonstrated that they are capable of movement and transformation. It seems to me that for anyone interested in the possibilities of a critical, nonimperialistic, feminist theory, *OBOS* deserves our most serious attention.

As a traveling theory, *OBOS* will be the subject of the remaining chapters of this book. After examining how its politics of knowledge was implemented practically through the interactions between the text and its readers, I will show how *OBOS* was taken up and rearticulated by readers in many different contexts both within and outside the United States. It will then become clear not only why *OBOS* deserves to be called one of the ten most influential books in the past twenty-five years but also how its critical knowledge and knowledge practices could circulate globally, thereby contributing to a transnational feminist body theory and a transnational feminist politics of health.

CHAPTER 5

Creating Feminist Subjects

THE READER AND THE TEXT

In the last chapter, I set out the ingredients of *OBOS* as feminist epistemological project. This project, as we have seen, involves understanding women's biological bodies (without falling into the trap of biological determinism and essentialism), mobilizing women's bodily experiences as a resource for criticizing medical knowledge (without treating this experience as a final arbiter of the truth), and treating women as epistemic agents (without forgetting that such agency is always discursively mediated by the culture in which the knower is located). As a feminist epistemological project, the aim of *OBOS* is to create critical knowledge and knowledge practices that can empower women individually and collectively.

This chapter explores how this epistemological project is accomplished in practice. How does *OBOS*—which is, after all, just a book—produce readers who are prepared to become embodied, critical, epistemic agents able to participate in a feminist politics of health? In other words, how does *OBOS* transform its readers into feminist subjects?

In order to answer these questions, I will be looking more closely at the relationship between *OBOS* as a text and its readers. Drawing on my own response as a reader, as well as other readers' responses in the form of letters written to the authors of *OBOS*, I will confront the "intentions" of the book with an analysis of how the text itself is constructed so that it can be read and interpreted in specific ways by its readers. I analyze how *OBOS* produces a certain kind of reader—an embodied, situated subject who can actively participate in the feminist knowledge project that it represents.

I will be drawing on the work of Dorothy Smith (1990a, 1990b, 1997, 1999), who has developed a sociologically informed methodology for text analysis[1]—an analysis that explores the active and constitutive relationship between texts and readers, as well as the role texts play in organizing and regulating power relations—or what she calls "relations of ruling." Smith is especially concerned with how texts are activated by the interpretative practices of individuals situated in specific historical, social, cultural, and political contexts. She assumes that readers do not simply absorb or passively respond to texts, nor that texts are static objects or assemblages of information. For any text to make sense, the reader must interactively draw on the interpretative methods and schemata that are to some extent "intended" by the text. In this sense, the relationship between the text and the reader can be understood retrospectively by "reading off" the interpretative procedures a reader will need to use in order to understand the meaning of the text. Like Foucault, Smith assumes that texts are embedded in powerful, institutionally structured discourses, which individuals draw on in making sense of the texts and themselves in relation to the texts.[2] Like Foucault, she is also committed to the possibility of subjugated or alternative forms of knowledge. However, in contrast to Foucault who tended to view the individual subject as little more than the discursive effect of the discourses in which he or she is embedded, Smith explores how self-consciously critical knowledge and knowledge practices can emerge in interaction with dominant discourses (Smith 1999, 94).[3] Her work, therefore, provides the methodological tools for analyzing how the text *OBOS* activates readers to become embodied, situated, feminist subjects willing and ready to participate in a feminist politics aimed at empowering women in matters concerning their bodies and health.

In order to show how *OBOS* as text produces feminist subjects, I will begin by analyzing my own interpretative practices as a reader. This is not because my reading of *OBOS* is necessarily typical (although for a certain generation of readers it may well be).[4] It is certainly not the only possible reading of the text and; indeed, it is not even my only reading, which has changed considerably since I encountered the book for the first time in the mid-1970s as a student and feminist activist.[5] However, by delineating how I go about making sense of the text, I can demonstrate, in "the proof is in the pudding" sense, that I have brought to it at least some of the interpretive schemata that the text "intended" (Smith 1990b, 121).

Reading *OBOS*

I open my most recent copy of *OBOS* to the chapter called "Understanding Our Bodies: Sexual Anatomy, Reproduction, and the Menstrual Cycle."[6] This is arguably the heart of the book and concerns the basics of women's health. I am told right off the bat what to expect—this is going to be a chapter about "the appearance and function of our sexual organs" (BWHBC 1998, 269). At this point, I'm expecting diagrams and a bone-dry description of how my hormones work, but instead I am invited as reader to get a mirror, a flashlight, and a speculum and see for myself. "Oh no," I think, "NOT the speculum" (remembering with mixed feelings how popular the practice of cervical self-help was among feminists in the seventies and how difficult it is to explain the practice to my students today). However, the wind is immediately taken out of my sails with an anecdote by another reader, which draws my attention because it is printed in italics.

> When someone first said to me two years ago, "You can feel the end of your own cervix with your finger," I was interested but flustered. I had hardly ever put my finger in my vagina at all and felt squeamish about touching myself there, in that place "reserved" for lovers and doctors. It took me two months to get up my nerve to try it, and then one afternoon, pretty nervously, I squatted down in the bathroom and put my finger in deep, back into my vagina. There it was, feeling slippery and rounded, with an indentation at the center through which, I realized, my menstrual flow came. It was both very exciting and beautifully ordinary at the same time. Last week I bought a plastic speculum so I could look at my cervix. (269–70)

It's pretty clear that the authors think it's a good idea to try this: "We find that the vagina is very clean and that normal touching, as in self-examination, is not painful or uncomfortable" (269). The personal account confirms this and is reassuring for the hesitant reader who isn't entirely sure she wants to go there. The result is an invita-

34 ✳ Self-examination. (Photo courtesy of Hazel Hankin.)

tion without pressure to explore the body, with or without a speculum.

This sets the stage for an account of the appearance and function of
women's sexual organs. The text is written for an audience of female
readers, that is, readers with female sexual organs, who are further
drawn into the text as active subjects, becoming informed and informing themselves about their bodies: "The following description
will be much clearer if you look at yourself with a mirror while you
read . . . as you spread your legs apart, you can see . . ." (270). The text
is accompanied by a photograph, which depicts a naked woman sitting on a bed looking at her genitals with a mirror.

The photograph and the text are meant to encourage the reader
to actively explore her body. This is not necessarily how it works, of
course. As we saw in chapter 4, Donna Haraway (1999) has criticized
the practice of using a speculum to view the cervix on no uncertain terms, calling it a misguided attempt by early feminist activists
to reclaim their bodies and comparing it to the European colonialist venture in which lands and peoples were "discovered" and "con-
quered" (67). This particular photograph, however, has also been an
eye-opener for many readers, perhaps because it is slightly shocking.

Since I have been doing this research, many women have told me that this particular photograph was, in fact, the first thing they remembered about *OBOS* ("That picture with the woman looking at her genitals in the mirror—I'd never seen anything like it before!").

The accompanying text focuses on what the reader can see unaided or with the help of her trusty mirror. When it finally turns to the inner organs, they are presented surprisingly under the rubric "Reproductive Organs You Can't See." For the first time, a diagram appears, depicting the uterus, fallopian tubes, and ovaries, not unlike the diagrams that are standard fare in most medical anatomy texts. As a reader, however, I have already been positioned in this text as an active and embodied subject, and it is now much more difficult for me to "read" this diagram as a disjointed assemblage of body parts.

As a feminist reader, I'm not surprised to discover that this text gives the clitoris pride of place. Most medical texts focus on the uterus and ovaries, thereby making reproduction rather than sexual pleasure central to women's sexual anatomy. In *OBOS*, however, the reader is led straight to the clitoris with a step-by-step account of how sexual arousal works. The clitoris, not the vagina, is compared to the penis—"Did you know that the clitoris is similar in origin and function to the penis? All female and male organs . . . are developed from the same embryonic tissue" (272)—thereby separating sexuality from (heterosexual) intercourse. The text is devoid of medical jargon that might alienate the reader or compel her to view her body from a distance as an object for medical interventions. The language is mundane and sensual, inviting the reader to imagine each body part and how it feels. For example, the shaft of the clitoris is described as "a hardish, rubbery, movable cord right under the skin. It is sometimes sexually arousing if touched" (271). Sight is not the only sense being mobilized, and here again the text departs from the tendency of modern science to privilege vision.[7] For example, the reader is urged to learn about her menstrual cycle by noting how the cervix changes, feeling the differences in vaginal secretions, and even tasting them: "They can be sour, salty, or sweet, changing during the cycle in a pattern typical for you" (277). It is very difficult *not* to be embodied when reading this text!

Stories abound about other women's experiences with their bodies and bodily functions.[8] These accounts are set apart from the rest of the text by italics, catching the reader's attention. Take, for example, the stories about menstruation, which occupy about half of this chapter. They range from the lyrical ("I like to think of the menstrual cycle as a symphony played by a hormonal orchestra" [276]) to the despairing ("A week before my period comes I go through a few days of feeling more helpless, stuck or down about things in my life" [282]) to the more practical and matter-of-fact ("I try to limit myself to using tampons only when I think I really need to" [278]). These statements attest to the diversity of women's experiences, underscoring, at the same time, that menstruation is more than a physiological event.

As I scan these stories, I can't help but remember my own. They come back in a rush, from the ambivalent feelings of getting my first period to the routine management and hassle of periods to the discomfort of menstrual cramps to—finally—the utter relief at being able to bid menstruation farewell. I find myself nodding in recognition at experiences that resemble my own ("As I entered menopause, my periods started coming less often. After several period-free months, another period would surprise me, and back I would be, scrambling for tampons and a heating pad. I'd feel 'Oh my God, isn't this finished.'" [280]) and astonished at others ("I'd feel nostalgic and a little sad, like this might be the last period I'd ever have" [280]). The sheer variety of the stories serves as a reminder of how varied women's experiences are and how each woman has her own story to tell.

At this point in the chapter, I'm beginning to wonder what happened to the medical story of menstruation, which was standard fare in most U.S. schools while I was growing up. Where are the complicated hormonal secretions, developing follicles, eggs awaiting fertilization, and endometrial linings building up and disintegrating? Like most white, middle-class, U.S. women, I had absorbed this story in my physical education classes at school.[9] *OBOS* tells the medical story, too, but in a language that reflects the long tradition of feminist critiques of medical discourse on women's bodily functions.[10] Susan Bell, one of the authors of the chapter on birth control in *OBOS*, describes how she incorporated these insights by replacing the metaphors of "failure" so prevalent in medical literature (menstruation as "failed" reproduction) with an account of menstruation as a creative process that varies enormously among women (Bell 1994, 57).

Thus, what remains of the medical story is an informative and accessible description of follicle development, cyclical changes in hormonal secretions, and transformations in the uterine lining during the menstrual cycle along with an appendix with the reassuring title "Hormones of the Menstrual Cycle Simplified." While I find myself reading with interest about the newly identified ovarian hormones, I am also gratified that the text acknowledges the complexity of hormones, thereby reassuring me that I may not be the only one who gets glassy-eyed at the thought of having to sort out which hormone is being secreted at which point in the menstrual cycle.

In *OBOS*, the medical story does not stand on its own, detached from the contexts of women's everyday lives. This story is situated instead in the context in which women live and includes the everyday management of menstrual flows (along with a critical discussion of tampons, feminine deodorant sprays, and toxic shock syndrome), cultural attitudes about menstruating women (from taboos about refraining from exercise, showers, or sexual intercourse during menstruation to the widespread belief that women who menstruate are "inherently instable" or subject to unpredictable mood swings), women's subjective feelings about menstruation, and—last but not least—menstrual problems. The list of menstrual complaints is long and includes everything from routine cramps, depression, anemia, and excessive bleeding to the absence of periods. Each problem is accompanied by a list of home remedies (herbal teas, improved nutrition, exercise, massage) or practical suggestions such as "Get support for yourself for times when you feel worst. Ask close friends to drop by, involve the rest of the family more in running the household, or ask someone to help with the kids" (282).

The focus of the text is on *healthy* bodies, on menstruation as a *normal* process, and on menstrual complaints as something *remediable* without recourse to the medical profession. It contrasts dramatically with medical discourse, which transforms even the most harmless complaints into objects for medical intervention. Nowhere is the critical stance toward medicine more apparent than in the way the text deals with premenstrual syndrome (PMS), a complaint that has received considerable medical attention in recent years.[11] The term *PMS* is placed in scare quotes in the text, underlining its status as a medical construct. The reader is immediately alerted that the term is just an interpretation and cannot be assumed to be factual or objective just because it belongs to the arsenal of medical knowledge. While the text reiterates that menstrual pain is a serious matter, the more pressing "concern" for the authors of *OBOS* is that medical professionals and drug companies "have picked up on PMS" and used it as an excuse to prescribe, and sell, more medications to women (281). Given that many of these treatments are expensive, have side effects, and do not necessarily do the job of eliminating menstrual complaints, the reader is advised, "If we help each other increase our self-esteem, and feel more comfortable with our moods as well as our anger, we may experience many of our premenstrual signs differently. We may also feel more empowered to define what our specific premenstrual problems are and to explore appropriate care for them without accepting a medicalization of the whole experience" (281–82).

It is here that my particular reading experience takes a more ambivalent turn. For me, it is the sudden act of being enfolded into an encompassing "we" that makes my internal red light begin to blink. Unconvinced that the "we" means "me," I find myself taking a more critical stance, prepared to read against the grain of the text. On the one hand, I agree *in theory* with the critique of medicalization that pervades the text. I know that PMS has been used to categorize all women as potentially unstable, sick, and even potentially homicidal. Moreover, the notions that women should accept a certain degree of "crankiness," or deserve special consideration or should be allowed to take time off from work "at that time of the month" are refreshing and even have a slightly subversive ring.[12] On the other hand, I remember all too well the debilitating menstrual cramps I used to have. While they were not labeled PMS at the time, I know how utterly relieved I was when my family physician took my distress seriously enough to give me a prescription for heavy painkillers. I doubt that I would have been satisfied—let alone felt empowered—with an admonishment to accept my moods or try some herbal remedies in the interest of avoiding medicalization. Thus, at the point in which a specific conception of shared experience and collective empowerment does not fit my knowledge of my own experiences, I find myself taking up a resistant position. While I may be prepared to accept that medicalization *in principle* is not a desirable framework for understanding women's health, I find myself balking at the assumption of a collective "we" in this *particular* instance. It is this "disjuncture"—as Dorothy Smith (1990a, 1990b) calls it—between my local knowledge and the collective ideology of the text that compels me to reject the antimedicalization stance for the time being—or at least regard it with some suspicion until I can see how it might include my particular experience.

This is, of course, just one reading of a fragment of *OBOS*, and it is, admittedly, idiosyncratic. While it shows how the text produces a certain kind of reader—embodied, sentient, using her experiences to critically interrogate both dominant and feminist discourses of women's health—the question remains of how the text is read by other readers—readers who are differently located than I am and will bring different experiences to the text. Given that *OBOS* has sold over four million copies during the past three decades and has been read by many more readers than that, learning how each and every reader responded to the book would be a "mission impossible." While I have no way of knowing what effect the book had on most of these readers or how it influenced their lives, some readers took the time and effort to write letters to the BWHBC. They wrote letters to explain what *OBOS* had meant to them and to share their bodily experiences, the problems they had encountered with health professionals, and the remedies they had tried. They did not hesitate to suggest new topics or advocate changes for future editions. While many readers expressed appreciation, recounting what *OBOS* had meant to them, others were critical of the book. But all indicated that they wanted to help other women learn from their experiences.

Not all of these letters have survived the ravages of time. Although the BWHBC always responded to these letters, neither the letters nor their responses were collected in a systematic way. Some letters were passed on to the authors of specific chapters for use in future revisions of *OBOS* and were incorporated on the pages of updated versions of the book. Still others found their way into filing cabinets or boxes, only to disappear when the files were finally transferred to an archive in 2000. However, a small corpus of letters has survived, and it is to these letters that I shall now turn.[13]

These letters are not necessarily representative of all the women (and men) who have read *OBOS* over the past three decades. They do not include the many women (and men) who briefly encountered the book at some point in their lives—perhaps while waiting in a clinic or taking a quick peek at a copy on the shelves of the local supermarket. They do not encompass the hundreds of women who called the office or contacted individual members of the group to relate their experiences and suggestions. Nor do they include the detailed comments from individual readers and groups, who specifically read the various versions of *OBOS*, paying particular attention to the exclusions of class, race, sexuality, able-bodiedness, or age.[14] The letters I discuss here were written by a fairly select group of readers—readers who were presumably inspired or concerned enough to want to write the authors of *OBOS* and had the opportunity and confidence in their ability to express themselves to do so. As a critical reviewer of *OBOS* once noted, the impoverished drug addict or pregnant teen would probably be unlikely to read the book. Its readers are more likely to be "educated, competent, mature, assertive women"—not unlike the authors of *OBOS* (Rooks 1985, 239).

However, even if these letters do not represent the impoverished drug addict or the pregnant teen, they provide a unique opportunity for analyzing how the text could generate a particular kind of reading, as well as a reader who could participate in the politics of knowledge that *OBOS* represents. It is my contention that this relationship between the text and the reader can also help us to understand the book's popularity and the significance of its epistemological project both within and outside the United States.

"Dear Collective . . .": Letters from the Readers

From the first edition in 1970 until the present, readers have written letters to the authors of *OBOS*. The letters came from all over the United States, from small towns in the South ("We're rather behind the times here") to large East Coast cities. While most of the letters were from North American women, some came from places as far away as Russia, Kenya, and Guatemala. Women wrote from their homes ("I write you on a Sunday night, it's late, I have just finished reading and my little daughter has fallen asleep and I give free rein to write this),[15] their workplaces, or prison ("Please keep writing and please stay in contact. Please").[16] Many of the letters were handwritten, especially during the seventies and early eighties. Others were typed. Later readers wrote to the BWHBC by e-mail. Some readers signed their names, and included addresses and telephone numbers, while others remained anonymous, ending their letters with initials or simply something like "A Florida Reader."

The Readers ✳ The letters came from women of widely different ages. Take, for example, a letter from a high school girl who is worried because she has been having sexual fantasies about her best friend, which reads, "I just want some input about my feelings and what you think I should do. Do you ever get letters like this with women not really sure of their identity. . . . I live with my parents, my mom would freak if a letter came back with a business name from a women's thing . . . [so] could you write a first and last name and a return address on it. Once I open it and read it, I'll realize who it's from. Thanks!"[17]

A middle-aged reader wrote that she had been married for more than twenty years without knowing anything about her body or sexuality: "This book inspired me to educate myself. . . . My girls and boys will not be married for *two* years before they begin to understand and not fear their bodies."[18] Some readers were married, others single; some had children, others did not; and some wanted to have them but couldn't. Readers were "women-identified," bisexual, heterosexual, or in some cases celibate. Although the letters were generally from women, occasionally a man would write to say that *OBOS* had helped him understand better what his girlfriend was going through (an abortion) or to thank the authors for having made a useful reference book. Many expressed a wish that a similar book for men was available. Some readers were students and others were full-time homemakers, but most were professional women (clerical workers, educators, nurses, social workers, parish counsellors, physicians). An occasional reader wrote from overseas where she was working as a Peace Corps volunteer, a missionary, or a worker in a governmental development project.

Most of the letters appear to have been written by readers with some education and a middle-class background. Race—one of the most fundamental categories of exclusion in the United States—was not addressed directly in the letters, and most readers did not identify themselves racially. In a racialized context where whiteness is treated by many white people as being without race, a condition of invisibility not available to people of color, this would indicate that many of the letters were probably written by white, Anglo-American women. The exceptional letter in which the reader mentions her racial background ("I'm 23, half Hispanic and white and am trying to pay off my college loans. . . . I would be forever grateful if you knew of a doctor I could see before my next pap tells me I might have cancer.")[19]

does not focus on race explicitly but rather on the problem of having had a "bad" pap smear and not enough money to pay a doctor's fees. Many letters, however, dealt with issues that have been of particular concern for women of color in the United States. For example, letters about sterilization abuse came from readers who felt that *OBOS* needed to stand up more for the rights of single mothers not to be forced to have tubal ligations just because they were on welfare.[20] One of the early critiques of the white women's health movement addressed its emphasis on abortion and neglect of the issue of sterilization abuse as central to women's reproductive rights. This does not mean that readers of *OBOS* did not, over the years, express their concerns about the way the text dealt with issues of race and racism. Many readers have been critical of the lack of attention paid to the perspectives of women of color and low-income women in early editions of *OBOS*, resulting in significant changes in later editions of the book. These changes were due to the active involvement of women of color in the overall conceptualization of the book, the writing of chapters, the editing, and the critical reading of every chapter to ensure that it was "as inclusive and accessible as possible for a wide variety of women."[21]

It is not surprising that many of the letters to *OBOS* came from feminists (or the daughters of feminists). A Chilean feminist living in exile, for example, wrote a lengthy letter about her political work with rural women in Colombia, which read, "In the provinces we go out on the roads and sit under a tree, surrounded by women with children, women who have never been able to learn to read, and tell them with love about *Nuestros Cuerpos, Nuestras Vidas*. It is necessary to break the barriers of idiom, language and inhibition; it is necessary to go out and give them—give ourselves—aid."[22]

More surprising, however, were the letters from women who were not feminists. Take, for example, a reader who described herself as a "born-again Christian." She had been warned by Jerry Falwell, the leader of the Moral Majority, about the dangers of *OBOS*, and he had urged his constituency to work to get the book banned from school libraries.[23] She wrote that she and her husband had been curious about what "all the fuss" was about and decided to have a look for themselves. She admitted that, while they didn't agree with everything in the book, they had found it, on the whole, to be useful and informative. She enclosed a letter that she had written to "Reverend

Falwell," in which she chastised him for his short-sightedness and informed him that the topics dealt with in *OBOS* were "far from immoral." In fact, as she put it, "the only immoral thing is the ignorance of them."[24]

The Letters * Most of the letters opened with an expression of appreciation. "Dear Wonderful Authors of OUR BODIES, OURSELVES," began one reader. "I have always read and . . . loved your book."[25] "I had to write you to let you know that the book is AWESOME and me & my friends are enjoying it."[26] Readers wrote that they had purchased every copy of the book they could find and had given them to friends and women in their families. "My husband likes your book, too," was a frequent postscript. Readers often expounded on how much the book had meant to them. "As I read your book," one related, "I was shocked at how ignorant I was about my body. . . . Thank you for publishing this book as I imagine it has helped many women, including myself."[27] In addition to having their eyes opened by what they read in *OBOS*, many readers expressed relief simply at discovering that they were not alone. A reader who had been suffering from bouts of depression wrote, "It may be hard for you to comprehend how your work could have such a profound effect on someone, but I've never felt so strengthened, purposeful, and serene. I know now that I'm not alone."[28] "When I realize how similar my feelings are to some of the letters in your book, it is indeed reassuring!" explained another reader, who had been struggling with the side effects of prolonged use of an intrauterine device (IUD) for contraception.[29] "It was the first book that told me I wasn't crazy, [that] there was something wrong with my cycles, and it gave me the tools to help the doctor figure it out."[30]

While readers often asked for advice or information about their health problems, they did not position themselves as passive recipients, nor did they approach the authors of *OBOS* as undisputed authorities on women's health. The letters were written as though *OBOS* (or its authors) were a good friend or family member ("I don't know who else to turn to" appeared in many letters). Or, as one reader confided, "You are the mother I never had."[31] Readers seemed to assume that *OBOS*—and, by implication, its authors—would want to hear about their experiences and would give them serious attention.

The letters often contained detailed accounts of the writer's bodily experiences: her feelings about sexuality, her health problems, and even her entire life history. Take, for example, this reader, who wrote at length about how *OBOS* helped her get through a particularly rough night during her second month of pregnancy. She described how she woke up in a panic and called her sister, who fortunately owned a copy of the book and read passages to her over the phone to calm her down. "It so perfectly reflected my feelings that I started to cry," she wrote, and "later she gave me your book which I have been gobbling up ever since."[32]

Many readers had medical "atrocity stories" to tell, tales about physicians who had treated them in demeaning or neglectful ways or about the inadequacies of the health care system in general. They described being dissatisfied with the lack of information about side effects of medications or the risks of various procedures. For example, a pregnant reader recounted how her physician diagnosed her as having an ectopic pregnancy and sent her home without telling her about the risks of rupture or internal bleeding.[33] Dissatisfied with this meager information, she looked it up for herself in *OBOS* and was able to admit herself to the hospital when she realized that her fallopian tube had ruptured. Other readers were angry at the arrogant or paternalistic attitudes of physicians. For example, a reader with severe vaginitis complained at length about her gynecologist, who had ridiculed her concerns about what was to him just "an everyday complaint."[34] "But," she wrote, "I just told him, '*I* itch, you don't.'"[35]

Readers seemed prepared to trust their own experiences with their bodies. In their letters to *OBOS*, they displayed unmistakable pride in how they were able to use these experiences to become informed about their bodies and their health or to ask critical questions. Their letters demonstrated that they were able to unmask and even reject definitions and treatments put forth by the medical profession as not always being "for their own good."[36]

Many letters contained requests for information about health problems. These problems ranged from herpes, depression, and pelvic inflammatory disease to sterilization procedures, prenatal screening, and cesarean births to breast cancer, substance abuse, and miscarriages. Some letters contained requests for an address of a female physician or a support group. But readers also frequently offered suggestions for remedies and treatments that they had tried themselves.

They recounted at length what had worked (or hadn't worked) for them. Some of these remedies were as mundane as the use of unscented soap to combat chronic urinary infections: "When I think of all the things doctors gave me to use for something so simple, I realize that if I simply [had] used my and my mother's and my sister's common sense, we would have solved the problem years earlier. They all knew to watch out for soaps."[37]

This reader also warns against too much reliance on medical authorities, emphasizing the importance of women's local knowledge about their bodies. Others provided detailed and assessable instructions on how to use home remedies. One suggested that women should "Take one or two tablets of Lactinex, grind them up (between two spoons is OK) and use them in a 1 quart douche. . . . When symptoms recur, repeat. . . . Adding a little (a glug) of vinegar to the douche water probably helps a smidgen (it would help a *lot more* if some women in college chemistry I worked out what the preferred solution should be; vinegar alone won't hold its acid pH for much time at all; no wonder it hardly works")."[38]

This letter combines a veiled critique of medicine and its lack of attention to women's complaints with an encouragement to women that they take their health in their own hands and experiment until they get it right. The reader's "recipe" concludes with an embodied reminder that is bound to speak to any woman who has tried to douche while standing in a cold tub: "The nicest way to douche is after a bath or shower with the drain closed so the tub doesn't freeze you to death."

Advice ranged from how to live with cervical polyps to staying "healthy with little money" and even how to masturbate: "It may surprise you but in talking to my women friends . . . I find a great ignorance of and desire for information—instructions, actually—on female masturbation! They would be delighted to find information on masturbating. . . . I am eagerly anticipating the release of your new *OBOS* and hope you will take into serious consideration my words."[39]

While the advice and remedies were varied, they were always represented as provisional, as something that had worked for a particular woman rather than as a blanket solution for all women. However, in sharing these experiences readers also made it clear that they had written precisely because they wanted their knowledge to be made available to a broader audience; they wanted it to help other women. The letters show how the readers of *OBOS*, through their experiences with their bodies and encounters with the health care system, situated themselves within a broader project. Many indicated explicitly that they hoped their letters would be included in further editions of *OBOS* ("You can use this letter if you want to" or "Maybe this information will help others").

Not all readers embraced *OBOS*. In fact, many were quick to express their criticisms of the book. Readers sometimes noted that the information provided in *OBOS* was not always complete or adequate. For example, one reader complained that cone biopsy had been described in *OBOS* as a routine diagnostic test for cervical cancer that "may lead to complications during future pregnancies." As she put it, this was both "gratuitous and irresponsible. Either explain it or don't say it, as far as I'm concerned."[40] The authors took her comments to heart in the next edition of *OBOS* and provided a more balanced account of the procedure and its value but also its risks.[41]

Another reader described her dismay at reading in the 1992 edition of *OBOS* that "ovarian cysts are relatively common and don't cause any symptoms of discomfort" and that a change of diet and acupuncture to reduce stress were recommended.[42] Incensed, she complained, "I came to you looking for practical, concise information and I feel as though I got a pat on the head and told to run along."[43]

Readers clearly expected *OBOS* to address their needs, and when it failed they felt called on to set the record straight. For example, one reader, disappointed with the way *OBOS* had dealt with women's decision to live without children, wrote, "I'd like to see that counted as a valid life choice in the next *OBOS*, so that other young women will know that it's okay to choose not to be a mom if they so desire."[44] While some readers felt that too much attention was given to particular groups (mothers), other readers felt that too little attention was being paid to their problems. For example, a reader who had just had a miscarriage wrote, "While I was reading about the *loss* of my babies, my peripheral vision was picking up your photos on page 176 of beautiful, fully pregnant women! Somehow it added to the envy and sadness I was feeling. . . . I write to you because perhaps you were unaware that the book is put together in this way. Your book is wonderful. My intent is to give you some feedback."[45]

Readers were not simply concerned that *OBOS* had given incomplete coverage to issues important to women's health or that they had been unsympathetic to how certain bodily experiences might feel to particular women. They were sometimes openly critical of its political perspective. For example, some readers took issue with its undisguised pro-choice standpoint. A college student wrote that, while she appreciated the concern for "everyday women's feelings" in *OBOS*, she was also worried about what she called its "oversights." She reminded the authors that many women find abortion "appalling and emotionally disturbing" and are not helped by the "bad rap" given to adoption as a valid choice for women. "Your slight to pro-life women is serious. . . . This oversight is an injustice, not only to your book, but to all your readers."[46] In a similar vein, another reader complained that *OBOS* had not given an "honest & fair sample of comments from women who have had an abortion." She proceeded to list the instances in the book where abortion was treated as "no big deal," thereby ignoring the "suffering and painful remorse" a woman might feel when she may have made the wrong decision. This reader also worried that a young woman reading *OBOS* might get the idea that abortion was an "easy answer." "Although abortion seems like a 'life saver' to women with an unwanted pregnancy, it also can harm women, too. I think this should be represented in your book."[47] The occasional reader was openly hostile, as, for example, in this letter, which was forwarded to the BWHBC from a local newspaper. This irate reader criticized *OBOS* for condoning "sexual promiscuity, lesbianism and abortion." While she acknowledged that the "scientific news" could be useful, it was "like hunting for palatable food in a garbage can, for the depravity described is beyond words. . . . I am strongly tempted to burn it."[48] However, most letters were milder in their critique and aimed toward improving rather than abolishing the book. Some readers worried that *OBOS* was equating sexuality too strictly with heterosexuality, while others were concerned about the missing perspective of the younger reader: "Keep in mind . . . there are lots . . . of young women that need this book as much as the women going through menopause. Keep it as a book for *all*, not just the maturing ones."[49]

Taken together, the letters demonstrate how readers used their experiences to engage critically with medical diagnoses and treatments and to develop interpretations and courses of action that made sense to them. They offered these experiences, interpretations, and courses of action as evidence of how reading *OBOS* had empowered them individually. They were not simply interested in providing individual testimonies, however. They also wanted their letters to help other women, and they saw themselves as part of a larger project of knowledge making—a project that was what *OBOS* was all about.

The Collective Responds ✳ The letters did not go unanswered. Most received an individual response from one of the members of the BWHBC. This was especially true during the first two decades of *OBOS*. Typically, their responses would provide information that had been requested about complaints or remedies, replete with lists of medical and other references and mailing lists of support groups for women with similar experiences. In some cases, collective members would bring in their personal experiences if they were relevant to the topic at hand ("I've had herpes, too"). More often than not, they would indicate the limitations of their knowledge ("I am far from expert on this subject") and would apologize to readers because their information was inadequate. They explained that they, too, were constantly stumbling over the problem of having to make sense of medical practices about which there was very little real evidence. However, they explained, they wanted to give each woman every possible resource for challenging medical and cultural dogmas about women's health. As one collective member put it, "So often there is no proof and so often women *can* with courage and determination (and the support of other women) triumph over these negative prognoses. . . . Women sometimes get stampeded into accepting an emergency treatment because a doctor feels he *must* do it in order to treat the condition responsibly and only afterwards do the women discover that there may be complications resulting from the treatment which they weren't told about or that alternative treatments were available."[50]

The authors of *OBOS* were effusive in their expressions of gratitude for readers' letters and often assured letter writers that their letters would be taken into account during the process of revising *OBOS*. Take, for example, a reader who complained that *OBOS* had "let her down at a crucial time" in her life (she had had a therapeutic abortion after testing positive for Tay-Sachs disease). She received the following response from one of the members of the collective.

> I feel very much humbled by your letter . . . and appreciate the time you took to help us make the abortion chapter of *OBOS* more careful and compassionate. It is letters like yours that help us make the book better, but it is always a sorrow for us that someone suffered for what we did or didn't say. In this case, it was both factual information that was missing *and* sensitivity to the emotional experience of someone who was not happy or at least relieved to end the pregnancy. Thank you very much for writing. We will try to improve the abortion chapter . . . Also enclosed are a few items you may find of interest.[51]

The letters from readers, along with the responses from members of the collective, had consequences for the development of *OBOS*. They ensured that new topics were put on the agenda of the collective's meetings, where they were discussed at length. Experiences were used—with the permission of the reader—in future editions of the book. In fact, the enormous expansion of the book's scope and length was directly linked to the ongoing input of readers and the collective's desire to be responsive to their concerns.

The collective's response to the letters represented a commitment to a specific politics of knowledge. It acknowledged the situated, partial character of all knowledge, warning not only about the limits and uncertainties of medical knowledge but about the limitations of their own knowledge as well. Ultimately, each woman was responsible for contextualizing knowledge and determining what was or was not relevant for the particularities of her own situation. This stance was in stark contrast to the objective neutrality adopted in medical discourse—what Haraway calls the "god-trick" (1991b, 189). It illustrated the feminist politics of location adopted by *OBOS*, which recognized the historical contingency of all knowledge claims and knowing subjects, while at the same time maintaining a commitment to a "faithful account of the 'real' world . . . one that can be partially shared and friendly to earth-wide projects of finite freedom, adequate material abundance, modest meaning in suffering, and limited happiness" (187).

It could be said that *OBOS* is a specific kind of text that creates a specific kind of reader. While not all readers will adopt exactly the same reading position in their encounters with *OBOS*, the text itself systematically generates a specific relationship between the text and the reader, mobilizing the reader as an embodied, situated subject who can use her experiences as a critical epistemic resource to take control over her own body and health. Based on my analysis of my own and other readers' responses to *OBOS*, I will now draw conclusions concerning three central features of this relationship.[52] The first concerns the "active" nature of the text, which not only regulates and organizes the experiences and local practices of its readers but is itself "activated" through their interpretative practices. The second concerns the way the text creates "disjunctures" between women's local knowledge and dominant forms of knowledge (medicine). And, finally, I will discuss how the disjunctures between the actualities of individual women's lived experience and the universalizing, disembodied discourses for thinking about these experiences can be exploited by readers, thereby opening up avenues for a critical feminist politics of knowledge.

Activating the Reader * Like any text, *OBOS* not only regulates and organizes the experiences of its readers but is itself "activated" through their interpretative practices (Smith 1990b, 121). The text is constructed in such a way that the reader is constantly compelled to consider her *own* body: its appearance, how it works, its regularities and idiosyncrasies, and what her particular embodiment means for the myriad practical contexts of her everyday life. This is done pictorially (through representations of women looking at themselves with speculum and mirror), as well as through textual references to the fleshy, sensual, sentient body (a body with weight and substance, a body that can be touched, smelled, tasted, perceived). In contrast to medical texts, which position the reader outside the text as a disembodied, disembedded subject who views the body as an object (Haraway 1991a), *OBOS* draws the reader into the text as an embodied, situated subject. It is from this position that she then embarks on a process of becoming knowledgeable. She is invited to think about her

own body at the same time she reads the text, to imagine her interactions with her body and through her body with the world around
her. The text activates her to become *both* an active knower *and* a
body to be known, subject and object, all in one.

In addition to imaginatively situating the reader in her own body,
the text instructs the reader to remember that her body—as well
as the bodies of other women—has a specific history and is located
in the specific circumstances of their life. This is accomplished
through myriad personal stories, offset in italics so that they immediately draw the reader's attention, in which differently embodied
and differently located women describe their bodily experiences,
interactions with others, and everyday living and working situations.
Written in the first person and full of contextual detail, these stories
include their authors' feelings and opinions about their bodies and
health, as well as the actions they have taken, what has helped and
what has not, and what this has meant to their overall well-being.
The reader cannot help but recall her own stories: how she experienced *her* first menstrual period, how *she* has felt about her sexuality,
or what menopause has meant to *her*. The stories of other women
also invite the reader to make comparisons. She automatically reads
her experiences back into the text, where they "flesh out" the already available testimonies of the other women. She may see her
experience as just one more instance of a shared concern. Or she
may regard it as the experience that has been left out but needs to
be mentioned. Or she may see her story as an important contrast
to the others. But, regardless of how she situates her story vis-à-vis
the others, she participates in one of the central features of *OBOS*'s
epistemological project, namely, the assumption that the acknowledgment of women's embodied experiences in all their diversity is
essential to a feminist politics of knowledge about women's health.

Debunking Medical Discourse * As a text, *OBOS* draws extensively
on medical knowledge concerning women's bodies and health. While
the reader is encouraged to inform herself, she is, at the same time,
instructed not to take medical knowledge at face value. Medical
knowledge is presented in such a way that the reader is reminded
of the "relations of ruling" inherent in the way medical knowledge
presents itself as unassailably factual and objective while hiding the
conditions, as well as the subjects (primarily white, heterosexual,

professional men), of its own production (Smith 1990b). The text accomplishes this in several ways.

To begin with, it debunks the privileged position of medical knowledge, by underlining the uncertainty inherent in all medical findings and stressing the limits of current medical knowledge. Controversies about treatments are acknowledged and left to the reader to judge. While undermining the logic of science that presents information as seamlessly factual, the text avoids paralyzing readers with so much confusion and uncertainty that they will be unable to make responsible decisions about their bodies and health (Bell 1994, 57). Information is therefore presented in an accessible fashion while at the same time health problems are treated as complex, often having complicated aetiologies as well as contradictory prognoses. There is never just one remedy for any given problem, and no remedy is ever a panacea. The reader is instructed to be wary of unnecessary treatments and to look for other courses of action before turning to more invasive procedures.

The text not only forces the reader to become aware of the limitations of medical knowledge, however. It also continually juxtaposes medical knowledge with women's local experiential knowledge, whereby neither is given absolute precedence over the other. Medical knowledge (and, for that matter, any form of knowledge) will always need to be interrogated against the specifics of the reader's own body and health needs because problems and remedies have different meanings for different women depending on their experiences and the circumstances of their lives.

It is through this juxtaposition of medical knowledge and local knowledge that the text creates the possibility of disjunctures—that is, moments when women's local knowledge fails to fit neatly into the powerful institutionalized discourses and practices of medicine (Smith 1990a, 92). This is not to say that experience is treated as an unproblematic criterion for assessing the truth. Just as the reader is frequently reminded of the ways in which medicine is fallible, she is instructed to view her embodied experiences as socially and culturally mediated, always embedded in the contexts in which they occur. Experience, however, can be a resource, a touchstone, or a starting point in the process of becoming knowledgeable (Smith 1990a, 104). While the process may begin with the retrieval and authorization of women's experience ("How does this apply to me?"), it is expected to continue as an ongoing, open-ended, and reflexive critical assessment of all forms of knowledge.

Empowering Knowledge Practices ∗ As a text, *OBOS* mobilizes the reader to take a critical stance toward medical knowledge and practice—a stance that is the sine qua non of any feminist politics of health. By creating a disjuncture between women's local knowledge about their bodies and the medical knowledge available to women for understanding their health, the text allows the reader to discover the "relations of ruling" (Smith 1990a, 1990b) that are produced and reproduced within institutionalized forms of knowledge. As we have seen, this is precisely what happened in the text's treatment of premenstrual syndrome as a medical construct rather than an objective fact. The reader is alerted to the ways in which this construct removes menstruation from the actualities of women's lives, transforming it into a feminine pathology requiring medical intervention.[53] The text redefines PMS as a "menstrual problem" and relocates it in the context of women's everyday embodied experience and the material conditions in which they live and work. Without minimizing the importance of getting professional help, the text demonstrates the variety and creativity of strategies available to women for helping themselves.

Even a cursory glance at *OBOS* makes clear that the text is not simply debunking medical knowledge as an ideological construct. It also expresses an explicit ideology of its own. For example, ideological is the stance *OBOS* takes against medicalization, making the unbridled authority of medicine over women's bodies seem inherently bad and disempowering for women. Like any ideology, this particular one works by displacing local knowledge (e.g., some women's desire for a more "medicalized" approach to their menstrual problems) with a generalizing and explicitly biased perspective (Smith 1990a, 32–33). While many readers undoubtedly share this ideology—or at least may become convinced of its merits in the course of reading the book—and while the authors of *OBOS* themselves would probably prefer to have their readers adopt it, it is not the *ideology* that is the most significant ingredient of the politics of knowledge expressed in *OBOS*. Indeed, I would argue that the critical impact of the text resides more in its ability to generate resistant readings. Nowhere is this more apparent than in the letters and comments of readers.

It is precisely those readers who do not agree with the text who—paradoxically—are the most active in their engagement with it. They are the ones who have felt compelled to write letters and share their comments with the authors of the book—not because they liked the book and agreed with it (although many of them did), but because they did *not*. In fact, it was precisely because their experiences were not included in the text or because they had been misrepresented that they felt compelled to take action. Through their critique of the text, they participated in the epistemological project that *OBOS* represented, a project that—at its very best—enables a critical and reflexive interrogation of all knowledge, including its own.

In conclusion, *OBOS* creates readers who are prepared to use their embodied experiences as a knowledge resource in the process of gathering and critically assessing information about their bodies and health. The text generates a set of knowledge practices—activating the reader, creating disjunctures between experiential and dominant forms of knowledge, and opening up spaces in the text for critical interrogation—that enable readers, even resistant ones, to become subjects who participate in a critical politics of knowledge aimed at empowering women to take control of their bodies and health. It is this politics of knowledge, mutually enacted in the interactions between the text and its readers, that accounts not only for the broad appeal of *OBOS* but also for its capacity to transform its readers into critical feminist subjects.

Part III ✳ TRANSNATIONAL BODY/POLITICS

CHAPTER 6

Oppositional Translations and Imagined Communities

ADAPTING *OBOS*

It was a sunny day in June 2001 in Utrecht, the Netherlands. Twenty women and one man had gathered around a table in the local women's health center to discuss their experiences and strategies in translating and adapting *OBOS*. This was not the first meeting of this kind; translators had also met at the United Nations Fourth World Congress on Women in Beijing in 1995.[1] This meeting was unusual, however, because the participants had a luxurious four days to devote to the translation projects. It had not been easy getting everyone there. The BWHBC had applied for funding, which arrived—predictably—much too late. Visa applications had been buried under bureaucratic paperwork, making it unclear whether some of the participants would be able to come. And, last but not least, finding a few free days amid the demands of family and work proved daunting for nearly everyone present. However, there we were—finally—ready to engage in a global dialogue face-to-face.[2]

For me, the meeting was a perfect opportunity to understand the process of translation and the kinds of problems facing those brave enough to take on the challenge of adapting *OBOS*. The participants came from different parts of the world: Mexico, Senegal, India, Japan, Serbia, Bulgaria, Poland, Armenia, and the United States. They were health activists, women's studies professors, translators, physicians, a bookstore owner, a journalist, a student, and a Tibetan nun. Some came alone, others in small groups. Some of the participants were just getting started with their adaptations (Tibet) and were inter-

35 * Participants in the Crossing Borders with *OBOS* conference, Utrecht, the Netherlands, June 2001. *Front, left to right*: Kornelia Slavova, Jane Pincus, Liana Galstyan. *Second row, right to left*: Marlies Bosch, Ester Shapiro, Lobsang Dechen, Toshiko Honda, Bobana Macanovic, Tatyana Kotzeva, Sally Whelan. *Back, left to right*: Chantal Soeter, Stanislava Otsavic, Norma Swenson, Miho Ogino, Codou Bop, Lourdes Ruiz, Toyoko Nakanishi, Kathy Davis. (Photo courtesy of Marlies Bosch.)

ested in any advice they could get. Others had successfully translated *OBOS* many years before and were looking forward to sharing stories about how the translation had become a national success (Japan).[3] Some had just finished adapting *OBOS* (Armenia) and were proud to display the finished product to the group. Many were prepared to share their—often harrowing—translation stories. (This could mean anything from having to complete the book in the midst of a conflict situation [Serbia] to having completed the manuscript but lacking the funds to get the book printed and distributed [Senegal].) Several participants had written papers in which they reflected on the process of translation. Others wanted to discuss creative ways to get the book distributed and ensure that it would be used by as many local women as possible. And still others were interested in how to sustain the book, once it was out, and keep it up-to-date and responsive to local conditions. The U.S. coordinator for the translation projects was present, along with two other founders of the BWHBC.

During those four days, something wonderful and—as we all agreed afterward—unusual happened. The participants had not only shared their translation stories; they had also engaged with one another in a dialogue about what it meant to do a cultural translation. This was not just a matter of how to deal with the inevitable "untranslatability" of languages, concepts, and discourses. For example, the Japanese translators described their struggles to come to terms with the fact that there was no language in which women could talk about their bodies. The vocabulary traditionally used to describe and diagnose the female body was either highly technical or negatively marked. Terms such as *pubic hair*, *pubic bone*, and *vulva* included characters that signified "shameful" or "dark and shady," thereby alienating women from their bodies. There was no language in which women could articulate their experiences of pain and pleasure regarding sexuality. The translators decided to engage in some linguistic innovation as a strategy for reclaiming women's bodies. They substituted characters meaning "sex" or "sexual" for more negatively nuanced characters (for example, "sexual lips" and "sexual hair"). The character meaning "blood," which marked bodily functions such as menstruation as polluted, was replaced with more straightforward characters meaning "monthly occurrence."[4] Using *OBOS* as a catalyst, the translators worked at developing a language that would allow women to talk to one another about their experiences, to express to their husbands why they weren't sexually satisfied, and to speak with physicians or lawyers without shame.[5] The Japanese example launched a more general discussion at the Utrecht meeting about the difficulties of finding positive language for women's bodies in other contexts; terms such as *shame hair* are not limited to Chinese and Japanese but can be found in Western European languages (German, Dutch) as well. We began to explore the linguistic possibilities for developing new, empowering ways to talk about women's bodies. The process of translation became an opportunity for cross-cultural

36 * Miho Ogino talking about the Japanese edition at the Crossing Borders with *OBOS* conference. (Photo courtesy of Marlies Bosch.)
37 * Codou Bop and Lobsang Dechen at the Crossing Borders with *OBOS* conference. (Photo courtesy of Marlies Bosch.)

comparisons and, more important, for discovering something about one's own culture while listening to narratives about another.

During these four days, several themes ran through our conversations. The first concerned the issue of how to contextualize translations of *OBOS* so that they could address the experiences and concerns of different readerships. The question was not so much how to make a faithful rendition of the original (i.e., the act of translation as we often think of it) but rather how to adapt the book so that it would be accessible and useful, as well as culturally sensitive for a new group of readers. The second theme involved the politics of translation. How could these translations be oppositional—that is, politically empowering—for women living in social, cultural, and geopolitical contexts very different from those of the United States?[6] In other words, how could they produce a new rendition of *OBOS* that would be different yet would politicize readers in such a way that they could say: "I read the book, and it changed my life."[7] Or, as one of the Japanese translators wrote in the preface of the Japanese *OBOS*, "From my first contact with this book until the completion of the translation, I have developed a much greater love for my own body. It is not merely that I have come to know it better but that I feel that I have learned new ways of experiencing the world differently. In this sense *Our Bodies, Ourselves* is not just a practical book but in fact a thrilling book and provocative work that will inevitably change the way of life of the reader" (Miho Ogino, translated in Buckley 1997, 209–10).

While the problem of negotiating differences was a central theme throughout these conversations, there was, at the same time and somewhat paradoxically, a noticeable attempt to establish a line of continuity between the U.S. *OBOS* and its translations. When the translators recounted the stories of their projects, they tended to situate their histories in the mythical tale, described in chapter 3, of how a group of young women met in Boston in the late sixties to talk about their bodies. Their stories would then move seamlessly from the U.S. context to their own—in Serbia, Japan, Armenia, Mexico, or Ladakh—where they would proceed to describe the trajectories that their own projects had taken. In this way, a shared history was constructed. This same history made its appearance in the preface of every translation, creating not only continuity between the U.S.

text and the translation but a community that encompassed both the original authors and their readers and the translators and their readers.

Nowhere was this "imagined community" more evident than at the Utrecht meeting when two of the founding members of BWHBC launched into a rendition of the mythical story of "how it all began." I watched women from Japan, Mexico, Armenia, Serbia, Senegal, Ladakh, and Bulgaria smiling and nodding. This was clearly a story that they had heard before. While it was clear that no one in the room had actually been present at the events in question, their smiles and nods indicated that they might as well have been. This story "belonged" to them. In re-creating *OBOS* in their specific historical and geographic locations, they were appropriating more than a book. They were also becoming part of the (mythical) feminist community that had made *OBOS* an icon not only for U.S. feminism but for transnational feminism as well.

This chapter explores some of the questions raised by the translation projects. I will show how the translators transformed the U.S. *OBOS* into a text that not only made sense in their local social, cultural, and political contexts but could be oppositional and politically empowering. To this end, I will draw on insights from critical (postcolonial) translation theory, which takes as its starting point that no translation is ever a faithful copy of the original.[8] Translations are, to some extent, always "faithless appropriations" (Tsing 1997, 253) whereby new meanings emerge through the complex interactions between the texts, the histories of their respective languages (concepts, discursive strategies), and the cultural and geopolitical contexts in which the texts are embedded. The translations of *OBOS* are perfect examples of such "betrayals" of the original and have invariably involved acknowledging often unbridgeable differences and incommensurabilities between the two texts. The very act of translation, however, also partakes in a necessarily utopian desire for mutual understanding and an "imagined feminist community."

In order to make my case, I will focus on two specific translation projects: the adaptation of the initial Spanish translation, *Nuestros Cuerpos, Nuestras Vidas* (*NCNV*), for Latin America (published in 2000) and the Bulgarian translation, *Nasheto Tyalo, Nie Samite* (published in 2001). I have chosen these particular translations for several reasons. First, because the translators were present at the meeting in Utrecht, I was able to talk with them about their translation experiences, as well as conduct interviews with several of the members of both translation projects. Second—and in contrast to many of the other translation projects—members of these particular teams had written about their translation process themselves.[9] But, most important, a comparison of these two projects was interesting because each had taken a very different approach to adapting *OBOS*, and these differences in translation strategies enabled me to explore how the oppositionality of a translation depends on the context in which it is produced and read. Taking a comparative approach, I will, therefore, be exploring how each project contextualized the U.S. text in order to make it accessible and useful for women in its specific locality, as well as how the U.S. text was adapted so that it would be oppositional and empowering for women in a very different social and political context. In conclusion, I will turn to the general issue of how cultural translations can create imagined feminist communities that are capable of recognizing differences among women while anticipating possible commonalities of struggle.

Critical Lessons from the South:
Nuestros Cuerpos, Nuestras Vidas

The project of translating *OBOS* into Spanish for Latin American readers spanned a period of more than two decades. It began as the only "homegrown" translation project when it was initiated by the BWHBC for Spanish-speaking women in the United States.[10] A team of Latinas, Amigas Latinas en Accion por Salud (ALAS) came together, under the auspices of the BWHBC, to work on making the translation more "culturally relevant" and sensitive to the needs of the Latina community. The project of adapting the book was met with some ambivalence. As was discussed in chapter 2, ALAS was not only frustrated with the quality of the initial translation, but it became increasingly concerned that the Spanish version was based on a book that had been written from a dominant, U.S., white woman's perspective. As Elizabeth MacMahon-Herrera, one of the founders of the group, put it, "When you're in another culture and you're seeing images of white women or you're being told, 'Oh, you have a right to this, that, and the other,' and you don't have that right in your country, it's confusing."[11] She also remembers feeling doubtful about whether a book meant to be read by an individual in her home was the best way to reach the Latina women who most needed information about their bodies and health. She and the other members of ALAS were much more inclined to use the book as a basis for developing brochures, videos, and television programs that would allow them and other health activists to more effectively address the health concerns of low-income Latina women. It is not surprising that the project of adapting the first Spanish edition of *OBOS* for women in other countries did not immediately become a priority. In the meantime, however, the initial Spanish translation had begun to "travel" and was already being widely read throughout Latin America. In the context of the burgeoning feminist and women's movements throughout Latin America, the Southern Cone, and the Caribbean, there was not only a need for the information provided by *OBOS*, but also an audience eager to hear about what was happening in U.S. feminism.

Despite its popularity, it wasn't until 1980 that the project of making a cultural adaptation of *Nuestros Cuerpos, Nuestras Vidas* was reinitiated. It was conceived of as a project that would address the specific needs and concerns of Latinas both in and outside the United States. It would also reflect the work being done around women's health and women's rights both inside and outside the United States. The idea was that U.S. Latinas and health activists from different countries in Latin America would collaborate to produce a well-translated and culturally relevant transcontinental *OBOS* in Spanish. As exciting as the project was, it remained on the back burner for another ten years in part because the feminist groups in Latin America lacked the economic resources to produce such a translation. As Elizabeth MacMahon-Herrera put it, "We want this book, but we want *you* to do it" pretty much summed up the messages the BWHBC was getting.[12]

In 1990 the Latin American adaptation project received a new impulse when two members of the BWHBC traveled to Argentina to attend one of its biannual feminist meetings (Encuentros), which attracted women from throughout Latin America, the Southern Cone, and the Caribbean.[13] They held a workshop in which health activists met to discuss the possibility of producing a cultural adaptation of *OBOS*. Nineteen groups with experience in women's health issues from Peru, Puerto Rico, Colombia, Chile, Cuba, Venezuela, Mexico, and El Salvador agreed to each translate and adapt at least one chapter of *OBOS*. The U.S. Latinas from ALAS would find funding for the project, do the coordination and editing, and ensure that the text would also be relevant for Latinas living in the United States.

In 1992, the Noyes Foundation provided a grant for the translation of the 1992 edition of *OBOS* into Spanish, and in 1993 the Ford Foundation offered a grant to finance the collaboration between groups working on adapting and editing *NCNV* for Latin America and the United States. Ester Shapiro, a Cuban feminist academic and health activist who grew up in the United States, was hired to coordinate the project. She not only had the organizational skills to direct such an ambitious project, but she provided a vision that pulled the disparate chapters together and gave the book its distinctive "voice." Given the enormous amount of work it took to coordinate and sustain the efforts of so many translators working in organizations that often had to struggle to stay afloat, it is not surprising that it was another seven years before *NCNV* finally appeared in print in 2000.

Like other foreign editions, *NCNV* consisted of a combination of direct translation and adaptation. In an attempt to correct the mistakes of the past, the editors ensured that the translation was not only "good" (i.e., linguistically accurate), in the traditional sense of the word, but that it would also be "poetic" enough to speak to Latina readers.[14] However, it was also a "faithless appropriation" (Tsing 1997) of the U.S. text, perhaps even more faithless than most. In addition to the usual strategy of replacing U.S. women's experiential accounts with *testimonios* of local women and changing the photographs to reflect a Latina audience, the editors radically changed the structure and methodology of the U.S. text.[15] As the coordinator of the project put it, "The book in English begins with body image and taking care of ourselves in this sort of individualistic, North American fashion. We didn't think the book in Spanish should start off that way. . . . It would be like trying to sell eating disorders as a North American product. Body image problems are not a major concern in Latin America."[16]

She explained that, while the image of a woman looking at her body in a mirror might make perfect sense in the U.S. context, where body image is a major concern for many women and eating disorders (obesity, bulimia, anorexia) have reached epidemic proportions, for Latin American readers another entrance into the text was required.

For Latin American women such a photo would not only be off-putting, because they had different problems and priorities than U.S. women, but it would be unacceptable to Latin American feminists, who had different ideas about what constitutes a feminist approach to body image.[17] As the introduction to *NCNV*, the editors took what had been the concluding chapter in the U.S. book (a chapter on the global politics of women's health) and made it the first chapter in their book. As one of them explained, "We didn't feel like we could start the book in Spanish any other way than to say, 'Well, as women, these are some of the concerns we share with all women in the world. We do most of the work and get the least amount of pay. We don't own property. We don't get an education. We do more and more with less and less. All we want is a roof over our heads, the resources to take care of the people we're responsible to, and, occasionally, ourselves.'"[18]

The Spanish translation borrowed the "consciousness-raising" approach of the U.S. *OBOS*, politicizing it through the introduction of Paolo Freire's liberatory pedagogy of participatory education, which had been popular among social movements and health educators in Latin America.[19] This methodology couples experiential learning with a social justice perspective. While it resonates with the politics of knowledge initially expressed in *OBOS*, whereby readers were invited to draw on their own bodily experiences to develop critical knowledge, the context is different. Gone is the lone woman reading *OBOS* in the privacy of her living room, which—according to the editors of *NCNV*—characterizes the U.S. book. In the spirit of more explicitly politicized, participatory education, the reader of *NCNV* is enjoined at the outset of each new chapter to make connections between her personal experiences and the social systems in which these experiences are embedded. To this end, each chapter of *NCNV* was given a short introduction specifically designed to help the Latina reader make these connections. While the Spanish translation provides information, just like its U.S. counterpart, there is less concern about being comprehensive than about enabling the reader to critically interrogate and reflect on her own experiences.[20]

In addition to changing the structure and "methodology" of the book, the Latin American adaptation of *OBOS* had three important additions. The first was a chapter devoted to religion, for, as the editor Ester Shapiro put it, "You cannot write a book for Latin American and Latina women without addressing the role of religion and spirituality. You just can't do it."[21] Whereas the U.S. book had mentioned religion solely in the context of the right-wing, antiabortion movement, the translators of the Spanish text acknowledged the significance of the Catholic Church in women's lives. They underlined the ways in which Catholic women were redefining the church, comparing it to the way other translations of *OBOS* had incorporated religion (e.g., the Egyptian adaptation). In addressing the issue of abortion, which is illegal in most Latin American countries, language was employed that specifically underlined the dilemmatic nature of the decision for Catholic women. The text subsequently reads, "Precisely because we recognize the sanctity of life, we want to make a decision that helps us nourish the lives of the members of our families and communities. Recognizing this wider context, we need to take into account the mother's life, the life of children already born, as well as those that might be born in the future."[22]

The second addition concerned spirituality and traditional healing practices. Traditional healing practices are both common and highly popular throughout Latin America.[23] The editors paid considerable attention to these practices, setting them apart from what they saw as the "completely Anglo, New Age approach" to spirituality in the U.S. *OBOS*. Their mission was not only to educate but also to transform traditions to meet their own needs. For example, they developed dedications to the women who had worked on the translation project using the style of Mexican religious folk art (*retablos*). Photographs of each woman were framed with personal stories describing why she had embarked on the translation project and what it had meant to her. In this way, the editors presented themselves as "grateful supplicants, awaiting a (miraculous) response" (Shapiro 2001, 7).

The third addition concerned the political situation in the South and the diverse and widespread activism among women in Latin America.[24] In sidebars replete with photographs and manifestos, readers were provided with examples from their local histories of social activism. One such passage reads, "We have all, as women of the world, learned from the heroism of the mothers of the 'missing' of Argentina, Chile and Uruguay, and of the Guatemalan Rigoberta Menchú, exiled for many years. All these women created political revolutions demanding justice for their children, brothers, fathers and family members . . . and transformed our ideas as to what is possible to achieve with political movements."[25] The Latin American translation assumed, and even expected, that its readers (unlike readers of the U.S. *OBOS*) would be sympathetic to women's movements or some form of feminism and that they would probably have some affiliation with other movements for social justice.

While all of these ingredients served to contextualize the translation for a Latin American audience, *NCNV* also transformed the politics of the U.S. text. Mindful of the "imperialistic" tendencies of U.S. feminism, the editors were especially keen to show that feminism was not simply a U.S. product. They did not believe that Latin American feminists must pattern themselves on feminism as it was practiced in the United States. On the contrary, they believed that U.S. feminists had a lot to learn from their Latin American "sisters," and they viewed the translation as a means of facilitating the flow of knowledge in both directions.[26]

> Many times the "experts" of the United States think that their knowledge of the "first world" [involves] concepts which are superior and which can be used to elevate the "Third World" from a primitive state to a superior level. We are quite clear on the fact that for our sisters in Latin America, their social and political relationships are a source of richness, in contrast to the United States, which is an individualistic country where everything is for sale, including social relationships which you must buy or reinvent. In words, we have a lot to share and a lot to learn together.[27]

The editors of the Latin American adaptation were critical of the U.S. *OBOS*, which they regarded as individualistic, consumer oriented, and insufficiently political. In their view, the U.S. text overemphasized the power of the individual woman to take care of herself as epitomized by the "completely Anglo" notion of self-help. Self-help ignored the support provided by other people in a woman's life (family, community), suggesting that women could become healthy in isolation. Such an image neither fit the circumstances of most Latina women nor corresponded with the politics that the editors envisioned for their book. According to Shapiro, "Nobody takes care of themselves by themselves. We have banished the term *auto ayuda* (self-help) from the book. We use words like *ayuda mutual* (mutual help) . . . because we want to make sure people understand that it's your relationships that keep you well and that it's in relationships that you gain all the things that make you well, including the energy for collective action, which is part of health."[28]

The Latin American translation, therefore, replaced aspects of the U.S. text, which were based on a consumerist health care system, with a community-based approach. The emphasis on understanding medical information, of making informed decisions, or even of navigating the health care system were deemed less important in the Latin American context. Thus, "If only about 10 percent of health outcomes for women in Latin America can be attributed to health care or physicians, while 90 percent are connected to economics, education, lifestyle, working conditions, or nutrition, a different conception of both health and health care politics is required."[29]

In line with their belief that health was not a "product" to be consumed but rather a responsibility and accomplishment of a community, the Latin American translation situated the individual woman in an extended network of people whose support made it possible for her to take care of herself (Shapiro 2001, 10). While the U.S. text had devoted an entire chapter to the U.S. medical system, *NCNV* replaced this chapter with a comprehensive section on community organizations and women's groups concerned with health issues, arguing that this information would be of more benefit to Latina women than information about the health care system. In general, they adopted a "gender justice" perspective, which shifted the focus from the individual woman and her body to a more encompassing perspective that included men and children. They stressed the importance of economic issues such as poverty, education, housing, and nutrition to women's health. While the U.S. *OBOS*—particularly in its later versions—also displayed an understanding of the connections between social inequality and health, *NCNV* made these connections its ideological centerpiece.

When the translators of *NCNV* emphasized the differences between the U.S. text and their adaptation, they were not simply contextualizing the text for a new set of readers. Their translation strategies were situated in a more encompassing political project, which involved building bridges between Latinas in the South and Latinas living in the diaspora in the United States. In line with contemporary U.S. Chicana feminist writings, *NCNV* constructed a panethnic or *mestija* identity, based on a shared history of the U.S. conquest in the South, as well as the contemporary experience of many Latinas of living "on the border":[30] According to Shapiro, "Women in Latin America, whether we are living in our own countries, living in exile in Latin America, or having emigrated to the U.S., for whatever combination of political and economic reasons, we are joined by both language and by certain cultural traditions and by the experience of having national sovereignty interfered with, first of all, by colonial powers and then by the United States."[31]

This new cultural space—a space formed by common *lenguas* (languages) and common *sitios* (situated locations)—was considered essential for coalition building among Latinas in the South as well as between Latinas in the South and the United States (Hurtado 2001).

Nowhere is this more clearly illustrated than on the cover of *NCNV*, which shows a group of Latina women united within a brightly colored sun (fig. 27). In the preface, the history of the book is recounted, however, without any of the iconic photographs of the U.S. authors that grace the U.S. edition. Instead a photograph shows a member of the U.S. Latina group ALAS proudly holding up the very first newsprint edition of *OBOS* (fig. 38). The message is clear: the history of the book did not come to a halt in the seventies, nor does it "belong" to the U.S. collective that authored the first editions of the book. She seems to be saying: "I am part of this history, too." In this way, a line of continuity is established between the U.S. book and the adaptation—a line that also underscores the agency of the Latina women who participated.

Given the enormous differences among Latin American women, *NCNV* was an ambitious undertaking. It is difficult to imagine that one book could ever appeal to an audience that encompassed such a diversity of women—ranging from the Guatemalan peasant, to the young assembly line worker in the *maquilladora* to the educated metropolitan feminist from Buenos Aires, not to mention the diversity of Latina women within the United States. While the editors acknowledged this challenge, their ideologically motivated desire to build transnational alliances between feminist health activists in the North and South took precedence.

This particular translation story does not have a happy ending. After the U.S. publisher transferred the book to a publisher in Spain

38 * Maria Skinner of ALAS holding up the first edition of
OBOS. (Photo courtesy of Kathleen Dooher.)

with the understanding that this would improve distribution in Latin America, the Spanish publisher decided to revise it. These revisions meant, in practice, cutting precisely those parts of the book that had been aimed at building bridges between women in the North and the South. The names of the translators and Latin American groups that had translated the various chapters were moved to the back of the book (where no one would read them) and a new preface was written in which a direct line was drawn between the Spanish edition of *NCNV* and the original U.S. authors of *OBOS*, the BWHBC. Thus, the attempt to build bridges between Latinas in the North and the South was circumvented. This demonstrates that translation involves constant negotiation about which community is to be addressed and how the book will be disseminated. This is never written in stone, but rather is a continuing and highly contested process. As Ester Shapiro, the coordinator, put it, the project was always "less about the book than about the shared projects that the book represents."[32]

"An Ongoing Dialogue": The Bulgarian *OBOS*

When Irina Todorova, a health psychologist from Bulgaria, was in the United States in 1996 and decided to get in touch with the BWHBC, she had no intention of translating *OBOS* into Bulgarian. She simply wanted to meet the women who had written it—a book she had read and that had resonated with much of what she was already thinking about women and health. However, after Sally Whelan, the coordinator of translation projects, told her about the "international life" of the book, Irina, laughing, remembered, "I said, 'Ha-a-a-h! This is *very* interesting. There isn't a Bulgarian edition of the book.' And things began to fit together."[33]

When she returned to Sofia, she became one of the initiators of the Women's Health Initiative (WHI), which was formed in Bulgaria in 1998. As one of its many projects, the WHI decided to translate the latest edition of *OBOS*, *Our Bodies, Ourselves for the New Century* (1998). With the help of a grant from the Global Women's Fund, as well as a translation grant from the Soros Foundation,[34] the women embarked on a translation and adaptation project, which took about two years to complete. The team included a feminist translator and philologist; a medical translator for the technical terms; a group of ten consultants, including members of the WHI and specialists in nutrition, drug abuse, occupational health, medicine, and alternative health practices; and activists in the fight against sexual violence.

Initially, members of the team agreed to translate about two-thirds of the book and adapt the rest. They wanted to produce a book that would be specific to the experiences and situations of women in postcommunist Bulgaria while remaining close to the "spirit" of the original book (Kotzeva 2001). It should sound "natural and inviting enough for a Bulgarian woman to identify with" but still provide a "faithful rendering" of the information and ideology of the original (Slavova 2001, 7).

While the Bulgarian women translated the core of the U.S. book, they adapted many of the chapters, expanding them with statistics and practical data relevant to the Bulgarian context. This was done primarily by adding explanatory footnotes, glossaries, cross-cultural commentaries, and additional paragraphs at the ends of chapters. This strategy of "thick translation" (Appiah 2000)[35] enabled them to contextualize the U.S. text, making it more accessible to Bulgarian readers (Slavova 2001). As Irina Todorova put it, "We didn't want to produce just an interesting book about what's happening in the U.S." They wanted a book that would be "maximally relevant to Bulgarian women." While she admitted that the goal was "far too ambitious" in retrospect, it was "ambitious in a positive way. . . . We didn't think we could come up in two or three years with a book that is a Bulgarian book. We didn't see it that way. We see it more as a topic for conversation or as an opening of an ongoing dialogue about what needs to be changed or added or reworded. That would be a much longer process."[36]

The translators did not feel that they needed to, or indeed could, make "major statements about how the book should sound to the plurality of groups and ethnicities and opinions in Bulgaria." They expected the Bulgarian readers to let them know if the text didn't work or if something needed to be changed. In this sense, the Bulgarian translation was conceived of from the beginning as a work-in-progress. Thus, "It wasn't terribly frightening to have a book which wasn't tailored 100 percent. I thought we could trust them [readers] to be critical if they needed to be. . . . They would take what is important and come back to us about what wasn't. . . . It's necessary to trust in the process."[37]

The belief that every reader—even "the grandmother who has lived in a village all her life"—would be able to understand the book and find something interesting or exciting in it for herself was central to the philosophy of the book and part of what the translators "borrowed" from the U.S. text. Describing this philosophy, Irina Todorova noted, "I looked up the word *outreach*. I realized it [the book] was being used as outreach to give out information while the original sense is outreach for information, for feedback, for interaction. . . . We don't want to give information; we want to get it back."[38] As part of the conception of the translation project, discussions with different groups of women were arranged in local community centers.[39] These groups were pragmatically intended to combine an evaluation of the book with its dissemination, as well as with gathering feedback for future editions.

In terms of content, adaptations of the book were directly related to the changes in, and in most cases the deterioration of, women's health in Bulgaria since 1989.[40] For example, the chapter on food addressed problems associated with the poor diet of most Bulgarians, for whom the preponderance of foods high in salt and fat has given rise to increasing rates of strokes, heart attacks, diabetes, and obesity. Bulgarian women currently have the highest rate of cardiovascular disease among women in Europe. The chapter on alcohol and drugs was revised to pay additional attention to the "hidden" problem of alcoholism among (elderly) Bulgarian women, a problem that is exacerbated by extreme poverty and the societal stereotype that older women don't drink in public. A new chapter was added on the history of women's organizations in Bulgaria both prior to and during communism. While women's health had not been an issue for these organizations, the translators felt that it was "symbolically important" to provide an image of a women's movement grounded in Bulgarian history and to highlight how this differed from the U.S. women's health movement.[41] Information about changes in the health care system since the transition was provided, along with guidelines for interpreting the proliferating and ever shifting new health legislation in Bulgaria.[42] A comprehensive list of resources was provided as well, including Bulgarian NGOs working in the field of women's sexuality and health, violence against women, or environmental issues; research findings about the situation of Bulgarian women; and an up-to-date guide to Internet resources on women's health.

Passages from the U.S. text that were deemed irrelevant for Bulgarian women were omitted. For example, the critique of conventional Western medicine found in the U.S. *OBOS* was deleted, particularly because references to the problem of medicalization, which, in a context in which the basic health needs of most Bulgarians were not being met, could have seemed cynical. Similarly, the centrality given to women relying on their "own sources of knowledge" was disregarded, as it seemed inadequate and even hypocritical in the Bulgarian context (Kotzeva 2001). At the visual level, nearly all of the photographs from the U.S. edition were replaced with photographs of Bulgarian women. The experiential accounts, which abound in the U.S. *OBOS* and played such a central role in its politics of knowledge, were also discarded. Interestingly, this decision was not based on the lack of importance given to women's experiences but rather to the translators' "intuitive" sense that the "voices" of Bulgarian women would sound awkward in a text that was not "Bulgarian made." Their strategy for drawing readers into the text involved, paradoxically, marking it explicitly as a foreign text written by women in the United States while making it "sound" (and look) like a Bulgarian text.[43]

An example of this balancing act is the way the translators dealt with parts of the U.S. text that were specific to the U.S. context. Many of the medications and procedures discussed in the U.S. text were unavailable in Bulgaria and were therefore omitted as being of little relevance to the Bulgarian reader. However, some exceptions were made. For example, a paragraph about the female condom was included. While it was unknown in Bulgaria, the translators felt that it provided a glimpse of what was possible ("It's nice to know it's out there even if you can't get it in Bulgaria and maybe wouldn't even want to use it if you could").[44] In a similar vein, topics that were controversial or taboo in Bulgaria—women's sexuality, masturbation, lesbian relationships—were kept in the text in order to open up discussions about sexuality, particularly among young people. The translators relied on the "balanced and positive stance" that the authors of the U.S. *OBOS* had adopted in order to "tone down" potentially negative responses from Bulgarian readers (Kotzeva 2001, 6).[45] The U.S. chapter on abortion was left basically intact, although abortion has had a very different history and different meanings in Bulgaria, where it has been legal for many years. As the primary method of birth control, abortion has been regarded as a medical intervention with limited consequences and none of the moral or religious discourse that surrounds abortion debates in the United States. Nevertheless, the translators reasoned that it would be instructive for Bulgarian readers to learn about the struggles of U.S. women against oppressive abortion legislation as a warning that women's reproductive rights, even in Bulgaria, are always in danger. In this way, the Bulgarian translation demonstrated that differences in abortion discourse and practice did not preclude the possibility of an inclusive (globally informed) understanding of what was at stake in abortion with regard to women's reproductive rights.[46]

While the Bulgarian translators grappled with the contextualization of *OBOS* for their readers, much more daunting than the content of the book was its ideological message. The greatest problem facing the translators was finding ways to introduce a gender-sensitive text such as *OBOS* into a context with little gender sensitivity and a nonexistent discourse of feminism. This required reworking the language, concepts, and rhetoric of the U.S. text in ways that would make it both accessible and oppositional in the Bulgarian context.

At the linguistic level, the challenge was to translate the U.S. *OBOS* into a language (Bulgarian) that was structurally hostile to gender. As with most Slavic languages, Bulgarian has rigid and pervasive markings of gender involving the frequent use of masculine and feminine forms—a usage that not only facilitates sexism but is exacerbated by the fact that most Bulgarian speakers are unaware of these usages let alone capable of imagining nonsexist alternatives (Slavova 2001). In this respect, Bulgarian and English are similar (e.g., both use a generic *he* to make universal references and both use masculine forms for professions, thereby excluding women). Both Bulgarian and U.S. feminists have engaged in linguistic strategies such as using the feminine gender as universal, screening language for gendered clichés and stereotypes, or putting scare quotes around "objectionable sexist phrases to show the translator's disapproval," a form of "feminist hijacking," as one of the translators noted (5). Translating *OBOS* into Bulgarian offered the opportunity to engage in a creative process of inventing a new language about gender. Thus, after struggling with the term *gender*, for which there is no Bulgarian equivalent,[47] the translators experimented with the neologism *sociosex*, which combines biological sex and social gender in one word, suggesting both continuity and difference.[48] They provided extensive explanations for such terms as *transgender, transsexuality, drag queen, queer, gender bending, homophobia*, and *gender blindness*. Some words were introduced into the Bulgarian context through the adaptation of *OBOS* (*surrogate mother, date rape, sexual harassment, coming out, domestic violence*, and *battered women's shelter*) and have since—five years later—been taken up in public discourse.[49]

The term *feminism* was more difficult to translate and involved more than finding an appropriate term or neologism that Bulgarian readers could understand. *Feminism* was not an innocent word in Bulgaria, where the popular representation of a feminist was "an aggressive, manly looking woman who hates men and even family and children . . . and who might also be a lesbian" (Kotzeva 2001, 5). In Bulgaria, even women well versed in feminist language and theory often avoided referring to themselves as feminists, claiming, "I am not a feminist and never will be one," "I am simply a woman," "I've had enough of this emancipation crap," or "I'll be your feminist, and now where is the money?" This refusal of feminism reflected the widespread allergy throughout Eastern Europe to anything that was reminiscent of the propaganda, ideology, political messianism, or big liberatory ideas that were rampant before 1989.[50]

> After fifty years of false equality and freedom under totalitarianism, some of the major objectives of [the] Western feminist movement reverberate cynically in our current context. The liberal concepts of "equality," "women's rights" . . . "feminists," [and] "feminism" itself— smack of Leninism and Marxism (considered now dirty words associated with leftist and unacceptable ideological projects and indoctrination). The same goes for some of the Western women's movement slogans (e.g., "the personal is political") or practices (such as "consciousness-raising groups," [and] "women's activism") or a more assertive collectivist mode . . . [which] also have negative connotations. . . . [This is] because of the long-term abuse of political institutions, the subjugation of the individual to collective practices, and groups [that were] forced upon [people] by the Communist Party in the past. (Slavova 2001, 3)

The translators and editors of the Bulgarian adaptation tried to find ways to avoid problematic associations with Western feminism, as well as the linkages between feminist and communist rhetoric. This involved more than deleting the "F-word," which, in fact, is noticeably absent throughout the Bulgarian text. It also required addressing Bulgarian readers as, first and foremost, individuals. Beginning with the title, *Nasheto Tyalo, Nie Samite*, which literally means "Our Body, Ourselves," the connotation of individuality and diversity was emphasized. In Bulgarian, "our bodies" would have suggested "depersonalized, multiple, undifferentiated bodies" and therefore would not have been appropriate after a historical period in which "bodies" were blended into a single, unitary collective of colorless entities.[51] Terms such as *self-understanding, self-confidence,* and *individual assertiveness* appear throughout the text.[52] The focus is on the individual woman, who in learning about her body can also learn how to protect her rights in the face of *any* form of power— whether of the state, her husband, her family, or even her children. "Knowledge is power" is a frequently repeated refrain. The aim is to initiate a process of consciousness-raising about women's rights (as human beings, consumers, patients, and citizens) that does not devalue women's caretaking but tries to expand it from taking care of others to taking care of oneself. As the translators wrote in the preface of *Nasheto Tyalo, Nie Samite*, "*Our Bodies, Ourselves* is . . . a guide toward loving, enjoying, appreciating and not being ashamed of our bodies, gifted with power and beauty. These are the messages of the book, which we hope will resonate with Bulgarian readers."[53]

The emphasis on the individual woman and her personal relationship to her body does not mean that the Bulgarian adaptation is devoid of any mention of collectivity. This would have denied the significance of *OBOS* as a catalyst for feminist health politics. The problem facing the translators was what to do about the ubiquitous "we" in the U.S. text, which is so central to its aim of encompassing the experiences and voices of differently located women within a collective feminist enterprise. They asked, "How can we render this most inclusive 'we' point of view in the book—uniting white and black women, Hispanic-American and other hyphenated Americans, men and women, lesbian and straight, young and old, healthy and disabled—in a form that sounds natural and inviting enough for a Bulgarian woman reader to identify with?" (Slavova 2001, 6). In other words, how could they adopt the notion of a "we" as one of intersecting differences without losing the individualism necessary to mitigate the rejection of collectivistic values so pervasive in postsocialist Bulgaria?[54]

> Reference to a *big* women's movement in Bulgaria would be something that women would resist. They'd say: 'Oh, no-o-o. All over again! They're trying to get us into this depersonified organism and idea remaining from decades of socialist ideals of everyone moving in the same direction.' . . . So if it's about a *huge* collective, integrating movement . . . at the same time . . . it's been such a creative time, there's been a striving to create organizations, *smaller* ones. There are so many organizations of one or two or three people."[55]

With great sensitivity to the contemporary cultural scene, the translators looked for ways to combine an individualistic discourse of "self-identification" with a vision of small groups getting together and thinking about ways to influence legislation and encourage social and cultural change. They tried to seduce the Bulgarian reader into accepting this message of collective action while taking into account her potentially allergic reaction to its ideology. To this end, the "we" of the U.S. text was not eliminated altogether but rather broken down into smaller "we's." Thus, the translators wrote in their preface:

In the book [the U.S. *OBOS*], the authors speak as "we"—which can be understood as all women around the world, "we"—the authors of the chapter, "we"—the women of a specific group (women with disabilities, women victims of violence, women from minorities, etc.). Thus the identification of "we" opens the book to its future authors who are ready to share their life experience and knowledge, not less valuable than the university medical science. Following the "by women for women" principle, the book is not only a medical encyclopedia, but also a significant companion and a partner for privacy in minutes of joy, sorrow and despair.[56]

The translators used the language of diversity in the U.S. text to engage with the socialist idea of sameness and pseudo unity ("We were all working class Bulgarian heroes: men and women, peasants and intellectuals, gypsies and ethnic Turks").[57] Bulgarian readers could be counted on to know that the gap between the haves and have nots, between the ethnically marginalized, and between the sexes was widening. However, these differences were not treated as abstract categories but rather as embedded in the individual woman's personal relationship with her body. Thus, *OBOS* was no abstract treatise on the "woman question" but a personal "companion," a "partner," to be read "in minutes of joy, sorrow, and despair." By selectively drawing on the U.S. text, the translators ensured that their version of *OBOS* would be empowering within their local circumstances. A discourse was borrowed and reworked to downplay notions of a common gender identity (while subversively creating a new, gender-related discourse) and a depersonalized, collective women's movement while at the same time mobilizing postcommunist women into an imagined feminist community. This imagined community was none other than the international community of readers, readers who were diversely located individuals unified not by virtue of their shared identity as women but by their shared quest for knowledge, which reflected their experiences and empowered them in their everyday lives.

Translating Oppositionality and Imagining Community

At the outset of this chapter, I raised the issue of how the translations of *OBOS* tackled the inevitable problem of creating a text that could speak to readers outside the United States. I examined two translation and adaptation projects in detail, drawing on the reflections of the translators concerning the complexities involved in such an undertaking. The strategies were discussed by which they made *OBOS* accessible and "culturally relevant" to readers with histories, circumstances, and political locations different from those of U.S. readers. I also showed how they made these translations oppositional—that is, capable of generating agency and a critical and politically engaged subjectivity among readers (Spivak 2000, 405). Gayatri Spivak views translations as cultural political practices that can be strategic in bringing about change.[58] While translations have the capacity to generate oppositional readings, oppositionality is not an inherent property of a translation. Texts invariably have different meanings in different locations and at different points in time. Depending on the cultural and political context in which the translation is produced, its political valence will change as well. What might seem to be resistant in an English text could well become reactionary in another language and vice versa (Spivak 2000, 404). Thus, any translator interested in producing an oppositional text will need to know more than what would make a translation "good" or "bad." He or she will need to understand how texts can "misfire" when they are taken up in other linguistic and cultural contexts, making it a complicated undertaking to transform the text so that it continues to be subversive but subversive in ways quite different from those of the original.

As we have seen, the translation of *OBOS* was rarely straightforward and inevitably involved a certain amount of "betrayal" of the U.S. text. In this sense, the translation had all the features of a "faithless appropriation" rather than a "faithful copy" of the original (Tsing 1997, 253).[59] Nor did the translators take for granted what Spivak (2000) has called a "too quickly shared feminist notion of accessibility" based on the assumption that women will automatically understand one another just because they have something (a female body?) identifiably in common (407). Rather the translators proceeded from the recognition of difference and the conviction that their text would have to be different from the U.S. text in order to make sense and be relevant in their local contexts. With great ingenuity and flexibility, they applied different strategies for contextualizing the U.S. text— from changing the appearance of the book (replacing the U.S. photographs with representations of local women or making their own distinctive covers) to ensuring that the translation would "sound" like a local product (flow) to adding explanations or glosses to make the text understandable for local readers (thick translation).

Of the two cases discussed in depth in this chapter, the Latin American text seemed at first glance to be the less loyal of the two. It not only radically restructured the U.S. text, but it explicitly set itself apart from its U.S. counterpart as part of its oppositional strategy. However, the Bulgarian translators, while apparently sticking more closely to the U.S. text, were also engaged in rearticulating *OBOS* to serve their own ends. Even when the U.S. text was perfectly rendered in the translation, it did not necessarily have the same meaning in the Bulgarian context. For example, ostensibly straightforward statements about the "female condom" or women's struggles in the United States against oppressive abortion legislation worked differently in the Bulgarian context; they were eye-openers or warnings rather than mere conveyors of information. In short, the translators did not simply "surrender" themselves to the U.S. text but rather adopted a "cannibalistic strategy" of using what was useful (Spivak 2000, 412).[60]

Interestingly, differences between the U.S. text and the context in which it was produced and the translation and the context in which it was produced were not treated as problems to be overcome, standing in the way of a "good" translation. On the contrary, the translators seemed more than willing to embrace these differences as an opportunity to produce a more oppositional text. For example, differences allowed them to open up controversial topics for discussion (homosexuality, masturbation, transgender), to celebrate local accomplishments (a more holistic or political perspective on health, a history of feminist struggle), or to warn about future dangers and suggest points for a coalition (reproductive rights). In short, the translators situated themselves—and, by implication, their readers,—as interested but critical subjects engaged in "friendly learning by taking a distance" (Spivak 2000, 412).

The translation projects adopted a politics of location to ensure that the translations would work as oppositional texts in a different social, cultural, and political context. Nowhere was this more clearly apparent than in the different ways the Bulgarian and Latin American translations rearticulated the political ideology of the U.S. text so that it would generate an oppositional consciousness among local audiences. In so doing, they demonstrated that feminist perspectives are neither universally shared nor universally empowering but need to be constantly rearticulated in order to "work" under different historical, social, cultural, and political circumstances. What might be oppositional in the U.S. context at a specific historical moment could prove to be reactionary in another context.[61]

As we have seen, the Latina translators rejected the political ideology of the U.S. text for its "individualism" in favor of a more "collective" perspective, which was considered more appropriate in the Latin American context. In contrast, the Bulgarian translators embraced the very same individualism, rejecting instead what they saw as the "collectivism" of the U.S. text, which would have been problematic in the postsocialist context of Bulgaria. The image of the individual woman with a "personal" relationship to her body was empowering for Bulgarian women, who had every reason to be suspicious of collectivism as ideology and practice. In a context in which gender was not considered salient for women's political subjectivity, the strategy of emphasizing the specificities of feminine embodiment was treated as a first step in women's politicization. It provided a way for Bulgarian women to begin thinking of themselves as embodied subjects and to imagine how they might become active in their own right and their own interests together (on a small scale) with other women. This same image of an individual woman and her body (with or without mirror and speculum!) was anathema to the Latina translators, who regarded it as symptomatic of the deep social, cultural, and political divisions between the North and the South. For them, this image needed to be replaced with a perspective that emphasized women in relation to their families and communities and situated political action within a broader range of existing movements for social justice. In the Latin American case, the oppositionality of their text lay in its capacity to generate linkages among Latina women across the globe. In contrast, the oppositionality of the Bulgarian text resided in its ability to generate sensitivity to gender issues and to lay the groundwork for new forms of political citizenship and public action.

While these translations gave very different meanings to the terms *individualism* (and *collectivity*), both differed from the U.S. text in their explicit emphasis on the necessity of using *OBOS* in communal settings rather than as a book to be read by an individual woman in the privacy of her home. In both cases, the translations were—from the outset—intended to be read in groups. Whether as an occasion for a "dialogue" in a small group (Bulgarian) or as a form of "participatory education" in a collective context (Latin American), the translations took up—or, as some would argue, "returned"—to the original intention of *OBOS* as a book that should be read, discussed, and shared among women. In this sense, the translation projects took up the collective process of knowledge making that had always made *OBOS* unique: the recurrent and collective "reading against the grain" that went into every new revision of the book and that involved hundreds of critical readers. The translators adopted this process of collective knowledge making, using their translations to generate similar discussions among women in their own contexts.

It is this feature of *OBOS*—more than its informational content, its format, or its specific feminist politics of health—that ultimately proved to be universally translatable. Despite the myriad differences between the U.S. text and the translations and among the various translations themselves, the commitment to the collective production and sharing of knowledge as central to women's empowerment remained the single feature that brought the disparate projects together under one umbrella, enabling *OBOS* to become a global feminist project.

Translations presuppose a desire to generate communication across boundaries—not just across boundaries between the United States and the rest of the world but also across social, cultural, and political divisions without the contexts in which the translations are undertaken. Venuti (2000) calls this the "utopian" moment of translation—the desire to create "zones of contact" between (as well as within) cultures. At their best, translations can lay the groundwork for alliances that, despite differences and hierarchies of power, can prove to be mutually beneficial (477). Drawing on Benedict Anderson's well-known metaphor, he suggests that translations generate "imagined communities." They bring together individuals who would never know one another or even meet but who might, nevertheless, through the practice of making and reading the translation, come to imagine common interests and struggles.

As we have seen, each new translation of *OBOS* enables differently located women to participate in a feminist project that has already inspired millions of women around the world. This "strange encounter" (Ahmed 2000) allows women who are separated geographically, as well as divided by unequal relationships of power, to imagine future reconciliations—a feminist community based not on identity or common experiences but on respect for difference and a desire to find commonalities of struggle. Through its translations, *OBOS* has become the occasion for a "global dialogue" in which the necessity of critical reflexivity is combined with the utopian desire for communication and community.

CHAPTER 7

Transnational Knowledges,
Transnational Politics

While I was in the final stages of writing this book, I gave a presentation about *OBOS* and its travels to an audience of feminist scholars. Afterward one of these scholars, well known for her work in postcolonial feminist theory, approached me. "You know," she said, "I can't tell you how nice it is to hear a story like this. It's so . . ."—she seemed to be struggling to find the right word—"it's just so *hopeful.*"

Her remark, I must admit, took me somewhat by surprise. I began this inquiry—as I set out in the introduction—with certain ambivalences, which were a reflection of my position as a feminist scholar. Within feminist scholarship, it is bon ton to situate oneself as a critic. Taking a critical and reflexive perspective is almost a kind of second nature, involving anything from debunking assumptions that are taken for granted in scientific discourse to exposing hidden inequalities and exclusions of power lurking within even seemingly benign practices and policies to being relentlessly vigilant concerning one's own blind spots and prejudices. While my experiences as a feminist health activist in the seventies made me embrace *OBOS*, my experiences as a feminist scholar in the nineties warned me to take a more cautious stance. Well versed in poststructuralist feminist theory, I was inclined to be suspicious of any text that glorified women's embodied experience as an unproblematic source of knowledge. Moreover, in the light of long-standing debates about "global feminism," I was disposed to be wary that any U.S. feminist export could exhibit imperialistic tendencies, which would obscure differences and hierarchies of power between U.S. feminists and feminists in non-Western contexts.

Throughout this inquiry, I have used these ambivalences as a resource for exploring the history and travels of *OBOS*, taking its trajectory within and outside the United States as an occasion to think critically about its politics of knowledge and its status as a transnational feminist project. As a result of my efforts to read *OBOS* through the critical lens of contemporary feminist scholarship, I find myself at the end of my own journey—much like the feminist scholar in my audience—left with an unfamiliar and yet unmistakably pleasant feeling that I can only describe as hopeful.

It is not my intention to romanticize *OBOS* as a feminist project, and, as I have shown throughout this book, it has produced its own problems and exclusions. Nevertheless, I will take the opportunity in this final chapter to explore some of the reasons for this strange and appealing sensation of hopefulness that the project has engendered, despite all its limitations. While I began this inquiry with the assumption that *OBOS* would have much to learn from contemporary feminist theory, in this chapter I will argue that it is contemporary feminist theory that may have just as much, if not more, to learn from *OBOS*. I will take the travels of *OBOS*—the scope and variety of its border crossings, the diversity of its multifaceted transformations, and the ways in which it has shaped encounters between feminists globally—as having implications for feminist scholarship and theory and, more specifically, for how we might begin to think about feminist history, feminist politics of knowledge, and transnational feminism.

Before I discuss these implications, however, I will return briefly to the questions that were raised at the outset of this inquiry: how a U.S. feminist book could resonate with women in such diverse social, cultural, and geographical locations; what happened to it as it traveled; and what these travels can tell us more generally about feminist knowledge and feminist politics in a transnational context.

Making *OBOS*

The present inquiry began with two somewhat unorthodox assumptions. The first was that *OBOS* should be regarded, first and foremost, as an *epistemological project* rather than a popular self-help book on women's health. Within feminist scholarship, the prevailing sentiment is that *OBOS* is historically important, practically useful, and undoubtedly well intentioned but has little of theoretical relevance to offer feminist scholarship. From the vantage point of postmodern feminist theory à la Donna Haraway, Joan Scott, Judith Butler, and many others, *OBOS* is regarded as theoretically naive and unsophisticated because it commits several cardinal theoretical sins: it naturalizes the biological female body, it valorizes women's experiences as authentic sources of the truth, and it glorifies the autonomous agency of individual women. Seen in this light, *OBOS* is at best old-fashioned and unsophisticated and at worst an object requiring critical deconstruction.

In the present inquiry, I have taken issue with this stance. I have argued that some of the assumptions made by postmodern feminist body theory, while helpful in deconstructing the problematic legacy of Western Enlightenment philosophy, have also become blinders, obscuring the analysis of *OBOS* as an epistemological project and, more generally, failing to engage seriously with feminist health activism. This theory gets in the way of exploring what has been the most distinctive feature of *OBOS*, namely, a politics of knowledge that invited individual women to use their own embodied experiences to engage critically with dominant practices of knowledge. This politics of knowledge was reflected in the book's distinctive format (accessible and accountable information, women's personal stories about their bodily experiences, and a critical framework situating women's health in a broader social, cultural, and political context). It was this politics of knowledge that enabled the readers of *OBOS* to become embodied, critical, epistemic agents.

The second assumption of the present inquiry was that in order to fully appreciate the impact and significance of *OBOS* as a feminist icon it would be necessary to connect the book's history *within* the United States with its travels *outside* the United States. This meant that I refrained from writing a straightforward history of *OBOS* as a U.S. feminist project. Instead I have taken the book's travels as a starting point for thinking critically about its impact during the past three decades, the myriad transformations it has undergone, and its worldwide significance as a transnational feminist knowledge project for transnational feminist health politics. This entailed situating the inquiry within contemporary theoretical debates about the politics of location. These debates explore how individuals use their material locations in the world as a resource for knowing what it means to be embodied as a particular kind of person in a particular social and cultural context. The politics of location is also a place from which to construct a critical subjectivity and political perspective for social change. In the present inquiry, I have used the politics of location (social, cultural, and geographical) to understand how *OBOS* as a feminist knowledge project has been able to circulate internationally, thereby generating a transnational feminist politics of the body.

The combination of an approach that treats *OBOS* as an epistemological project and a perspective that decenters it as an exclusively U.S. feminist project has brought me to the following insights.

First, the politics of knowledge represented by *OBOS* was particularly suited to crossing borders of class, race and ethnicity, sexual orientation, and generation, allowing the book to speak to a wide diversity of women. The reason for its success in addressing different women was that it did not assume that women would automatically have identical experiences, needs, or interests simply by virtue of having a female body. Indeed, the book recognized differences in women's embodiment (experiences, social location, and circumstances), and this recognition had consequences for the process in which each new edition of *OBOS* was made. It assumed that this would not be a one-time affair but would require the ongoing critical interrogation of each new version of the book. Through the collaborative method of knowledge production, whereby different women were invited to "read against the grain" and to think critically about the text from their specific embodied location, *OBOS* was not only able to include a variety of perspectives on women's health, but it used these different perspectives to enable readers to think critically about their own embodied experiences, as well as become sensitized to the circumstances of women in social, cultural, and political locations different than their own.

Second, the politics of knowledge represented by *OBOS* not only allowed it to cross the borders of class, race and ethnicity, sexual orientation, and generation within the United States, but it also enabled what was otherwise a local product—a typically U.S. book—to travel. One of the unique features of *OBOS* was that its content, form, and politics did not remain intact in the course of its border crossings. It invited women across the globe to rewrite the book and, ultimately, transform it in ways that would make it accessible and relevant in their own social, cultural, and geopolitical contexts. This required something other than a straightforward translation; it required a feminist translation strategy of "friendly learning by taking a distance" (Spivak 2000). The translators of *OBOS* invariably participated in a collective process of contextualizing and critically reworking the U.S. text, whereby they creatively used differences between their own context and the U.S. context to open up controversial topics, celebrate local accomplishments, or suggest points for political coalitions. The same process of reading against the grain that had been instrumental to the widespread popularity of *OBOS within* the United States proved to be its most translatable feature *outside* the United States. In the course of translating *OBOS*, women from widely divergent locations were able to appropriate this collective, critical process of knowledge production, using *OBOS* as an occasion for developing their own brand of oppositional feminist politics of knowledge.

Third, the travels of *OBOS* have implications for how we think about the circulation of feminist knowledge and politics in a global context. One of the most notable features of the translations is that they were not simply transported from the "West to the rest" (Hall 1992) or imposed as a kind of feminist cultural imperialism. The international trajectory of *OBOS* suggests that the circulation of feminist knowledge is much more complicated and contradictory. When feminist knowledge moves from place to place, it is reworked and rearticulated, allowing new configurations of the original to emerge. Thus, while *OBOS* emerged initially in the United States, its flows were not unidirectional. The text not only moved from place to place, but its translations traveled as well, providing the basis for new translations or returning—literally—to the United States, where they were taken up and used by diasporic communities there. Thus, *OBOS* should be viewed less as a U.S. book with multiple translations than as an ongoing transnational feminist knowledge project.

Fourth, as a catalyst for transnational feminist politics, *OBOS* has created a global feminist imagined community. This community is not based on shared gender identity or common interests or even identical political goals. It has emerged through the engagement of women from different locations with *OBOS*, predicated on their willingness to engage in a shared politics of knowledge. Through the act of making, reading, or translating *OBOS*, women in different locations and at different points in time were able to participate vicariously in that first mythical discussion group "where it all began." The story of the first meeting in 1969 in Boston when a group of young women met to talk about their bodies not only became a foundational myth for U.S. feminism. This myth also traveled, capturing the minds and hearts of women across the globe, who imaginatively situated themselves within the mythical history of *OBOS*, making it their history, too. Thus, the very myth that created *OBOS* as a U.S. feminist success story has, through its travels, enabled *OBOS* not only to continue but to become much more than the original project. As transnational feminist project, *OBOS* has taken on a life of its own, becoming a feminist icon for women across the globe.

Having looked at the making of *OBOS* and how it traveled, I will now turn to the implications of this transnational knowledge project for feminist scholarship—in particular, for feminist history, knowledge politics, and transnational practice.

Feminist History

The making of *OBOS* and the ways it has traveled have implications for how feminist history should be written. In recent years, U.S. feminist historians have devoted considerable attention to what has been called "second-wave feminism."[1]

Written against the backdrop of a widespread feminist backlash in the United States (Faludi 1992), these histories exude a sense of urgency—a desire to set the record straight before it is too late. There is a palpable sense that feminism has come and gone, leaving us with no other choice than to patiently await the next "wave"—a new generation that will pick up the torch and carry on where "we" left off. While many historians lament its passing, expressing an unmistakable nostalgia for the "good old days," others have been more critical, pointing to its mistakes and failings. However, in either case, feminism is treated very much as a U.S. phenomenon. Both its emergence and its demise seemed to occur without reference to what happened outside the United States. The implicit assumption is that what happens in the rest of the world is dependent on what happens to feminism in the United States. It is as if without U.S. feminism there would be no feminism at all.

The history of *OBOS* refutes the assumptions made by this particular brand of feminist historiography. It disrupts the notion that feminism is a thing of the past. While many of the projects of the so-called second wave of U.S. feminism may be over, *OBOS* is not only still around but feminism itself is very much alive and kicking in many different locations around the world. The longevity and the success of *OBOS* are inextricably linked to its capacity to transform itself so that it can speak across shifting lines of difference. Its resilience raises questions concerning the claim that feminism is dead or at least on its last legs. U.S. feminist history has been criticized for its "time-charged terminologies" (first wave, second wave, third wave), which marginalize the activism and worldviews of women of color.[2] Ironically, the very period that white feminist historians typically treat as the moment of decline is the time when women of color began to develop as a new political subject. From the point of view of multiracial feminism in the United States, feminism gained momentum in the eighties and its best days are yet to come (Thompson 2002, 344).

But, even more powerfully, the transnational trajectory of *OBOS* demonstrates that feminism is not limited to the United States and, indeed, may presently play a more significant role outside the United States. U.S. feminism has often situated itself (and been situated by others) as the standard against which all women's struggles across the globe are to be measured. Ironically, even so-called international or comparative studies of feminism tend to treat the United States as the undisputed center of feminist history. Precedence is given to events and struggles occurring within the borders of the United States. A discourse of the Western Enlightenment is reproduced, whereby notions of progress and development are privileged so that what comes after is automatically better than what came before. This version of feminist history tends to leave non-Western women's movements "stuck" in an earlier and "less advanced" stage (Shih 2002, 98). The translations of *OBOS* demonstrate that, while notions about what might constitute a feminist politics of the body may differ, there is a broad interest among women's groups in widely divergent locations about issues of women's health. The international women's health movement is not only one of the most vibrant of the contemporary social movements, but it has become a force to be reckoned with in the terrain of international politics. The global interest in women's health, reproductive rights, and sexual integrity demonstrates that worries about the demise of feminism may be, in fact, little more than ethnocentric myopia, that is, the failure of U.S. feminism to look beyond its own backyard. A more accurate and politically viable vision of history would encompass the wide diversity of feminist histories and women's struggles across the globe.

The global dissemination of *OBOS* shows why—when it comes to the state of feminism in the world—there may be considerably more reason for optimism than despair. It provides a case in point for the importance of what Susan Stanford Friedman has called "thinking 'geographically'" (2001), that is, for replacing the "overdeveloped historical contextualization" of U.S. feminist scholarship with a better-developed "spatial and geographical imagination" (16). This not only means acknowledging and learning about feminist histories of struggles in other parts of the world. At a time when the accelerating pace of globalization and transnational cultural traffic has made national borders increasingly porous, it also makes sense for contemporary feminist historiography to explore the ways in which the global is already implicated in local histories, as well as the diversity of feminist struggles across the globe.[3] By tracking the migratory and transcultural formations, feminism can become viewable as both more ubiquitous (global) and more historically specific (local), that is, as emerging in specific geographical locations and at specific historical moments.

Politics of Knowledge

The making of *OBOS* and its travels also have implications for how we should think about feminist knowledge and knowledge politics. Postmodern feminist scholarship, particularly under the influence of critical race and postcolonial theory, has devoted considerable attention to the production and dissemination of feminist knowledge in the context of global hierarchies of power. Many scholars have criticized the problematic legacy of Western Enlightenment philosophy, along with its humanistic conception of identity, its arrogant claims to universalist knowledge, and its notion of modernity, which locates progress and development squarely in the West, while the non-Western world remains mired in ignorance and tradition (Grewal and Kaplan 1994; Mohanty 2003). Attention has increasingly been paid to the unequal circulation of feminist knowledge, whereby feminist theory (with a capital *T*) is situated in the United States (or France) while non-Western women become the objects of that theory, the "subalterns" in whose name white, already emancipated, First World feminists may speak (Spivak 1988a).

While this critique has been extremely important in uncovering the relationship between power and knowledge in a transnational context, it has tended to focus—somewhat paradoxically—on feminist theory in the West.[4] Postcolonial feminist theorists have directed their critical energy inward, preferring to deconstruct the humanistic, modernist, or ethnocentric assumptions of Western feminist theory (John 1996). The unintended consequence of these critiques has been a centering (rather than a decentering) of feminist theory in the metropoles of the First World rather than an exploration of what actually happens when feminist knowledge and knowledge practices flow from the West to other parts of the globe and how "Western" feminism gets taken up outside the United States. It seems to be assumed that Western feminist conceptions and knowledge practices are automatically irrelevant for or even harmful to feminists in non-Western contexts. But, as Roy (2001) has noted, the assumption that universals are simply the outcome of First World hegemonies makes it difficult to imagine "careful and responsible modes of universalization" in feminist knowledge practices. In short, while sophisticated theoretical reflections on the feminist politics of knowledge in a global context abound, little attention has been paid to the vicissitudes of feminist knowledge practices on the ground and to how feminist knowledge travels and is transformed in ways that might make it oppositional in different locations.

One look at the international impact of *OBOS* as a feminist knowledge project belies the assumption that feminist knowledge that is relevant in the West will automatically be irrelevant for non-Western women. Aside from the fact that it is unclear why the modernization projects of other nations should not be subjected to the same critical scrutiny as the modernization projects of the West (Narayan 1998), the notions of modernity, humanism, and ethnocentrism are hardly limited to the West. The translations of *OBOS* suggest that a more complicated approach is needed. For example, the fact that discourses of equality originated in the West and many exclusions have since been enacted in their name does not mean that these discourses cannot be rearticulated outside the United States in ways that will make them oppositional. The notion of women's reproductive rights—which provides the undisputed ideological lynchpin of *OBOS*—obviously draws on Western notions of equality (with all their drawbacks). Nevertheless, the notion of reproductive rights has proved to be an effective rallying cry for feminist health activism internationally and has been strategic in empowering women in many contexts outside the United States (Petchesky 2003, 1995). It would be shortsighted to dismiss it with the "poison skull" label of ethnocentrism merely because it employs a modernist discourse and politics of rights, equality, and collective struggle (Pfeil 1994, 224).

In the present inquiry, I have shown how non-Western feminist scholars and activists from very different social, cultural, and geopolitical locations have freely borrowed from the U.S. *OBOS*, including its concepts of individualism, choice, and informed consent. While these concepts were clearly modernist in origin, they could easily be used (albeit flexibly and strategically) to empower women in the context of their own (often very different) modernization projects. A case in point is the Bulgarian *OBOS*, which I discussed in chapter 6, in which the individualism of the U.S. book is embraced and rearticulated into a strategy for gendered citizenship and social change as an oppositional response to the postcommunist legacy of collectivist ideologies and state-imposed equality between the sexes. The Bulgarian case illustrates that rather than summarily dismissing Western feminism it makes more sense to explore how feminist concepts and practices associated with the West (e.g., the language and politics of rights, equality, and collective solidarity) are taken up and rearticulated as potentially useful discourses within the contested terrain of oppositional feminist politics.

In other words, rather than viewing *OBOS* as just another typically U.S. feminist book about women's health, it should be regarded as a traveling theory par excellence. It is a prime example of how feminist knowledge and knowledge practices can travel in ways that both take up and reinscribe, but also transform and decenter, Western theory. By looking at how women in other contexts appropriated *OBOS*, a valuable site for theoretical exploration is opened up, offering an opportunity for analyzing how and why feminist knowledge can become oppositional at specific moments in time and in particular locations. Ironically, paying closer attention to the diverse sources and character of non-Western feminist knowledge practices might do more to revitalize Western feminist theory than the most "rigorously reflexive meta-theoretical ruminations" on its own intellectual practices (Stacey 2001, 102).[5]

As Edward Said (1983) argued in his seminal essay on traveling theory, what happens to a theory when it travels is at least as interesting as the "original" for what it can tell us about the limitations and problems, but also the possibilities, of the original. As traveling theory, *OBOS* has shown that it has a unique capacity to generate endless alternatives—a capacity that is, when all is said and done, what critical consciousness is all about (Said 1983, 247). For those theorists interested in decentering First World feminist theory, it may well be time to stop focusing on those theories that are most firmly embedded in the context that is being criticized (the U.S. academy and Western philosophy) and begin considering theories that have demonstrated that they are capable of movement and transformation. For anyone interested in the possibilities of a critical, nonimperialistic, feminist theory on a global scale, any theory with such a capacity clearly deserves our most serious attention.

Transnational Feminist Practice

Finally, the making of *OBOS* and its travels have implications for how transnational feminist practice should be theorized. This inquiry has critically engaged with the ideological commitment to internationalism that assumes that feminism can encompass all women regardless of nationality, uniting them against the masculine aberrations of fascism, imperialism, and war.[6] In its most recent incarnation, this dream of international feminist solidarity has come to be known as transnational feminism. This version of international feminist politics rejects binaries such as the West and the rest, global and local, and center and periphery, assuming instead that women are linked by globally structured relations of power that influence their lives at every level in ways that are both varied and historically specific (Grewal and Kaplan 1994, 13). Women are viewed as having different experiences, different needs, and different struggles depending on the particularities of their local circumstances, as well as their location within a global nexus of power. This conception of transnational feminism assumes that, while feminist alliances are necessary and desirable, they are also invariably infused with inequalities and hierarchies. It is essential, therefore, that feminists do not assume a natural affinity based on a shared gender identity but rather acknowledge their complicities in national histories of imperialism, colonialism, and slavery. Differences rather than similarities among women should be drawn on as an occasion for global dialogues about common issues and common struggles. That these alliances are complicated and often fraught with contradictions is illustrated by the recent emergence of feminist NGOs that adopt agendas inspired by the United Nations and engage in international coalitions aimed at helping Third World women. These coalitions can involve mainly urban, middle-class, white feminists ("globetrotting feminists") from different parts of the world who meet at international megaconferences to set feminist agendas, often to the detriment of the local activism of community-based women's groups (Alvarez 1998; Thayer 2000). While these transnational feminist alliances are undoubtedly undertaken out of a desire for international feminist solidarity, in practice they sometimes exacerbate inequalities among women at a local level and even deradicalize local feminist politics (Mendoza 2002). Thus, transnational feminism requires constant vigilance in order to ensure that global linkages between women remain mutually empowering (Mohanty 2003). However, by looking at how feminists actually work across lines of difference in the context of transnational alliances, some of the pessimism of this important critique can be tempered by a more realistic and simultaneously more hopeful perspective on transnational feminist politics.[7]

In the present inquiry, I have shown how the alliances generated in the course of translating *OBOS* bear many of the features of what might be called *good* transnational feminist practice—that is, practice based on the acknowledgment of differences among women, on an awareness of privilege and complicity in national histories of domination, and an attempt to discover common concerns and struggles.

As we have seen, *OBOS* went from an almost exclusively U.S. project to a transnational feminist project with offshoots across the globe. The "center" of *OBOS* gradually moved to the "periphery," whereby the translations increasingly became the raison d'être for the project as a whole. In the wake of waning sales and uncertainties concerning future editions of *OBOS* within the United States, the translation projects clearly were instrumental in the longevity and success of *OBOS* as feminist project. In this context, the U.S. collective increasingly took on a supportive role, facilitating the adaptation of the book in other contexts. The help provided was of the "no strings attached" variety, sometimes interventionist, sometimes "hands off," depending on the needs of the local groups doing the translations. Members of the U.S. collective was consistently mindful of their status, using their financial and organizational resources, international status, expertise, and substantial international network to help local women's groups do what they wanted to do. Moreover, the groups involved in translating and disseminating *OBOS* did not passively adopt the agenda set out by their U.S. "sisters" but rather used the project in ways that fit their own needs and political agendas, sometimes explicitly in opposition to the U.S. project. Thus, *OBOS* provides a promising example of how U.S. feminism can be decentered while maintaining an awareness of and responsibility toward the unequal division in resources (financial, institutional, and informational) between First and Third World feminists. It shows how feminist political practice can recognize and (re)dress global power hierarchies while remaining mutually beneficial for all parties concerned.

However, *OBOS* is not simply an illustration of how transnational feminism works in practice. It also suggests some directions in which contemporary scholarship on transnational feminist politics should be elaborated. While postcolonial feminist scholarship tends to highlight difference as the sine qua non of any feminist alliance across national borders, the transnational alliances around *OBOS* indicate that the similarities or commonalities among women may be equally important.[8] Despite its commitment to the struggles of non-Western women, postcolonial feminist scholarship has not paid sufficient attention to the actual practices of activists from the First and Third Worlds who are already working across lines of difference. As a result, the lessons that these practices might teach us have been foreclosed in advance by a perspective that commits itself to "unbridgeable distance between differently constituted individuals or groups" (Pfeil 1994, 226).

Ultimately, a political perspective of "unity in difference," a determination to remain "full of hope," may be just as—or even more—important for a transnational feminist politics than the recognition of the many differences and conflicts that divide us (Pfeil 1994, 227).

The efforts of feminist activists already working across borders to create workable coalitions attest to an awareness of conflict but also to a belief in the possibility of solidarity. As we have seen, this unity in difference does not have to be of the "common world of women" variety that has been so perceptively criticized by Mohanty (2003) and others. Nor does it require a shared identity, a common experience of oppression, or even a collective political ideology. As the translation projects have shown, community can be constructed imaginatively as a common history that begins with a small group of Boston women meeting in 1970 to talk about their bodies and continues through space and time to include Serbian activists, Japanese feminist scholars, Armenian physicians, and even Tibetan nuns. Incommensurable differences in personal history, social and cultural contexts, and geopolitical circumstances are not forgotten but momentarily transcended in order to create a liminal unity. The global feminist imagined community that is generated through working together on *OBOS* is a shared political project—a project aimed at developing empowering knowledge practices concerning women's bodies, sexuality, and health.

On a Hopeful Note

Up until now, I have dealt with the reasons for a hopeful assessment of *OBOS* and its travels. It's unlikely that *OBOS* could have emerged at a different time or in a different place than during the exuberant activism of the sixties in the United States. Nor could it have happened without a group of women (the "founders") with the vision and motivation to launch such a project and the stamina to persevere through several more decades. It required a mass audience eager to read and be inspired by what the book had to say. But the success and longevity of *OBOS* cannot be attributed to these historically specific conditions alone. Processes of globalization have enabled knowledge and information to circulate around the globe. People are on the move (willingly or unwillingly), making the borders between nations and cultures more permeable and creating opportunities for cross-cultural exchange. Information and communication technologies make global connections possible across time and space. The global expansion of capital has done much to increase disparities between the postindustrial nations of the First and the Third Worlds. However, while the threatening cloud of globalization has given us ample reason for pessimism, it has also provided cause for optimism, particularly because it has enabled what Appadurai (2000) has called "grassroots globalization" or "globalization from below."

It is my contention that the global dissemination of *OBOS*—its seemingly unstoppable ability to cross borders—is just such an example of grassroots globalization. Despite its limitations, it has—through its myriad transformations—invariably provided opportunities for dialogue among differently embodied and differently located women. While these dialogues are hardly a sinecure for the global empowerment of women, they offer the possibility of understanding points of divergence and intersection among women across multiple borders, whether personal, cultural, national, or political.

Throughout this inquiry, I have been puzzled over the willingness of many feminist groups to undergo enormous hardship in order to get a mere book translated. I have wondered at the equanimity with which they struggled to finish the book only to have their publishers balk at giving it proper distribution. And I have observed with growing despair how foundations are more than willing to finance translation projects under the banner of international feminism and yet have no interest in the less sexy and more mundane task of keeping these projects afloat once the book has come out. And yet, despite all odds, those women involved in *OBOS*, both within and outside the United States, seem prepared to carry on, taking difficulties in stride in order to produce new editions of the book. It is, ultimately, the process of collaboration rather than the outcome that justifies the enormous expenditure of time and effort and makes the project worth doing.

The process of transforming *OBOS*, whether updating it for a new generation of readers or translating it for another audience, involves getting women together and discussing the book against the backdrop of their specific experiences. It involves finding ways to make the book interrogate and speak across lines of difference shaped by class, race, ethnicity, sexual orientation, and more. This process invariably entails introducing feminist discourses and initiating collective forms of political activity that can make sense in specific locations. This project of cultural translation—in the broadest sense of the word—is an occasion for what can become a transnational, cross-cultural dialogue among women loosely united under the banner of a shared, but differently conceived, feminist political project. Such encounters inevitably provide an opportunity for what Lugones (1990) has called "world traveling"—the delight and pain of entering another's world, in learning "what it is to be them and what it is to be ourselves in their eyes" (401).

It is, of course, an open question whether such encounters will provide the kind of dialogue necessary for mutually empowering and reflexive transnational feminism. It may not always be possible for future editions of *OBOS* to maintain a commitment to the critical politics of knowledge that made it oppositional and translatable to other contexts: its commitment to women's embodied experience as critical resource; its critical engagement with dominant forms of knowledge; and its conviction that all knowledge is situated and partial, requiring ongoing reflection and critique. However, based on the present inquiry into the making of *OBOS* and its travels as an epistemological project, my inclination is to end this book on a note of optimism and an appreciation for the hopeful glimpse that this particular feminist project provides of what might someday become a better world.

❋ **APPENDICES**

Title	Language/Country Published	Date Published/Current Status	Coordination/Publisher
Our Bodies, Ourselves for the New Century	Korean/South Korea	2005	Alternative Culture Publishing Co. in collaboration with the Korea Sexual Violence Relief Center
Nasze ciała, nasze życie (Our Bodies, Our Lives)	Polish/Poland	2004	Network of East/West Women, Polska
Մենք ու մեր մարմինը Menk ou Mer Marmine (We and Our Body)	Armenian/Armenia	2001	Charitable Foundation on Population Development in collaboration with the Armenian for Family and Health Association
Tu Si Corpul Tau Pentru un Nou Secol (You and Your Body for Moldova a New Century)	Romanian/Moldova	Summer 2002	National Women's Studies and Information Center, Moldova
Нашето Тяло, Ние Самите Nasheto Tyalo, Nie Samite (Our Body, We Ourselves)	Bulgarian/Bulgaria	Summer 2001	Women's Health Initiative with help from the Open Society Foundation and the Global Fund for Women
Naša Tela, Mi (Our Bodies, We)	Serbo-Croatian/Serbia	Summer 2001	Autonomous Women's Center against Sexual Violence with help from the Soros Foundation
Nuestros Cuerpos, Nuestras Vidas (Our Bodies, Our Lives)	Spanish/United States	2000, 1977/translation out of print	Collaboration between Latina groups in the United States and groups in Latin America, published in collaboration with BWHBC

Title (translation)	Language/Country	Printing history	Publisher/notes
Unser Körper, Unser Leben (Our Bodies, Our Lives)	German/Germany	Vols. 1 and 2, 1980; revised, 1988/ Vol. 1 in 19th printing (1999); Vol. 2 in 15th printing (1996)	Rowolt Verlag in collaboration with a group of feminist health activists
我们的身体 我们自己 (Our Bodies, Ourselves)	Mandarin/China	1998; 3rd printing 1999/in print, adaptation currently on hold	Translated by the Chinese Women's Health Network and the Women's Studies Institute of China and printed by the Encyclopedia Publishing House of China, Science and Technology Department
ร่างกาย ของเรา ตัวตนของเรา	Thai/Thailand	1996/out of print, adaptation currently on hold	Self-published by the Women's Health Education Network in collaboration with the Population Council of Bangkok
О Вас и Вашем Теле (About You and Your Body)	Russian/Russia	1995/out of print	Progress Publishing Co., out of business. A women's health group in St. Petersburg is currently working on a new edition.
Our Bodies, Ourselves	English/United Kingdom	1978, 1988/in print	Published by Penguin Books
からだ・私たち自身 (Bodies, Ourselves)	Japanese/Japan	1975, 1988/out of print	松香堂, published by Shokado Women's Bookstore, Osaka
Notre corps, nous-mêmes (Our Bodies, Ourselves)	French/France	1977, 1987/in print	Published by Albin Michel, Paris
הגוף שלנו חיינו (Our Bodies, Ourselves)	Hebrew/Israel	1982/out of print	Published by Second Sex Publishing House, out of business

Title	Language/ Country Published	Date Published/Current Status	Coordination/Publisher
Nuestros Cuerpos, Nuestras Vidas (Our Bodies, Our Lives)	Spanish/Spain	1982/out of print	Published by Icaria Editorial, Barcelona
Je Lichaam, Je Leven (Your Body, Your Life)	Dutch/the Netherlands	1981/out of print	Published by Bert Bakker/Prometheus, Amsterdam
Εμεις Και Το Σομα Μας (We and Our Body)	Greek/Greece	1981/out of print	Published by Ipodomi Books, Ltd., out of business
Våra Kroppar Våra Jag (Our Bodies, Ourselves)	Swedish/Sweden	1980/out of print	Published by Gidlunds
Noi e il Nostro Corpo (We and Our Body)	Italian/Italy	1974/out of print	Published by Feltrinelli Editore

Source: The *Our Bodies, Ourselves* Web site, www.ourbodiesourselves.org.

Note: A seven-volume Braille edition was produced from the 1973 edition; all editions except that of 1970 have appeared in audio versions.

APPENDIX TWO * Books Inspired by *OBOS*

Title	Language/ Country Published	Date Published/Status	Coordination/Publisher
Healthy Body, Healthy Mind	Tibetan/India	2005	Coordinated and published by the Tibetan Nuns Project with funding from the Global Fund for Women
Notre corps, notre santé (Our Bodies, Our Health)	French/Senegal	2004	Coordinated by Groupe de Recherche sur Les Femmes et Les Lois au Sénégal. Published by La Santé et la Sexualité des Femmes en Afrique Subsaharienne
Taking Charge of Our Bodies: A Health Handbook for Women	English/India	2004	Coordinated by the Hyderabad Women's Health Group at the Anveshi Research Centre for Women's Studies. Published by Penguin
Kvinde Kend din Krop (Woman Know Your Body)	Danish/Denmark	1st edition, 1975; 4th edition, 2001	Coordinated by K. Vinders Fond. Published by Tiderne Skifter
The South African Women's Health Book	English/South Africa	1996/in print	Coordinated by the Women's Health Project and published by Oxford University Press
A Hundred Thousand Questions about Women's Health	Telugu/India	1991/in print; an English adaptation (see entry above) was recently published.	Coordinated and published by the Hyderabad Women's Health Group at Anveshi Research Centre for Women's Studies
حياة المرأة وصحتها Hayāt al-mar'a wa'sihatuhā (The Life of a Woman and Her Health)	Arabic/Egypt	1991	Coordinated by the Cairo Women's Health Book Collective. Published by Sina li'n-nashr, a woman-owned publisher in Cairo

Source: The *Our Bodies, Ourselves* Web site, www.ourbodiesourselves.org

APPENDIX THREE * Translations and Adaptations of *OBOS* in Progress

Language	Country	Coordinating Group/Publisher	Status
Albanian	Albania	Coordinating group: Women's Center Tirana Publisher: The Book and Communication House International Cultural Center	The coordinating group is currently working on a direct translation of *OBOS*.
Indonesian	Indonesia	Coordinating group: Consumers Union of Indonesia	The Consumers Union has adapted and illustrated two editions of *OBOS* with support from the Ford Foundation. The first book focuses on reproductive health, the second on reproductive rights. The latest edition is stalled at the production/publishing stage and has not yet been distributed.
Turkish	Turkey	Coordinating group: Mavi Kalem (Association for Social Assistance and Charity) Publisher: Citlembik	Mavi Kalem is currently working on the adaptation and is creating a companion Web site to accompany the book. It has created a brochure titled "Why on Earth a Turkish Adaptation of *Our Bodies, Ourselves?* Let Me Explain . . ."
Hausa, Yoruba, Igbo, Pidgin English, Shante, Fante, Egun, and English	Nigeria	Coordinating group: Women for Empowerment, Development, and Gender Reform	Although the coordinators have not yet raised funds to fully implement the project, they have begun to translate sections for use in community-based outreach on HIV/AIDS and sexually transmitted infections.

Source: The *Our Bodies, Ourselves* Web site, www.ourbodiesourselves.org.

APPENDIX FOUR * Translations and Adaptations of *OBOS* Seeking Funds for Start-up

Language	Country	Coordinating Group/Publisher	Status
Arabic	Unknown	A network of women in Jordan are seeking to identify an appropriate group to coordinate this project.	The network is seeking funds to produce an Arabic adaptation. They plan to involve other organizations in the region.
Hebrew	Israel	Women and Their Bodies (WATB)–The Association of Women for Health Action and Responsibility	This project is a collaboration among women of many ages, occupations, and ethnicities. The goal is to produce *OBOS* in both Hebrew and Arabic, with the Arabic focusing on the health issues and conditions of Palestinian women.
Russian	Russia	Women's Health in Saint Petersburg	This project is in the planning stage, and the group is seeking funding.
Portuguese	Brazil	Mulher e Saúde (MUSA)	This project is in the planning stage, and the group is seeking funding.
Nepali	Nepal	Women's Rehabilitation Centre	The group is seeking funding.
Vietnamese	Vietnam	Institute for Social Development Studies	The Institute conducts social science research on gender, health, and sexuality, and the coordinators plan to produce a comprehensive self-help book and a series of informational booklets based on *OBOS* for specific audiences.

Source: The *Our Bodies, Ourselves* Web site, www.ourbodiesourselves.org.

1 See the afterword in the 2005 updated edition of *For Her Own Good*, by Barbara Ehrenreich and Deirdre English, in which they chronicle some of the changes that have taken place in medicine since their path-breaking book on women's historical relationship with the medical profession and medical knowledge was published in 1978.

2 The study not only showed that medical allegations that HRT prevented heart disease and Alzheimer's and kept women soft skinned, sexually vital, and emotionally balanced were incorrect but that women on hormones suffered higher rates of breast cancer and were twice as likely to develop dementia than women who were not taking hormones. See Landau and Cyr 2003; and Seaman 2003.

3 See Davis 1995, 1997, 2003.

4 The oral history part of my inquiry, initially its raison d'être, is now contained in chapter 3.

5 See Moi 2002 for an interesting discussion of the international reception of this well-known feminist classic.

6 See Bell and Reverby 2005.

7 I discuss this in chapter 7.

8 Obviously, I am using border here to encompass more than national borders. Throughout this inquiry, I have dealt with the ways in which *OBOS* has crossed (and sometimes failed to cross) the metaphorical and material borders of class, "race," ethnicity, religion, sexuality, age, and able-bodiedness.

9 "I need to understand how a place on the map is also a place in history within which as a woman, a Jew, a lesbian, a feminist I am created and trying to create" (Rich 1986, 212). Rich was primarily interested in white U.S. feminists' becoming more reflexive about their location in the world. While acknowledging the importance of this intervention, Kaplan (1996) has criticized Rich for remaining "locked into the conventional opposition of the global-local nexus as well as the binary construction of Western and non-Western," thereby reducing the issue of accountability between women in the North and South rather than between women within the United States as a whole (166).

10 Frankenberg and Mani (1993) use a politics of location to criticize Eurocentric periodizations that reproduce the temporal logic of domi-

nant histories, advocating instead a conception of historical processes as uneven and discontinuous. Criticizing the too hasty use of postcoloniality within contemporary feminist and postcolonial theory, they note that at "given moments and locations, the axis of colonialization/decolonialization might be the most salient one, at other times, not so" (304).

11 Nancy Hartsock (1983, 1998) deserves credit for this important intervention in feminist knowledge politics. It has since been taken up and elaborated by many others. See, for example, Keller 1985; Harding 1986, 1991, 1998; Smith 1987, 1990a; Haraway 1991b; Moya 1997, 2001; and Collins 2000. For a constructive discussion of the significance of standpoint thinking for feminist theory, see the discussion in the winter 1997 issue of the journal *Signs* (Heckman 1997a, 1997b; Hartsock 1997; Collins 1997; Harding 1997; Smith 1997).

12 See Henwood et al. 1998 for an illuminating discussion of the similarities and differences between feminist standpoint thinking and feminist discussions of differences in the ways women are situated in terms of race, class, sexuality, and nationality.

13 Some of the best-known and most frequently cited examples include Davis 1981; Smith 1983; hooks 1981, 2000; Moraga and Anzaldúa 1983; Anzaldúa 1987, 1990; King 1988; Spelman 1988; Crenshaw 1989; Sandoval 1991; and Mohanty 2003.

14 In describing this "vision of feminism," I have adopted Friedman's (2001) use of feminism in the singular, rather than feminisms, as encompassing "myriad and often conflicting cultural and political formations in a global context" (4). In her view, it was the specific U.S. context of identity politics that demanded the diversification of feminism. However, the risk of pluralization is a fetishization of difference—a point to which I will return in chapter 7. As Audre Lorde (1984) wisely noted, "It's not our differences which separate women, but our reluctance to recognize these differences" (122).

15 Ahmed (2000) uses the metaphor "strange encounter" to think about global alliances among feminists that are not based on a false universalism, nor on an irresponsible cultural relativism, but rather on a dialogue that "must take place, precisely because we don't speak the same language." A strange encounter occurs when "one has a close encounter, where something happens that is surprising, and where 'we' establish an alliance through the very process of being unsettled by that which is not yet" (180).

16 While Grewal and Kaplan view transnational feminism as a more helpful term than global feminism, they are aware that it is not a panacea. As they put it in a later publication, no term is ever authentic or pure but needs to be examined in terms of its various articulations and the rhetorical imperatives underlying its uses in different institutional sites (2001, 664).

17 The term founders is contested, as I will discuss in chapter 3. I use

it here, however, in the same way that the members of the BWHBC do to refer to members of the "original group" (formally constituted in 1972) and three additional members who were taken into the group and given the title founder at a later date.

18 Most of the founders lived in or near Boston. The exception was Elizabeth MacMahon-Herrera, who lived in the southwestern United States. We had a long interview by phone, which I also taped and transcribed. All of the interviews have been released to the Schlesinger Library at the Radcliffe Institute at Harvard University.

19 This material provides the basis for the first three chapters of the book: the history of *OBOS* in the United States, the history of the translation projects, and the collective history of the BWHBC.

20 This is the subject of chapter 4.

21 I received a Berkshire History Summer Fellowship from the Radcliffe Institute of Advanced Study, which enabled me to spend several months in these archives. Before that, I had worked—somewhat sporadically—in the library of the BWHBC, which was disbanded shortly after the organization's papers were donated to the Schlesinger Library.

22 I also discovered great quantities of blank paper, doodles on notepads, and the occasional half-empty ballpoint pen. The files have since been processed and are considerably more user friendly than they were, thanks to the able work of Kathy Kraft of the Schlesinger Library.

23 This is the subject of chapter 5.

24 Vilunya Diskin, Judy Norsigian, Norma Swenson, and Jennifer Yanco provided considerable background information. Sally Whelan, the current director of translation and adaptation projects, has been my most constant informant, keeping me abreast of all recent developments, as well as sharing her vision about *OBOS* as a transnational project.

25 In recent years, the prefaces of the translations have been translated and posted on the *Our Bodies, Ourselves* Web site. They provide an invaluable resource for understanding why different groups decided to make the translations, how they changed the U.S. text (and why), and how they situated themselves in *OBOS* as a transnational feminist project.

26 I describe this meeting in chapter 6.

I *OBOS* in the United States

1 The 2005 edition of *OBOS* was published as I was in the process of finishing this inquiry. While I have discussed it briefly in this chapter, the analysis in the remainder of the book is based on earlier editions.

2 In addition to the founders (see note 13), I interviewed Heather Stephenson, who was the editor of the 2005 *OBOS*. The group interview

described in this chapter was conducted with Judy Norsigian, Jane Pincus, and Wendy Sanford on July 21, 2000.

3 For the history of this period of the women's liberation movement, see Evans 1979, 2003; Echols 1989; DuPlessis and Snitow 1998; Brownmiller 1999; and Rosen 2000.

4 Interview, Paula Doress-Worters (December 2, 1998).

5 Interview, Jane Pincus (January 20, 1999).

6 See Freeman 1971; and Shreve 1989.

7 Interview, Wendy Sanford (December 4, 1998).

8 Jane Pincus in group interview (July 21, 2000).

9 Considerable attention has been given to the neglect of differences among women in the early stages of "second-wave" feminism. See, for example, Bell et al. 1981; hooks 1981; Moraga and Anzaldúa 1983; Smith 1983; Alarcón 1990; Mohanty et al. 1991; Wing 1997; and Ruiz and DuBois 2000, just to name a few.

10 See Ginsburg 1998; and Solinger 1998.

11 Interview, Joan Ditzion (October 28, 1998). She is quoting from an angry letter that was sent to the New England Free Press after the group transferred the book to Simon and Schuster.

12 Later this contract was expanded to include foreign-language translations, which could only be undertaken by local women's groups approved by the BWHBC. All royalties would go to those groups.

13 The original BWHBC members included Ruth Bell, Pamela Berger, Vilunya Diskin, Joan Ditzion, Paula Doress, Nancy Hawley, Judy Norsigian, Jane Pincus, Esther Rome, Wendy Sanford, and Norma Swenson. The twelfth member, Mary Stern, left after the first year. I will be returning to the way the group evolved in chapter 3.

14 The BWHBC records at the Schlesinger Library (no. 154.12) contain numerous reviews praising *OBOS*, including scholarly reviews in medical journals as well as reviews in national newspapers from the *Wall Street Journal* to small town dailies to feminist publications and popular magazines such as *Parade* and the *Ladies' Home Journal*.

15 See Sanford and Dorress 1981 for an account of these censorship attacks.

16 Interview, Norma Swenson (October 29, 1998).

17 Interview, Joan Ditzion (October 28, 1998).

18 For a nostalgic look at these early discussions, see Abbott and Love 1972; and Johnston 1974.

19 Interview, Jane Pincus (January 20, 1999).

20 In 1979, Sally Whelan was hired to develop the Women's Health Information Center, which later became a comprehensive library devoted to women's health issues.

21 See Ruzek 1978; Moss 1996; Norsigian 1996; Clarke and Olesen 1999; Ruzek, Olesen, and Clarke 1997; Ruzek and Becker 1999; and Morgen 2002.

22 Between 1974 and 1980 the bwhbc provided financial assistance to many other women's health groups—for example, to Cambridge Documentary Films for the production of the feminist film on women's health (*Taking Our Bodies Back*), the Boston Area Rape Crisis Center, the translators of the French *OBOS*, the Philadelphia Women's Health Concerns Committee, the Association of Radical Midwives, Casa Myrna Vasquez, Women Organized for Reproductive Choice, the Twelfth National Conference on Women and the Law, and the Rising Sun Feminist Health Alliance. See bwhbc Records 1972–1997 [#7.1], Schlesinger Library, Radcliffe Institute, Harvard University, Cambridge, Massachusetts.

23 Interview, Judy Norsigian (October 27, 1998).

24 Depending upon how substantial the changes were and how much new material was included, the new editions of *OBOS* were called updates (15 to 20 percent new material without substantial changes in content), revisions (30 to 60 percent new material and the same basic outline but with new discussions of issues and the removal of outdated material), and rewrites (total revisions of the book). Updates were published in 1979 and 1992 and revisions in 1973, 1976, 1984, and 1998. The 2005 edition was the only "rewrite" (data from the "*OBOS* Update Manual," which was written by the bwhbc for the editors of future editions of *OBOS*).

25 The acknowledgments in the 1984 edition of *OBOS* cover three pages with four columns of names in small print, including groups and individual contributors.

26 Interview, Jane Pincus (January 20, 1999).

27 Later this chapter became so extensive that Paula Doress-Worters, a founder, and Diana Siegel turned it into a book, the popular *Ourselves Growing Older*, which was published in 1987 and updated in 1994.

28 Interview, Paula Doress-Worters (December 2, 1998).

29 Interview, Wendy Sanford (December 4, 1998).

30 Interview, Wendy Sanford (December 4, 1998).

31 See Hayden 1997 for an interesting discussion of how the rhetoric of *OBOS* changed over the years.

32 Interview, Norma Swenson (October 29, 1998).

33 See, for example, the collection of the controversial and widely read papers that were presented at the "sex wars" conference held at Barnard College in 1982, Vance 1984.

34 See, for example, Chesler 1973; and Smith and David 1975 for classic renditions of this argument.

35 Interview, Nancy Miriam Hawley (January 21, 1999).

36 I will return to how this intersectional strategy worked in terms of mobilizing critical readings of the text in chapter 5.

37 Interview, Joan Ditzion (October 28, 1998).

38 Morgen's (2002) work is particularly useful for understanding the context in which the BWHBC and other grassroots collectives attempted to negotiate the dream of a multiracial feminism with the hard realities of giving up class and racially based privilege and forging workable alliances across lines of difference in the workplace. The story of the BWHBC does not stand alone but is part of a larger story of the politics of race and class in U.S. social movements.

39 In 1992, an update was done in which the organizational format of the book remained unchanged, but outdated information was eliminated and replaced with more up-to-date material and references. New topics like AIDS, new birth control methods, and special disorders that effect primarily women were added. For the 25th anniversary of the BWHBC in 1996, a new edition of *OBOS* was published with a new cover and prefaces by well-known feminists Byllye Avery, founder of the Black Woman's Health Project, Helen Rodriguez-Trias, a physician active in the Committee to End Sterilization Abuse (CESA), and Gloria Steinem, the founder of *Ms.* magazine and long-time activist. This "update" caused considerable upheaval among authors and readers. While it "looked like a new edition," it was, in fact, an old edition in a new package. As Wendy Sanford put it: "I just felt it was a marketing ploy and it really bothered me. And we got some complaints. People called: 'I bought your new book. It's not new. It's the same book.' Ughhh. It really upset me. I was embarrassed." Interview, Wendy Sanford (December 4, 1998).

40 Interview, Jane Pincus (January 20, 1999).

41 I will discuss these conflicts in more detail in chapter 3.

42 Interview, Wendy Sanford (December 4, 1998).

43 Interview, Norma Swenson (October 29, 1998).

44 Despite this intention, *OBOS* has always been less successful in its treatment of health issues among low-income women. While it has discussed the effects of lack of education, poor jobs, and inadequate housing on women's health in a general way, it has had less to say about the effects on women's lived experience with poverty. A more successful book on women's health that addresses both class and race in conjunction with women's health experiences and draws on a politics of knowledge very similar to that of *OBOS* is *The Black Women's Health Book: Speaking for Ourselves* (1990). For black feminist perspectives on women's health, see also Smith 1995; and Springer 1999.

45 Interview, Wendy Sanford (December 4, 1998).

46 Interview, Jane Pincus (January 20, 1999).

47 Ibid.

48 The editorial group consisted of Judy Norsigian, a founder and now the director of the BWHBC; Kiki Zeldes, who was responsible for the accompanying Web site; and Zobeida Bonilla, who was to check on "tone and voice."

49 Bonilla (2005) describes the attention that went into ensuring that the language of the 2005 book was "inclusive" enough to speak to differ-

ent groups of women. For example, the editors avoided the use of "us" and "them" pronouns and constructions of specific women as "other" and strove to include representative personal experiences, as well as an accessible presentation of medical information.

50 Interview, Heather Stephenson (April 7, 2005).

51 Interview, Judy Norsigian (April 7, 2005).

52 Ibid.

53 This narrative strategy is analyzed in more depth in chapter 5.

54 See Goodman 2003; Fox 2005; and Helfland 2005.

55 Interview, Judy Norsigian (April 7, 2005).

56 In contrast, Davis-Floyd (1994) draws on differences in embodied experience to understand the desire of pregnant professional women for elective C-sections. Her critique of the medicalization of childbirth resonates with *OBOS*. She does not treat C-sections merely as a matter of informed choice, but draws instead on the earlier politics of knowledge expressed in *OBOS*, which seeks to understand why certain women might choose to have a C-section despite its drawbacks.

57 See Morgen 1995, 2002; Simonds 1996; Weisman 1998; and Taylor 1999.

58 To date, the organization survives on a combination of 50 percent foundation subsidies, 15 percent royalties, 25 percent individual contributions, and the rest from miscellaneous sources. It is interesting that individual contributions often come from readers who want to "give back" something to a book that meant so much to them in the past.

59 See Ehrenreich and English 2005 for a classic rendition of this critique. See also Riessman 1983; Davis 1988; Todd 1989; and Lorber 1997.

60 Beginning in 1970, when just under 8 percent of U.S. physicians were women, the percentage of female physicians began to steadily increase—to nearly 12 percent in 1980 and 17 percent in 1990 (American Medical Association, *Women in Medicine: An AMA Timeline*, http://www.ama-assn.org/ama1/pub/upload/mm/19/wimtimeline.pdf [accessed March 19, 2007]).

61 As Judy Norsigian put it, public health education had always been their "natural ally," and yet, somewhat ironically, only recently have the editors begun to direct their attention explicitly to how *OBOS* could become part of the public health school curriculum. Interview, Judy Norsigian (April 7, 2005). In contrast, the Spanish edition of *OBOS* had always been explicitly used for community outreach and public health education programs.

62 Susan Love's *Dr. Susan Love's Breast Book* (1990) and Christiane Northrup's *The Wisdom of Menopause* (2001) are two of many well-known self-help books on women's health.

63 The German feminist historian Barbara Duden (2002) has argued that the women's health movement has played a role in this development. The quest for knowledge, together with the expansion of tech-

nology, leaves feminists no other choice than to engage critically with these technologies. This also resonates with Donna Haraway's (1997) "modest witness," who cannot stand outside the technologies he or she critiques.

64 Copies of the book have, of course, been donated to clinics all over the world, where they have been used as educational tools. In this sense, *OBOS* does reach women who would otherwise be unable to afford it. Moreover, the BWHBC has invariably been engaged in community outreach projects. The problems of making the book available to low-income women or women without literacy skills have been dealt with creatively by many of the translation projects—a subject to which I will return in later chapters. It is here, perhaps, that the U.S. *OBOS* has the most to learn from its translations.

2 *OBOS* Abroad

1 Interview, Marlies Bosch (December 2, 2000). Most of the participants were young Tibetan nuns between the ages of 18 and 22, who had been living in nunneries in Ladakh, often brought there by parents escaping persecution in Tibet.

2 Interview, Marlies Bosch (December 2, 2000). The Tibetan edition has recently been completed. Under the title *Healthy Body, Healthy Mind*, by the Tibetan Nun Project, it focuses on teaching basic health issues, body awareness, nutrition, and hygiene and is intended for distribution throughout the Himalayan region.

3 For an updated look at the translations, see www.ourbodiesourselves.org. This list contains the projects that maintain an active contact with the BWHBC. There are, however, countless "unofficial" translations, cases in which a local group translates a chapter or two for its own purposes. Recently, a colleague told me that she had left her copy of *OBOS* at a clinic in Burma where local health workers translated the pregnancy and childbirth chapters for use by their patients.

4 The term Third World is problematic for various reasons. It separates the "First" from the "Third" Worlds in ways that belie their interconnectedness, and it provides no space for regions that are emerging from communism and no longer belong to a "Second World." While I will often be contrasting "Western"—that is, U.S. and Eurocentric feminism—with non-Western feminisms, this, too, is problematic as it seems to efface the divide between North and South. Keeping in mind that there is no completely satisfactory terminology that captures the complexity of global power relations, I will be using all these terms somewhat interchangeably throughout this book. For a discussion of some of the issues of finding the right terminology to speak about global power relations, see Grewal and Kaplan 1994; Jaggar 1998; and Mackie 2001.

5 For the seminal discussion of cultural imperialism, see Edward Said's pathbreaking *Culture and Imperialism* (1994). Many feminist scholars have employed the concept of cultural imperialism to criticize U.S. feminism. It goes beyond the scope of this chapter to deal with this discussion at length, although I have done so in an article (Davis 2002). The interested reader is referred to Lugones and Spelman 1983; Anzaldúa 1987; Enloe 1989; Mohanty et al. 1991; Grewal and Kaplan 1994; Kaplan 1996; Alexander and Mohanty 1997; and Mohanty 2003.

6 Interview, Norma Swenson (October 29, 1998).

7 See the list of foreign-language editions in appendix one.

8 While many of the European editions went through several printings, most are now out of print. The Danish *Kvinde Kend din Krop* (Woman Know Your Body), which was not a translation but a book inspired by *OBOS*, went through four printings, the last one in 2001. A revised French *Notre Corps, Nous-Mêmes* appeared in 1987 and a new *OBOS* for the United Kingdom in 1988. There were several reissues of the two-volume German *Unser Körper, Unser Leben* in 1980 and, based on the 1984 *OBOS*, again in 1988; there was also a nineteenth reissue of volume 1 in 1999 and a fifteenth reissue of volume 2 in 1996.

9 Interview, Norma Swenson (March 19, 1999).

10 This was a particularly circuitous translation story, involving various editions that circulated throughout the southern hemisphere before a comprehensive adaptation involving the efforts of several feminist Latina groups in the North and South was published in 2000. I will be returning to the complexities of this adaptation later in this chapter, as well as in chapter 6.

11 This edition is currently out of print, but a new project under the auspices of a women's health nongovernmental organization (NGO) in St. Petersburg is currently under way.

12 For a thoughtful account of this project, see the group's project proposal, "Why on Earth a Turkish Adaptation of Our Bodies, Ourselves?" posted on the *Our Bodies, Ourselves* Web site, http:// www.ourbodiesourselves.org/programs/network/funding/turkish.asp (accessed March 20, 2007).

13 I will be discussing this translation and adaptation in more detail in chapter 6.

14 By the time this book appears, the list of translations and adaptations will undoubtedly be much longer.

15 Interview, Norma Swenson (October 29, 1998).

16 Letter, Norma Swenson (November 7, 1976), BWHBC Records, 1972–1997 (no. 78.15), Schlesinger Library, Radcliffe Institute, Harvard University, Cambridge, Massachusetts. For those readers unfamiliar with this episode in feminist history, the term Mouvement de Libération des Femmes was legally registered with a small splinter group calling itself Psych et Po (short for Psychoanalyse et Politique). This action was hotly

contested by other feminist groups in France, which mobilized media support and enlisted Simone de Beauvoir to help them win their case. Ultimately, Psych et Po came to be seen as *the* women's movement.

17 See, for example, Petchesky 2003; Petchesky and Judd 1998; and Ginsburg and Rapp 1995.

18 Various members of the BWHBC traveled to Mexico, New Zealand, Australia, the Philippines, Hong Kong, Malaysia, Thailand, Bangladesh, China, and India.

19 While NGOs have been successful in getting women's issues on state and international agendas and have often provided much-needed institutional and financial support for local feminist initiatives, they have also been greeted with some skepticism. Lang (1997), for example, worries about what she calls the "NGO-ization" of feminism, whereby NGOs inadvertently undermine state-sponsored welfare programs for women by doing "social repair work" themselves (health care, social services, community education). They may also weaken local feminist politics by watering down a broader feminist agenda to single issues and state-oriented action. See also Scott et al. 1997; Alvarez 1998; Thayer 2000; and Naples and Desai, 2002.

20 The publication coincided with Hillary Clinton's visit in 1995 in Beijing and was the subject of an unusually frank public forum with representatives of the Chinese women's movement (*New York Times*, June 28, 1998). In the *New York Times*, Liu Bohong, the coordinator of the Chinese translation, presented the translation as "revealing about how far discussion had come" in a situation where political debates had often been stalled. "No matter that the final product was missing the American edition's sections on lesbianism and masturbation or that a number of pictures were not reproduced. At last, the book was out." While this remark may have been strategic, it ignored the work of local Chinese feminists, who were already busy translating the "missing sections" and adapting the rest of the book.

21 In addition to raising funds in order to provide small grants for translation and adaptation projects, the BWHBC was often approached by individuals interested in supporting specific projects. Some examples include an anonymous donor who contributed funds to help distribute the Serbian adaptation to areas heavily populated by Muslim women in Bosnia-Herzegovina; a male hospital worker who had "always followed the collective's work with great interest" and, after reading about the francophone African edition in the BWHBC newsletter, donated a surprisingly large sum toward its distribution in Africa; and several U.S. donors of Armenian descent who wanted to make sure the Armenian *OBOS* got off to a good start.

22 An interesting example concerns a recent project in which a group of Palestinian women in East Jerusalem, together with activists in Jordan and Lebanon, developed a plan to update the 1991 Arabic edition

to create a pan-Arabic *OBOS*. About the same time, a group of Israeli academic women contacted the BWHBC with a proposal to update the Hebrew *OBOS* and include materials in Arabic on Palestinian women's health issues, paying particular attention to the disparities in Palestinian and Israeli women's health. As Sally Whelan put it, "Our first impulse is always to put groups who want to work on *OBOS* in touch with one another. . . . Who knows how it will turn out?" Interview, Sally Whelan (May 17, 2005).

23 Interview, Sally Whelan (July 25, 2000).

24 I will be returning to the issue of translation in more detail in chapter 6. While I did not have access to all the "translation stories," I was able to draw on the correspondence between the translators and the BWHBC in which translators kept the collective posted—at least in a cursory way—about how they adapted the book. They invariably sent copies of the finished version, which were sometimes passed on to "native speakers" who gave assessments about what had been left out. Each translation has a preface, which provides an explanation by the translators of how the book was adapted to fit the local context, and these prefaces are now being translated into English and posted on the U.S. Web site. The translators frequently gave interviews—in local newspapers or during their visits to the United States—in which they explained some of the difficulties they had encountered, and some wrote accounts of the adaptation for academic journals (see, e.g., Farah 1991 on the Egyptian version; Shapiro 1999, 2001, 2005 on the Latin American version; and Yanco 1996, one of the first articles about the importance of the translations of *OBOS* for the international women's health movement).

25 For example, the sentence "We don't all want to sleep together, but we don't want to limit our friendships because of fear of homosexuality" in the original became "We don't say we agree with homosexuality." In another instance, an anecdote about a woman in a bathtub touching her clitoris (in the section "Lovemaking") was cut, along with other references to touching, apparently a taboo subject. Memo from Paula Doress-Worters (March 25, 1983), BWHBC Records, 1972–1997 (no. 74.12), Schlesinger Library, Radcliffe Institute, Harvard University, Cambridge, Massachusetts.

26 Interview with Liu Bohong, coordinator and primary translator of the Chinese translation, *Boston Globe*, December 12, 1998.

27 See *Japan Times*, September 3, 1990. Critics of censorship have argued that the controversy should be seen as a symptom of Japan's history of isolationism and an attempt to curtail women's international contacts.

28 In an interview with Sandra Buckley, Saitō Chiyo, the founder of the feminist journal *Agora*, criticizes Western feminists for assuming that feminism in Japan was simply a result of the influence of the

women's liberation movement in the West. The notion that feminism is an exportable commodity ignores how Western feminism influences but does not determine the shape feminism will take in different national contexts. In a world of permeable borders, information about feminism is imported and exported, influencing local feminisms in such a way that it is impossible to speak of a purely indigenous national movement. However, it would be not only inaccurate but arrogant to assume that a foreign feminism simply takes root as the basic ideology of a movement in another country. She argues for the need to look more closely at the origins and currents of "Japanese-style feminism"—a feminism that is shaped by the specific history and conditions of patriarchy in Japan and by a long-standing maternalist tradition of thought. Buckley 1997, 257–271. See also Uno 1993; and Khor 1999.

29 Nakanishi Toyoko, quoted in Buckley 1997, 192–93.

30 Hantrakul 1996.

31 Interview, Elizabeth MacMahon-Herrera (March 5, 1999).

32 Interview, Elizabeth MacMahon-Herrera (March 5, 1999).

33 I will discuss this process in more detail in chapter 6.

34 Cited in BWHBC Minutes, Sept.–Dec. 1978, BWHBC Records, 1972–1997 (no. 2.3), Schlesinger Library, Radcliffe Institute, Harvard University, Cambridge, Massachusetts.

35 Preface, *Je Lichaam Je Leven*, 1975, 12.

36 Correspondence from one of the translators of the German edition with Norma Swenson and Judy Norsigian, August 5, 1977, BWHBC Library, private files.

37 See Whelan and Pincus 2001.

38 See preface to the British edition of *OBOS* by Angela Phillips and Jill Rakusen (1978, 9–10).

39 In chapter 6, I will explore in more detail several cases in which the politics of the original were changed in the translation.

40 Cited in Whelan and Pincus 2001.

41 Interview, Ester Shapiro (February 24, 1999). See also Shapiro 1999.

42 An interesting example is the Bulgarian cover, which shows a woman's body (without a head) swathed in a gauzy green material (see fig. 21). While the BWHBC took issue with this cover, worrying that it played into stereotypes of the "mysterious veiled woman," the Bulgarian translators argued that it had a different symbolic meaning in the Bulgarian context. Given the proliferation of hard-core pornography throughout Bulgaria, they felt that this image was a potentially empowering alternative. Interview, Irina Todorova (June 4, 2003).

43 Quoted in Whelan and Pincus 2004, 3.

44 When asked how the Danish book differed from the original *OBOS*, Gerd Winther, one of the members of the collective, explained that it became more and more experiential and grass roots. "We were all

professional women at the time—journalists, therapists, academics—so it had a much more scientific slant. Just imagine—we even had some Masters and Johnson in it at first!" Conversation with Gerd Wintner (June 5, 1998).

45 Cited in *Telegraph India*, July 20, 2004.

46 *Hindu*, July 13, 2004.

47 Preface, *The South African Women's Health Book* (1996, ix), written by Margaretha Goosen and Barbara Klugman for the Women's Health Project.

48 Barbara Klugman, in written comments submitted to the Crossing Borders with *Our Bodies, Ourselves* meeting in Utrecht in 2001, which she was unable to attend. Interestingly, members of the new translation project in Nigeria have, for similar reasons, decided not to make a book at all, opting instead for multilanguage pamphlets for use in radio programs, street theater, and—most innovatively—posters in the canoe transport system, which brings women from their farms to the marketplace.

49 Codou Bop, quoted in Whelan and Pincus 2001.

50 For a good discussion of the debates and what is at stake for transnational feminist alliances around the issue of female circumcision and genital cutting, see James and Robertson 2002.

51 Although female circumcision was officially banned in Egypt in 1959, it continues to be performed, particularly in rural settings, where it is estimated that 90 percent of women are circumcised regardless of whether they are Christian or Muslim. While the most severe forms of circumcision (infibulation) occur in neighboring Sudan, in Egypt clitoridectomies are widely practiced. The reasons women give for engaging in the practice range from wanting to be "pure" to the belief that it is more "aesthetic" to fearing dependence on a man through sexual desire to wanting to be part of a collective coming of age ritual, not unlike the ritual surrounding male circumcision. See Dorkenoo 1994; Abdalla 1982; and Assad 1980.

52 "Imagined community" is borrowed from Benedict Anderson's (1983) influential study on nation building. Anderson applies the term to the process by which people who have never met, and who may be embroiled in relations of inequality or exploitation, nevertheless imagine that they know one another or are linked in some "deep, horizontal comradeship" (9). I will be using this term throughout the present inquiry for thinking about the kind of feminist alliances that *OBOS* as a global project generates.

53 The story is usually transmitted in the form published by Nadia Farah (1991).

54 Robertson's (1995) term glocalisation has been taken up by many contemporary globalization theorists to express the interconnections between the local and the global. See also, for sophisticated theoriza-

tions of cultural globalization that take up the contradictory interconnections between the local and the global, Grewal and Kaplan 1994; Appadurai 1996, 2000; Hall 1996, 1997; and King 1997.

55 Interview, Norma Swenson (March 19, 1999).

56 Quoted in Chen 1996, 393.

57 Examples included the dumping of dangerous pharmaceuticals and contraceptive devices on unsuspecting women in the Third World, the exploitative role of multinationals, international sex tourism, and more. The authors were critical of development discourses that assume that modernization only occurs according to a Western model, arguing that women in every country need to be involved in designing programs to meet their needs. They placed population control in a critical perspective and argued for the validation of traditional healers and the importance of simple, preventative services for people in rural areas (BWHBC 1984, 611–25).

3 Between Empowerment and Bewitchment

1 In fact, my study is not the only one on the BWHBC. In addition to several unpublished theses (Blumenthal 1987; Diskin 1990; Hayden 1994; Mayer 1996; Werner 2001), the story has been included in numerous articles (Eaton 1979; Beckwith 1985; Hayden 1997), including articles written by members of the group (Sanford 1979; Norsigian and Sanford 1987; Norsigian et al. 1999; Pincus 2002), as well as chapters or parts of chapters in books about U.S. feminism or the women's health movement (e.g., Ruzek 1978; Brownmiller 1999; Ruzek et al. 1997; Weisman 1998; Rosen 2000; Morgen 2002).

2 *OBOS* was not only of interest to white, middle-class, well-educated women. Byllye Avery, the well-known founder of the National Black Women's Health Project, has acknowledged on various occasions her debt to the BWHBC, referring to *OBOS* as the "bible of women's health," which allowed women "across ethnic, racial, religious and geographical boundaries to start examining their health from a perspective that will bring about change" (Preface, BWHBC 1992, 9, my italics). However, as I will argue in this chapter and later in this book, both *OBOS* and the history of the BWHBC have had different meanings for women who are differently located in terms of class, ethnic or "racial" background, and other categories of difference.

3 There is a broad literature on the myths within literary criticism as well as history. In this inquiry, I have drawn on the work of oral historians, particularly those concerned with the use of myth in social movements. See, for example, Samuel and Thompson 1990; Passerini 1990, 1996; and Portelli 1990, 1991, 1997. Morgen 2002 also provides an ex-

cellent account of the role feminist "foundational stories," including the story of the BWHBC, played in the U.S. women's health movement.

4 See, for example, Riger 1994; Taylor and Whittier 1995; Ferree and Martin 1995; Simonds 1996; and Morgen 2002, 1995.

5 This was published as an open letter in the widely read feminist newspaper *Sojourner* (Bonilla et al. 1997, 4).

6 During the first twenty years of the project (1970–90), each founder spoke at meetings, conferences, women's group gatherings, libraries, schools, and hospitals or testified before legislatures, where she would invariably give some rendition of the group's history. For each new edition of *OBOS*, the founders went on publicity tours, where they would tell their story to numerous newspaper reporters and radio and TV hosts. Even today the founders are asked as many as five times a year to tell the story.

7 This accounts for the somewhat unequal distribution of quotations from the various founders in the account that follows. I have often drawn on quotes from founders who were—at least at the time of the events in question—less centrally involved and therefore, perhaps, more willing and able to reflect on them. The fact that I have made more use of these reflexive comments to help me make sense of the history is, therefore, not intended as a denial of the importance of the underrepresented founders in the collective history.

8 To this end, I have drawn on recent literature in what has been called whiteness studies that explores how whiteness as structural privilege is implicated in racism. See, for example, Frankenberg 1993, 2001; Fine et al. 1997; and Rasmussen et al. 2001.

9 It wasn't until I was at the Radcliffe Institute for Advanced Studies in 2004 that one of the fellows told me she was "the woman at the blackboard" and that the incident had taken place not at the initial meeting but at one of the later courses at MIT.

10 Interview, Nancy Miriam Hawley (January 21, 1999).

11 Interview, Vilunya Diskin (December 2, 1998).

12 Interview, Jane Pincus (January 20, 1999).

13 Interview, Wendy Sanford (December 4, 1998).

14 Interview, Nancy Miriam Hawley (January 21, 1999).

15 See chapter 1, note 13.

16 Interview, Pamela Morgan (December 3, 1998).

17 *Shaking the Tree* (dir. Kim Powers, 1993).

18 The photograph was taken in 1972 by Phylis Ewen.

19 This photograph was taken during a retreat in 1996 by Judith Lennett. Ironically, it is the same retreat at which three members of the BWHBC, who had worked in the organization for many years, were finally—and after considerable discussion—granted the official status of founder. I will discuss this in more detail later in this chapter.

20 Interview, Jane Pincus (January 20, 1999).

21 While this sentiment was by no means universally held within the U.S. women's movement and, indeed, had historical roots linked to the way U.S. feminism emerged in the seventies, it is a sentiment that traveled, influencing the image of U.S. feminism both within and outside the United States. As we will see in chapter 6, many of the translation projects were forced to counter this sentiment in their local contexts, where U.S. feminism was decried as "antiman" or "antifamily." They were no doubt helped by the approach that *OBOS* took toward mothering, which was both celebratory and cognizant of the burdens and ambivalences of motherhood.

22 Interview, Norma Swenson (October 29, 1998).

23 The BWHBC did pay contributors to and editors of the various editions of *OBOS* a nominal fee, but no one was paid a salary just for her work on the book.

24 I was often surprised when the first question founders would ask me during the interviews was whether or not I had children. This would be followed by a question about my partner. They showed considerably more interest in my personal life than my academic career, as though the former were more relevant to the task at hand.

25 Interview, Vilunya Diskin (December 2, 1998).

26 Interview, Norma Swenson (October 29, 1998).

27 Interview, Joan Ditzion (October 28, 1998).

28 Interview, Paula Doress-Worters (December 2, 1998).

29 Interview, Vilunya Diskin (December 2, 1998).

30 Interview, Ruth Bell Alexander (March 20, 1999).

31 Interview, Paula Doress-Worters (December 2, 1998).

32 When I gave a talk recently in Cambridge, one of the founders came with her daughter and her granddaughter. She approached me afterward, announcing proudly, "You see, here we are, three generations!"

33 See, for example, Sanford 1979, 92. Under the title "They Talked and Talked, and Then Wrote a Classic," the *New York Times* published an article on June 22, 1997, that includes a rendition of this history with an update on the personal lives of the collective's members.

34 Interview, Pamela Berger (January 19, 1999).

35 Ibid.

36 Ibid.

37 Interview, Ruth Bell Alexander (March 20, 1999).

38 Ibid.

39 Interview, Nancy Miriam Hawley (January 21, 1999).

40 Interview, Sally Whelan (October 30, 1998).

41 Ibid.

42 Interview, Elizabeth MacMahon-Herrera (March 5, 1999).

43 See, for example, Joeres 1994; Weisser and Fleischner 1995; Wing 1997; hooks 2000; and Ruiz and DuBois 2000.

44 Interview, Judy Norsigian (October 27, 1998).

45 Ibid.

46 Ibid.

47 Minutes from a meeting of September 17, 1973, BWHBC Records, 1972–1997 [no. 1.16], Schlesinger Library, Radcliffe Institute, Harvard University, Cambridge, Massachusetts.

48 These minutes have been displayed at the Schlesinger Library in an exhibit of some of the most memorable artifacts of U.S. feminism.

49 Interview, Pamela Morgan (December 3, 1998).

50 Interview, Ruth Bell Alexander (March 20, 1999).

51 Ibid.

52 For good discussions of nostalgia in feminism, see Huffer 1998; Brown 2001; Adkins 2004; and Hemmings 2005.

53 Interview, Wendy Sanford (December 4, 1998).

54 Ibid.

55 Interview, Sally Whelan (October 30, 1998).

56 Ibid.

57 Ibid.

58 Ibid.

59 Interview, Pamela Morgan (December 3, 1998).

60 Interview, Paula Doress-Worters (December 2, 1998).

61 See Simonds 1996; Morgen 1998; Scott 2000; and Zajicek 2002.

62 Interview, Paula Doress-Worters (December 2, 1998).

63 Interview, Nancy Miriam Hawley (January 21, 1999).

64 Interview, Wendy Sanford (December 4, 1998).

65 Interview, Jane Pincus (January 20, 1999).

66 Interview, Joan Ditzion (October 28, 1998).

67 Interview, Pamela Morgan (December 3, 1998).

68 See also Roof 1995, 1997; and Brown 2001.

69 Despite the conflicts, the updated *Our Bodies, Ourselves for the New Millennium* was published in 1998, and, ironically, it was by all standards the most attentive to issues of racism and multiculturalism of all the editions up to that point.

4 Reclaiming Women's Bodies

1 Other books were Theda Skocpol's *States and Social Revolutions*, Harry Braverman's *Labor and Monopoly Capital*, Clifford Geertz's *The Interpretation of Cultures*, Pierre Bourdieu's *Outline of a Theory of Practice*, William J. Wilson's *Declining Significance of Race*, and, as the only other "feminist" contribution, Nancy Chodorow's *The Reproduction of Mothering*. As the editor of *Contemporary Sociology* noted, the selection process had been agonizing but had ultimately given rise to a surprising degree of agreement among the board members about the books with

the notable exception of *Our Bodies, Ourselves*. In that case, he ended up making the decision on his own "at the urging of some but to the dismay of others" (Clawson 1996, ix).

2 This is not to say that *OBOS* is not used in women's studies courses. It often appears on required reading lists for undergraduates. However, it tends to be presented as a useful handbook on women's health rather than a book of scholarly interest.

3 See Kapsalis 1997; Morgen 2002; Murphy 2004; Bell and Reverby 2005 for discussions on the conflicting perspectives on self help within the U.S. women's health movement.

4 This has been done at much greater length by others and goes beyond the scope of the present inquiry. Several of these critiques of Haraway's work are worth a brief mention, however. Moore and Clarke (1995) disagree with Haraway's conflation of *OBOS* with the "medical gaze." Referring to the well-known photograph in the text of a woman looking at her own vulva and clitoris in a mirror, they suggest that this practice can hardly be seen as an instance of women "objectifying" their bodies, analogous to the medical pelvic exam. The woman in the picture is not only looking at herself but is allowing the reader to look, too. For this reason, the trope of women "discovering" their bodies "dramatically challenges the subject/object distinction so rigorously constructed in almost all traditional anatomies since the Renaissance" (276–77). In a similar vein, Kapsalis (1997) argues that Haraway's treatment of the speculum as outdated and "symbolically inadequate" does not acknowledge its significance, symbolic and otherwise. The speculum was a particularly potent symbol for the women's health movement because of the nefarious role it played within U.S. gynecology, where it was initially employed by J. Marion Simms (the "father of American gynecology") in his surgical experiments on unanaesthetized slave women. The symbolic appeal for feminists of appropriating what had originally been an instrument of oppression to help women "take back their bodies" was obvious. The stresses and pains of routine pelvic exams continue to make the speculum relevant for feminist health activism, however high tech gynecology may have become. Haraway's critique does not do justice to the importance of the practice of self-help in turning pathology-oriented medicine on its head and replacing it with a well-woman approach to medicine. Scudson (1997) is more generally critical of Haraway's rhetorical strategy, which divorces the object of her critique (in this case, the U.S. women's health movement) from the specific social, cultural, and historical context in which it emerged. The effect of this strategy is to distance readers from the lived realities of the actors involved, as well as the ambivalences and conflicts that were inevitably part of their practices. And, last but not least, Moya (1997) takes issue with Haraway's authorization of herself as the proper person to "speak for" poor women and women of color, while at the same time dismissing their experiences

and practices as inconsequential for the feminist politics of health that she envisions.

5 Like any feminist epistemology, *OBOS* is also a political project. However, for the purposes of this chapter I will be focusing on its epistemological features. The consequences for feminist politics of the body, particularly in a transcultural, transnational context, will be the subject of the subsequent chapters.

6 Even women who do not menstruate, have vaginas, or bear children will be influenced by societal expectations of what it means to have a female body. See, for example, Hall (2005) who, drawing on insights from queer theory, criticizes the taken for granted linkage of vaginas with feminine embodiment, which excludes disabled or differently embodied women.

7 In her experientially based epistemology, Patricia Hill Collins (2000) calls this the "wisdom to know how to deal with educated fools," something that is often the key to their survival (257). While her epistemology is based specifically on the experiences of U.S. American black women as a framework for black feminist thought, the centrality she gives to women's embodied experience as source of critical knowledge is very similar to that of *OBOS*.

8 Young (1990a) provides an insightful analysis of this process, referring to it as the "aesthetic scaling of difference." She views it not only as one of the primary ways difference is constructed but also as a mainstay of modern processes of power and domination.

9 Marshall (1996) draws upon Grosz's work in an interesting way to analyze the corporeality of pregnancy as both defying and embodying the mind-body split. She draws on the metaphor of the Mobius strip, which enables the external (biological) body and the internal (social) self to appear distinct at a given moment while being seamlessly united overall.

10 The lack of attention to bodily integrity in contemporary feminist body theory has been a source of concern for feminist biologists like Birke 1999 and Fausto-Sterling 2005. See also Bordo 1993, 71–98.

11 This resonates with feminist phenomenological approaches to the body that explore the contradictions in women's embodiment (see, e.g., Bartky 1990; Young 1990b; Marshall 1996; Lindemann 1997; and Alcoff 2000).

12 This perspective resonates with the concern expressed by feminist biologists, who worry that the emphasis on the transformability of the body without a concomitant sense of the body's integrity can open the floodgates for a total manipulation of human and nonhuman nature. As Birke (1999) puts it, the literal dismemberment of bodies in modern medicine in organ transplantations, hysterectomies, and plastic surgery has already reduced the body to "a set of bits" that can be removed or manipulated (171). It is important that feminist body theory does not replicate this.

13 This perspective is very much in tune with critical disability studies (Breckenridge and Vogler 2001). For women living with chronic illness or disabilities, for example, a certain amount of splitting or "transcendence" (mind over matter) is not simply a reprehensible relic of masculinist philosophy in need of immediate deconstruction but may be a welcome—and even necessary—resource, enabling an individual to better cope with the limitations of her body (Wendell 1996, 169).

14 Asserting the primacy of women's experience became the "sine qua non of any feminist project of liberation," serving as the foundation for the knowledge claims for marginalized groups more generally (Kruks 2001, 132). See also Harding 1998; Hurtado 1998; Mediatore 2003; and Mohanty 2003.

15 One of the most widespread effects of this particular essay, in addition to its compelling attack on the validity of experience, was that the term could no longer be used without putting it in scare quotes.

16 Alcoff (2000) regards this choice as little more than an unproductive replaying of "tired modernist debates between empiricism and idealism" (45). It reflects the more general problem that postmodern feminist theory is too caught up in the project of deconstructing Enlightenment philosophy—an issue to which I will return in chapter 7.

17 Moya (1997) refers to this as the "cognitive component" and uses this to frame her call for a more "realist" feminist epistemology, one that will be more relevant to the material concerns of Chicana women. While I agree with many of her arguments, I don't believe that it is necessary to separate the cognitive from practical consciousness or the discursive from the real in order to retrieve women's experiences as a critical resource. See Mohanty 2003 for a similar argument.

18 I do not wish to imply that Foucauldian feminist theorists employ identical conceptions of agency, and, indeed, there have been many debates concerning the problem of agency in feminist theory. Bordo (1993) has, for example, criticized Butler's conception of agency as being overly playful, emphasizing and celebrating resistance, subversion, and the instabilities in current power relations rather than their recuperative tendencies. While they both share an appreciation of Foucauldian notions of power, Bordo sees a danger in Butler's placing certain forms of transgressive subjectivity (transgendered sexuality, drag queens) on an equal footing with historically dominant forms, thereby romanticizing the degree of cultural challenge taking place (292–95). See also Bordo 1998; and Hekman 1998. Bordo and Butler both emphasize the importance of (feminist) praxis, but neither offers a way to think about women as actors capable of envisioning feminist courses of action. See Davis 1995, 2003; and McNay 2000.

19 The term cultural dope is borrowed from sociology, where it was developed as a critique against deterministic and functionalist perspectives on human agency in which human actors have so completely in-

ternalized the norms and values of the society in which they live that their activities become limited to acting out a predetermined script. See Giddens 1976 and Davis 1995.

20 This approach to epistemic agency resonates with recent U.S. and Third World feminist critiques of poststructuralist feminist theory. Lugones (2003), Mohanty (2003), Moya (1997), and others have been skeptical of the abandonment of epistemic agency in favor of a more discursive notion of agency. They have argued that U.S. and Third World women have been constantly engaged in reflecting on and renaming their experiences—a process ultimately leading to the development of alternative forms of knowledge.

21 See Bartky 2002 for a similar argument.

22 Haraway's critique of *OBOS*—and, more generally, the women's health movement—was also motivated by political considerations. She was not only worried that the project was theoretically misguided and hopelessly outdated as a feminist critique of science but also that it did not adequately address the health needs of poor women and women of color in the United States, as well as health disparities on a global scale. While this concern is well taken, because Haraway does not seriously engage with the knowledge practices of health activists—including feminist health activists of color—she is forced to turn to mainstream science—and, in particular, statistics about differences in morbidity and health outcomes—to make her case. This not only leaves the problems inherent in statistical knowledge unaddressed, but it ignores the ways in which health activists in the United States have grappled with global and local disparities in women's health.

5 Creating Feminist Subjects

1 There are obviously other ways of doing text analysis. For example, I could have treated *OBOS* as a cultural product, a representative of a genre (e.g., self-help literature), which could then be analyzed using literary techniques of text analysis. Alternatively, I might have subjected *OBOS* to a content analysis, a method that is much beloved by practitioners in communications and media studies. This would entail assembling and counting the topics presented in the book and searching for underlying communicative messages and verifying them with surveys among readers. However, while these methods could be applied to an analysis of *OBOS*, they are less suited to explaining how readers could become embodied, knowledgeable, feminist subjects just from reading a book. See Kline 2005 for an excellent example of a content analysis of readers' letters to *OBOS*.

2 See, in particular, Foucault's *The Archaeology of Knowledge* (1972), as well as Foucault 1978, 1980.

3 The reader is referred to McNay 1992 and 2000 (chapter 1) for a critique of Foucault's work, with particular attention paid to the problem of agency and feminist politics.

4 Interestingly, the chapter of *OBOS* I will be analyzing has proved popular among a very diverse readership. In the next chapter, I will show how a group of young Tibetan nuns became inspired to translate *OBOS* after encountering the chapter on anatomy and physiology.

5 See the introduction to this volume.

6 As I set out in chapter 1, I wrote most of this book before the last edition of *OBOS* appeared in 2005. This analysis is, therefore, based on the 1998 edition of the book. The chapter in question has gone through many changes throughout the years, moving from its position as first chapter of the 1971 edition to becoming chapter 12 in 1998. Its title changed as well, from "Anatomy and Physiology" in 1970 to "Anatomy and Physiology of Sexuality and Reproduction" in 1976 and 1984. See chapter 1 for a brief description of how this chapter changed in the 2005 edition of *OBOS*, indicating that, while the format is different, it is written very much in the spirit of the original.

7 See, for example, Laqueur 1990; Haraway 1991a; Moore and Clarke 1995; and Martin 2001.

8 Initially, experiences were provided by women who participated in group discussions, becoming the basis for the first *OBOS*. Later experiential accounts were based on letters or telephone calls from readers. Some were collected by the authors of the various chapters during the many revisions of the book, and, of course, the members of the BWHBC included their own experiences as well as the experiences of their friends and family members. See chapter 1.

9 According to Martin (2001), this "medical story" tends to be adopted by white, middle-class, U.S. women while it meets with more resistance among low-income women and women of color. They are more likely to talk about menstruation in phenomenological terms (how it feels, the hassles involved in coping with it) or in terms of its status as rite of passage into womanhood.

10 Keller 1985, 1992; Jacobus et al. 1990; Jordanova 1989, 1999; Lacqueur 1990, 2003; Haraway 1991a, 1997; Clarke and Olesen, eds. 1999b; Creager et al. 2001; Martin 2001, 1991; Schiebinger 2004.

11 For a good overview of feminist critiques of the medicalization of PMS, see Lorber 1997; and Swann 1997.

12 Martin (2001) also views such strategies as discursive and discusses at length the possibilities for disrupting masculinist notions of efficiency by refusing the discipline of the workplace, taking it easy, expressing irritation, or taking time off from work because of menstrual cramps.

13 I read some of these letters in the BWHBC library, which has since closed. Later the letters, along with other papers (minutes, correspon-

dence) from the BWHBC were donated to the Schlesinger Library at the Radcliffe Institute at Harvard University in Cambridge, Massachusetts (BWHBC Records, 1972–1997). While many of the more recent letters were held back for use in the next update of *OBOS*, there are more than 250 in the Schlesinger Library currently available to the public. A small number of letters dealing with sensitive topics have been placed in closed files and will be available at some later date.

14 See chapter 1 for a discussion of this process of intersectional reading.

15 Letter (4.6.1980), BWHBC Records, 1972–1997 (no. 112.14), Schlesinger Library, Radcliffe Institute, Harvard University, Cambridge, Massachusetts.

16 Letter (7.24.2000), BWHBC Library. One of the projects sponsored by the BWHBC was sending free copies of *OBOS* to women's prisons. In this context, several members of the collective corresponded regularly with some of the inmates.

17 Letter (9.6.1993), BWHBC Records, 1972–1997 (no. 72.6), Schlesinger Library, Radcliffe Institute, Harvard University, Cambridge, Massachusetts.

18 Letter (5.16.1985), BWHBC Records, 1972–1997 (no. 110.29), Schlesinger Library, Radcliffe Institute, Harvard University, Cambridge, Massachusetts.

19 Letter (9.14.1993), BWHBC Records, 1972–1997 (no. 72.6), Schlesinger Library, Radcliffe Institute, Harvard University.

20 See Kline 2005, 102.

21 Wendy Sanford to Carolivia Herron, editor for tone and voice, January 26, 1997, BWHBC Library.

22 Letter (4.6.1980), BWHBC Records, 1972–1997 (no. 112.14), Schlesinger Library, Radcliffe Institute, Harvard University.

23 See chapter 1 for a discussion of the backlash against *OBOS* in the 1980s. See also Sanford and Doress 1981.

24 Letter (12.23.1981), BWHBC Library.

25 Letter (11.19.1993), BWHBC Records, 1972–1997 (no. 72.6), Schlesinger Library, Radcliffe Institute, Harvard University, Cambridge, Massachusetts.

26 Letter (7.24.2000), BWHBC Library.

27 Letter (7.30.1998), BWHBC Library.

28 Letter (1.4.1988), BWHBC Records, 1972–1997 (no. 71.10), Schlesinger Library, Radcliffe Institute, Harvard University, Cambridge, Massachusetts.

29 Letter (11.25.1979), BWHBC Records, 1972–1997 (no. 107.11), Schlesinger Library, Radcliffe Institute, Harvard University, Cambridge, Massachusetts.

30 Letter (9.30.1999), BWHBC Library.

31 Letter (9.14.1993), BWHBC Records, 1972–1997 (no. 72.6), Schlesinger Library, Radcliffe Institute, Harvard University, Cambridge, Massachusetts.

32 Letter (3.18.1994), BWHBC Library.

33 An ectopic pregnancy is one in which the fertilized egg implants itself outside the uterus, most often in the fallopian tube, which can be life threatening if the tube ruptures and requires immediate treatment.

34 Vaginitis is vaginal inflammation caused by a fungus, bacteria, or virus. It usually causes vaginal discharge and may be itchy or painful.

35 Letter (9.23.1979), BWHBC Records, 1972–1997 (no. 107.12), Schlesinger Library, Radcliffe Institute, Harvard University, Cambridge, Massachusetts.

36 This phrase was coined by Ehrenreich and English ([1978] 2005) in their popular critique of the history of medical advice to women.

37 Letter (3.18.1994), BWHBC Library.

38 Letter (12.30.80), BWHBC Records, 1972–1997 (no. 107.12), Schlesinger Library, Radcliffe Institute, Harvard University, Cambridge, Massachusetts.

39 Letter (10.30.1981), BWHBC Records, 1972–1997 (109.22), Schlesinger Library, Radcliffe Institute, Harvard University, Cambridge, Massachusetts.

40 Letter (5.17.1976), BWHBC Records, 1972–1997 (no. 107.10), Schlesinger Library, Radcliffe Institute, Harvard University, Cambridge, Massachusetts.

41 "A cone biopsy involves some risk of future infertility because it may weaken the cervix. A hysterectomy permanently ends a woman's reproductive capacity. Both surgeries can be appropriate and save women's lives. However, if such a treatment is recommended, it is important to seek a second or even a third opinion on whether it is appropriate and what other treatment options may be available, especially for severe CIN [cervical intraepithelial neoplasia] or cancer in situ" (BWHBC 1984, 574–576).

42 BWHBC 1992, 598.

43 Letter (1.22.1993), BWHBC Records, 1972–1997 (no. 72.6), Schlesinger Library, Radcliffe Institute, Harvard University, Cambridge, Massachusetts.

44 Letter (9.30.1999), BWHBC Library.

45 Letter (1.15.1981), BWHBC Records, 1972–1997 (no. 70.14), Schlesinger Library, Radcliffe Institute, Harvard University, Cambridge, Massachusetts.

46 Letter (2.21.1995), BWHBC Library.

47 Letter (9.2.1997), BWHBC Library.

48 Letter sent originally to the Bangor Daily News, March 15, 1979, BWHBC Records, 1972–1997 (no. 156.6), Schlesinger Library, Radcliffe Institute, Harvard University, Cambridge, Massachusetts.

49 Letter (1.22.1993), BWHBC Records, 1972–1997 (no. 112.13), Schlesinger Library, Radcliffe Institute, Harvard University, Cambridge, Massachusetts.

50 Letter, Norma Swenson (3.27.1979), BWHBC Records, 1972–1997 (no. 107.10), Schlesinger Library, Radcliffe Institute, Harvard University, Cambridge, Massachusetts.

51 Letter, Wendy Sanford (8.14.1980) BWHBC Records 1972–1997 [#107.5], Schlesinger Library, Radcliffe Institute, Harvard University, Cambridge, Massachusetts.

52 I am drawing, in particular, on Smith 1990a, 61–106; Smith 1990b, 12–52, 120–158; and, more generally, Smith 1999.

53 See Smith 1990b for an interesting analysis of how the diagnosis of mental illness is constructed textually. She shows how it requires separating a person's feelings and actions from the context in which they occur and make sense, thereby establishing them as *not* making sense and *only* explainable as a symptom of mental pathology (12–52).

6 Oppositional Translations

1 See Yanco 1996.

2 For a delightful account of this meeting, see Whelan and Pincus 2001.

3 In addition to translating *OBOS*, the participants from Japan were translating *Sacrificing Ourselves for Love*, a book about eating disorders, violence against women, and cosmetic surgery that was written by Jane Hyman and the late BWHBC member Esther Rome.

4 Ogino 2001. See also Nakanishi 1997, 185–225.

5 Nakanishi 1997, 196. The Japanese translation of *OBOS* not only sold six thousand copies but is available in libraries and women's centers throughout Japan. It has generated research on women's health issues and compelled hospitals to pay more attention to women's complaints about inhumane ways of giving birth (Ogino 2001). Interestingly, some of the terms introduced by the translators of *OBOS* were later taken up by standard Japanese dictionaries. Many thanks to Daniel Morales for discovering this small but significant proof of the translation's impact in Japan.

6 I am using the term oppositional in the sense employed by the political theorist Jane Mansbridge. She uses oppositional consciousness to refer to the ideational resources required by groups that have historically been marginalized or socially subordinated to create a legitimacy and perception of injustice, anger, solidarity, and belief in the group's power. While it does not guarantee collective political action, it is a necessary prerequisite (Mansbridge 2001, 7). See also Sandoval 1991 for a somewhat different reading of oppositional consciousness as a capacity (*faculdad*) for holding on to multiple perspectives while simultaneously maintaining a concrete center around which material forms of oppression revolve.

7 This quote was taken from a memo about a Brazilian adaptation of *OBOS* produced by the Mulher e Saúde (musa) Centro de Referéncia de Educação and illustrates the expectations many of the translation projects of *OBOS* have.

8 Mainstream translation theory tends to assume that foreign texts can—and, indeed, should—be translated in such a way that the original meanings are left intact. Indeed, the task of any good translator is to produce a text that "sounds" as if it were originally written in the new language. In contrast to this view, critical translation scholars, along with postcolonial theorists from a variety of disciplines, have argued that such an undertaking is a "mission impossible." See, for example, Said 1983; Hall 1997; Appiah 2000; Spivak 2000; and Venuti 1995, 1998, 2000.

9 See Shapiro 2005, 2001, 1999; Kotzeva 2001; and Slavova 2001.

10 This first edition of *Nuestros Cuerpos, Nuestras Vidas* was translated by Raquel Scherr-Salgado and Lenora Taboada. It was published in 1977 and reprinted in 1979.

11 Interview, Elizabeth MacMahon-Herrera (March 5, 1999).

12 Ibid.

13 See Sternbach et al. 1992; and Alvarez et al. 2003 for an excellent history of these biannual meetings, held in different countries, which drew large numbers of feminists, members of indigenous women's groups, and later women working in NGOs to discuss the most significant feminist questions of the day.

14 They added many poems, often political in nature, producing a political framework that "seduced" the reader to enter the text. This resonates with the thinking of U.S. Chicana feminists (Norma Alarcón, Gloria Anzaldúa, María Lugones, and Cherríe Moraga) who advocate combining theory with a poetic language designed to draw the reader into the text rather alienating her. See Anzaldúa 1990; and Lugones 2003.

15 Despite these radical changes, the adaptation was only about two-thirds as long as the U.S. *OBOS*.

16 Interview, Ester Shapiro (February 24, 1999).

17 The editors engaged with body image later in the text by presenting "a wonderful poem by Daisy Somora . . . who was a Sandanista fighter, who then became one of the ministers of culture in the Sandanista government. And she has a poem called 'My Body,' which does the same kind of thing [as the woman looking at her image in the mirror, which opens the "Body Image" chapter in the U.S. *OBOS*]. It does an inventory of a woman's body, but . . . rather than focusing entirely on image, it . . . shows you a beacon of how one's body could be different." Ibid.

18 Ibid.

19 See Shapiro 2001; and Walters and Manicom 1996.

20 Shapiro is highly critical of the fact that the U.S. *OBOS* has become "intimidatingly information based" (2001). While this does not necessarily preclude the reader from engaging in "participatory education," it may well be that *NCNV* is closer in its approach to earlier versions of *OBOS*.

21 Interview, Ester Shapiro (February 24, 1999).

22 Shapiro, in the chapter "Introduction to Health and Reproductive Rights," *Nuestros Cuerpos, Nuestras Vidas* (BWHBC 2000, 305). Quotations are based on English translations by Shapiro herself, which are available on the BWHBC Web site.

23 Traditional healing practices are the most common form of health care throughout rural Latin America, the Southern Cone, and the Caribbean. However, urban women are also likely to seek the services of a traditional healer in addition to visiting medical practitioners. My thanks to Lynn Stephen for her insights on this subject.

24 The women's movement in Latin America has a long history and includes women of various class and ethnic backgrounds—feminist groups (often consisting of white, middle-class, educated women), popular women's movements devoted to practical issues, and a burgeoning black feminist movement. More recently, NGOs with a feminist agenda and strong ties to governmental policymakers have also sprung up throughout the South. See Safa 1990; Sternbach et al. 1992; Jacquette 1994; Alvarez 1998; Caldeira 1998; Jacquette and Wolchik 1998; and Alvarez et al. 2003. While not every women's group would call itself "feminist," there is an awareness of gender among Latin American women and a history of women organizing around issues of concern to them as women. In Latin America, feminism historically has and continues to have strong ties to other progressive social movements and in the popular imagination is clearly linked to opposition to dictatorial regimes and advocates for democratic change of the oppressive regimes of the past. Despite failing economies and widespread poverty, women have managed to meet regularly and form alliances around issues of reproductive rights, sexual violence, and health. It is not surprising that U.S. Latinas, having experienced exclusion or marginalization within white-dominated feminism in the North, would look to the South for inspiration and practical alliances.

25 Shapiro in the preface to *NCNV* (BWHBC 2000, 15).

26 Thayer (2000) argues that the focus in Latin American feminism is more toward gendered or "corporeal citizenship" and less toward knowledge about women's bodies. She criticizes U.S. feminism—and *OBOS* in particular—for not having borrowed this perspective, an example of how women's movements in the North might benefit from feminist discourses and practices in the South.

27 Shapiro in the preface to *NCNV* (BWHBC 2000, 15–16).

28 Interview, Ester Shapiro (February 24, 1999).

29 Ibid.

30 Many theorists have argued that borderlands are the space from which Latinas can understand their situation. The history of U.S. imperialism demonstrates how one nation was forcibly imposed over existing ones, thereby giving Latino people a strong sense of the temporality of the nation-state. Moreover, the political border between the United States and Mexico does not correspond with the cultural and everyday experience of families living on both sides of the divide. See Anzaldúa 1987; Lugones 1990, 2003; Sternbach et al. 1992; and Hurtado 1998.

31 Interview, Ester Shapiro (February 24, 1999).

32 Ibid.

33 Interview, Irina Todorova (June 4, 2003).

34 See chapter 2.

35 Writing in the context of a critic of U.S. hegemony in translation politics, Appiah (2000) uses the notion of "thick translation" to encourage critical (U.S.) translators to take the activity of translating texts of the "Other" more seriously. Capturing the meanings of a text as it was intended within a specific historical, cultural and political context requires much more than a linguistically correct translation. A "thick" description which illuminates some of this context is not only necessary for a "genuinely informed" and "respectful" rendition of the text, but also addresses the "need to extend the American imagination—an imagination that regulates much of the world system economically and politically—beyond the narrow scope of the United States" (427–428).

36 Interview, Irina Todorova (June 4, 2003).

37 Ibid.

38 This philosophy was explicitly borrowed from the U.S. *OBOS*, and the editors' hopes for the Bulgarian edition are in line with the history of the original book. Thus, Todorova expressed the hope that they would "get the same wonderful letters [from readers] that they do" (ibid).

39 Community centers—or *Chitalishte*—are a remarkable tradition in Bulgaria dating from before the era of Soviet control. These centers provide libraries and space for different generations and social and ethnic groups to meet, have discussions, and learn from one another. Always enormously popular, they are one of the few institutions to have survived the transition from Soviet control. See Women's Health Initiative in Bulgaria 2003. At present, the WHI is in the process of conducting and evaluating discussions with different groups of readers (interview, Irina Todorova [October 1, 2004]).

40 One of the most dramatic changes in world health in the late twentieth century has involved the decline in life expectancies in the former Soviet Union and Eastern Europe. In Bulgaria, this deterioration can be attributed to the fact that more than one-third of Bulgarians live below the poverty line and, of female-headed households, 64 percent live in absolute poverty (especially elderly women and single mothers). Un-

employment rates are also considerably higher among women, while women continue to bear the brunt of the care of other family members (children, men, and the elderly). In the wake of the 1989 transition, the previously existing health care system has been dismantled, but the new one is not fully functioning, making it very difficult for many women to exercise their "right" to health care. See Women's Health Initiative in Bulgaria 2003; Einhorn 1993; and Todorova 1994.

41 Krassimira Daskalova wrote this chapter. See Daskalova 1997 for an illuminating overview of the history of the "women's movement" (her quotes) and the present state of women's organizations in Bulgaria.

42 There has been a shift in Bulgaria from a protectionist state, which treated women patients as irresponsible and requiring compulsory medical treatment, to a situation in which "anything goes," private initiatives abound, and medications are obtainable through the Internet without a prescription. In 2004, a new Health Law was enacted to regulate health care in Bulgaria. While regulation was obviously necessary, it is often done in a way that continues to treat women as irresponsible and in need of compulsory measures regarding their health. Compulsory testing for cervical cancer by general practitioners (GPs) is a case in point. Since many women regard GPs as primarily pediatricians, and therefore not competent to address their gynecological needs, initiating compulsory measures without consulting them did not sit well. In contrast to this top-down approach to reform, women's health groups (including WHI) advocate health legislation that treats women as embodied subjects with reproductive rights (interview, Irina Todorova [October 1, 2004]).

43 This suggests that in practice translations are not the either-or affairs they appear to be in translation theory, where fierce debates are waged about the desirability of "translator invisibility" (the text reads as though it were originally written in the language rather than translated) and the refusal to force the text into another language and preserving its foreignness—the strategy that many critical translation theorists advocate. See Venuti 2000.

44 Interview, Irina Todorova (June 4, 2003).

45 Interestingly, Bulgarian women in discussion groups indicated that, while the book's "direct" approach to women's bodies, sexuality, and medical procedures made it seem "American," this did not detract from its usefulness. The personal and frank language employed in the U.S. text may have been especially attractive to readers who were used to totalitarian discourses, which were often boring, predictable, and ideologically marked. During this period, there was no foreign borrowing except from Russian (personal communication, Kornelia Slavova, May 2005).

46 This displays awareness of how fragile even the most unassailable reproductive rights can be, as well as of the utility of situating struggles for reproductive rights in an international context. It also raises the issue

of the importance of treating abortion in a culturally informed way. For example, Susan Gal (1997) criticizes Western feminists for erroneously assuming that when women from Eastern Europe speak of abortion they are worried about the same kinds of issues that trouble U.S. feminists, that is, a woman's right to control her own body. In Bulgaria, women's rights are less the issue than the expansion of women's reproductive choices to include other forms of contraception.

47 Like English, Bulgarian has a separate term for biological sex (*pol*) and linguistic gender (*rod*). As in English, the biological term is frequently used, and, as in English, Bulgarian feminists were faced with the difficulty of finding ways to convey gender as a social and cultural construction (see Daskalova 1997). Different strategies were employed. *Gender* was sometimes left in English (thereby underlining its foreignness); in other cases, *rod* was used, which is the linguistic term for gender but also means "family order"—ironically, one of the targets of U.S. secondwave feminism.

48 In view of the seemingly interminable Anglo-American debates about the sex and gender distinction, a little cross-cultural borrowing might be in order here. See Fraser 1997; and chapter 4 in this volume.

49 Personal communication, Kornelia Slavova (May 2005). This terminology also resonates with the burgeoning gay and lesbian movement in Bulgaria.

50 Many authors have addressed the antifeminist stance of Eastern European women and their skepticism toward U.S. feminism in particular. See Marody 1993; Todorova 1994; Goldfarb 1997; Busheikin 1997; Watson 1997; and Nikolchina 2002.

51 Personal communication, Irina Todorova (May 2005).

52 See Petchesky 1995 for a perceptive discussion of the inapplicability of Western feminist critiques of individualism in a Central or Eastern European context.

53 Translated preface to *Nasheto Tyalo, Nie Samite*, http://www.ourbodiesourselves.org/programs/network/foreign/bulgpr1.asp (accessed March 23, 2007).

54 It is worth noting here that the discourse of difference, which focuses on the triad "race-class-gender," is also a transatlantic traveler and has been adopted by many feminists outside the United States, where the intersectional differences and inequalities among women are very different from what they are in the United States. See Knapp 2005 for an interesting critique of the temporal and epistemic economy connected with these appropriations.

55 Interview, Irina Todorova (June 4, 2003).

56 Translated preface to *Nasheto Tyalo, Nie Samite*, http://www.ourbodiesourselves.org/programs/network/foreign/bulgpr1.asp (accessed March 23, 2007).

57 Personal communication, Kornelia Slavova (May 2005).

58 A few well-known examples of "translations" that have been instrumental in international social movements are Karl Marx's *Das Kapital* for the workers' movement, Simone de Beauvoir's *The Second Sex* for second-wave feminism, and Harriet Beecher Stowe's *Uncle Tom's Cabin* for antislavery abolitionist movements.

59 Tsing, in fact, uses the translations of *OBOS* as an illustration of this point.

60 Given the global hegemony of the English language and the very real danger of cultural imperialism, Spivak (2000) advocates different strategies for translating English texts into the languages of the Third World than the other way around. She is skeptical of the growing interest among First World feminists in translations of the writings of Third World women, suggesting that it is motivated by the "desire to speak for" the postcolonial subject. The "cannibalistic strategy" that makes sense for Third World translators of English texts would clearly not be in order here. Instead she suggests that humility and a willingness to learn from the "other" would be more appropriate strategies for the Western feminist translating non-Western texts. See also Spivak 1985.

61 And, indeed, as the politics of the U.S. text have changed dramatically during the past three decades (see chapter 1), it becomes clear that oppositionality remains an issue that needs to be addressed anew with every edition of *OBOS*, whether it is produced within or outside the United States.

7 Transnational Knowledges

1 See DuPlessis and Snitow 1998; Brownmiller 1999; Rosen 2000; Freedman 2001; and Evans 2003, just to name some of the more widely cited histories. See also the more "classic" renditions of second-wave feminism: Evans 1979; Echols 1989; and Davis 1991. There have also been countless autobiographies and memoirs by feminists who had been active in the U.S. women's movement during the sixties and seventies.

2 Sandoval (2000) refers to this version of feminist history as "hegemonic feminism."

3 For a similar argument applied to the field of ethnography, see Burawoy et al. 2000.

4 The same argument can be made concerning poststructuralist feminist body theory, which has also tended to focus on deconstructing Enlightenment notions of the autonomous self or the authenticity of experience rather than engaging with the embodied practices of women in their everyday lives.

5 This remark was made in the context of a longer discussion instigated by the journal *Feminist Theory* concerning the separation between feminist theory (writ large) and feminist scholarship. Many of the contributors felt that feminist theory had become too abstract and esoteric, divorced from the social and political realities of everyday life. Stacey (2001) was not arguing for a return to activism but rather to a longing for a feminist inquiry that might contribute to feminist action. Her models for this kind of inquiry were Barbara Christian, Audre Lorde, and other "prematurely fallen activist-theorists" (102).

6 This is encapsulated most succinctly in the oft-quoted statement by Virigina Woolf, "As a woman, I have no country. As a woman, I want no country. As a woman, my country is the whole world" (1938).

7 Mendoza (2002) is one of the pessimists. She is skeptical of transnational feminism as a fashionable buzzword in the U.S. academy because it so often remains attached to liberal multiculturalism and a "newfound cosmopolitanism," while inequalities between women at a local level may be exacerbated. She suggests that the path toward political solidarity among feminists remains problematic and requires more than good intentions (309–10). See also Haggis and Schech 2000 for an interesting discussion of what "good manners" might entail for global feminism. In the authors' view, respectful collaborations entail giving up the attempts to be "good feminists" (i.e., "Lady Bountiful") and acknowledging instead the epistemological incommensurabilities and inequalities of power that are inherent in any global feminist project.

8 Pfeil (1994) has criticized the uniform emphasis on difference among contemporary postcolonial feminist scholars as a "disabling fetish." The preoccupation with differences between feminist projects across the globe may obscure the "long work and deeper pleasure of constructing 'structures of affinity' now, in theory and practice" (228). Bartky (2002) makes a similar point, observing that it may be more important for multicultural, transnational feminist politics to focus on the role of sympathy in creating relations of solidarity than in finding ways to further theorize difference.

Abbott, Sidney, and Barbara Love. 1972. *A Liberated View of Lesbianism: Sappho was a Right-on Woman*. Chelsea: Scarborough House.

Abdalla, Raquiya Haji Dualeh. 1982. *Sisters in Affliction: Circumcision and Infibulation of Women in Africa*. London: Zed.

Adkins, Lisa. 2004. "Passing on Feminism: From Consciousness to Reflexivity?" *European Journal of Women's Studies* 11, no. 4: 427–44.

Ahmed, Sara. 2000. *Strange Encounters: Embodied Others in Post-Coloniality*. London: Routledge.

Al-Ali, Nadje. 2000. *Secularism, Gender, and the State in the Middle East: The Egyptian Women's Movement*. Cambridge: Cambridge University Press.

Alarcón, Norma. 1990. "The Theoretical Subject(s) of This Bridge Called My Back and Anglo-American Feminism." In *Making Face, Making Soul: Creative and Critical Perspectives by Feminists of Color*, edited by Gloria Anzaldúa, 356–69. San Francisco: Aunt Lute Books.

Alcoff, Linda Martin. 2000. "Phenomenology, Post-structuralism, and Feminist Theory on the Concept of Experience." In *Feminist Phenomenology*, edited by Linda Fisher and L. Embree, 39–56. Dordrecht: Kluwer.

Alcoff, Linda, and Elizabeth Potter. 1993. "Introduction: When Feminisms Intersect Epistemology." In *Feminist Epistemologies*, edited by Linda Alcoff and Elizabeth Potter, 1–14. New York: Routledge.

Alexander, M. Jacqui, and Chandra Talpade Mohanty. 1997. "Genealogies, Legacies, Movements." In *Feminist Genealogies, Colonial Legacies, Democratic Futures*, edited by M. Jacqui Alexander and Chandra Talpade Mohanty, xiii–xlii. New York: Routledge.

Alvarez, Sonia E. 1998. "Latin American Feminisms 'Go Global': Trends of the 1990s and Challenges for the New Millennium." In *Cultures of Politics, Politics of Cultures: Re-visioning Latin American Social Movements*, edited by Sonia E. Alvarez, Evelina Dagnino, and Arturo Escobar, 293–324. Boulder: Westview.

Alvarez, Sonia E., Elisabeth Jay Friedman, Ericka Beckman, Maylei Blackwell, Norma Stoltz Chinchilla, Nathalie Lebon, Marysa Navarro, and Marcela Ríos Tobar. 2003. "Encountering Latin American and Caribbean Feminisms," *Signs* 28, no. 1: 537–80.

Anderson, Benedict. 1983. *Imagined Communities: Reflections on the Origin and Spread of Nationalism*. London: Verso.

Anzaldúa, Gloria. 1987. *Borderlands/la Frontera: The New Mestiza*. San Francisco: Aunt Lute Books.

———, ed. 1990. *Making Face, Making Soul: Creative and Critical Perspectives by Feminists of Color*. San Francisco: Aunt Lute Books.

Appadurai, Arjun. 2000. "Grassroots Globalization and the Research Imagination." *Public Culture* 12, no. 1: 1–19.

———. 1996. *Modernity at Large: Cultural Dimensions of Globalization*. Minneapolis: University of Minnesota Press.

Appiah, Kwame Anthony. 2000. "Thick Translation." In *The Translation Studies Reader*, ed. Lawrence Venuti, 417–29, London: Routledge.

Assad, Marie B. 1980. "Female Circumcision in Egypt: Social Implications, Current Research, and Prospects for Change." *Studies in Family Planning* 2, no. 1: 3–16.

Bartky, Sandra Lee. 2002. *"Sympathy and Solidarity" and Other Essays*. Lanham, Md.: Rowman and Littlefield.

———. 1990. *Femininity and Domination: Studies in the Phenomenology of Oppression*. New York: Routledge.

Beauvoir, Simone de. 1953. *The Second Sex*. Trans. H. M. Parshley. New York: Knopf.

Beckwith, Barbara. 1985. "Boston Women's Health Book Collective: Women Empowering Women." *Women and Health* 10, no. 1 (spring): 1–7.

Bell, Patricia, Gloria T. Hull, Patricia Bell Scott, and Barbara Smith, eds. 1981. *All the Women Are White, All the Blacks Are Men, but Some of Us Are Brave: Black Women's Studies*. New York: Feminist Press, City University of New York.

Bell, Ruth, ed., with other members of the Boston Women's Health Book Collective. [1987, 1991] 1998. *Changing Bodies, Changing Lives: A Book for Teens on Sex and Relationships*. New York: Three River Press.

Bell, Susan E. 1994. "Translating Science to the People: Updating *The New Our Bodies, Ourselves*." *Women's Studies International Forum* 17, no. 1: 9–18.

Bell, Susan E., and Susan M. Reverby. 2005. "Vaginal Politics: Tensions and Possibilities in *The Vagina Monologues*." *Women's Studies International Forum* 28, no. 5: 430–44.

Bell Alexander, Ruth, Pamela Berger, Cassandra Clay, June Cooper, Vilynya Diskin, Joan Ditzion, Paula Doress-Worters, et al. 1997. "Response from the Board and Founders of the Boston Women's Health Book Collective." *Sojourner* 23, no. 4: 5.

Birke, Lynda. 1999. *Feminism and the Biological Body*. New Brunswick, N.J.: Rutgers University Press.

Blumenthal, Leslie. 1987. "The Transformation of a Feminist Ideology." B.A. thesis, History and Science Program, Harvard University.

Bonilla, Alba, April Taylor, Mayra Canetti, and Jennifer Yanco. 1997. "An

Open Letter to the Board of Directors, Boston Women's Health Book Collective." *Sojourner* 23, no. 4: 4.

Bonilla, Zobeida E. 2005. "Including Every Woman: The All-Embracing "We" of *Our Bodies, Ourselves.*" *NWSA Journal* 17, no. 1 (spring): 175–83.

Bordo, Susan. 1998. "Bringing Body to Theory." In *Body and Flesh: A Philosophical Reader*, edited by Donn Welton, 84–98. Malden, Mass.: Blackwell.

———. 1997. *Twilight Zones: The Hidden Life of Cultural Images from Plato to O. J.* Berkeley: University of California Press.

———. 1993. *Unbearable Weight: Feminism, Western Culture, and the Body.* Berkeley: University of California Press.

———. 1987. *The Flight to Objectivity: Essays on Cartesianism and Culture.* Albany: State University of New York Press.

Bourdieu, Pierre. 1986. "The Forms of Capital." In *Handbook of Theory and Research for the Sociology of Education*, edited by John G. Richardson, 241–58. New York: Greenwood.

———. 1977. *Outline of a Theory of Practice.* Cambridge: Cambridge University Press.

Brah, Avtar. 1996. *Cartographies of Diaspora: Contesting Identities.* London: Routledge.

Braidotti, Rosi. 1999. "Signs of Wonder and Traces of Doubt: On Teratology and Embodied Differences." In *Feminist Theory and the Body*, edited by Janet Price and Margrit Shildrick, 290–301. Edinburgh: Edinburgh University Press.

———. 1991. *Patterns of Dissonance.* New York: Routledge.

Braverman, Harry. 1976. *Labor and Monopoly Capital: The Degradation of Work in the Twentieth Century.* New York: Monthly Review Press.

Breckenridge, Carol A., and Candace Vogler. 2001. "The Critical Limits of Embodiment: Disability's Criticism." *Public Culture* 13, no. 3: 349–57.

Brown, Wendy. 2001. *Politics out of History.* Princeton: Princeton University Press.

Brownmiller, Susan. 1999. *In Our Time: Memoir of a Revolution.* New York: Dial.

Buckley, Sandra. 1997. *Broken Silence: Voices of Japanese Feminism.* Berkeley: University of California Press.

Burawoy, Michael, Joseph A. Blum, Sheba George, Zsuzsa Gille, Teresa Gowan, Lynne Hanley, Maren Klawiter, Steven H. Lopez, Sean O'Riain, and Millie Thayer, eds. 2000. *Global Ethnography: Forces, Connections, and Imaginations in a Postmodern World.* Berkeley: University of California Press.

Busheikin, Laura. 1997. "Is Sisterhood Really Global? Western Feminism in East Europe." In *Ana's Land: Sisterhood in Eastern Europe*, edited by Tanya Renne, 12–21. Boulder: Westview.

Butler, Judith. 1993. *Bodies That Matter: On the Discursive Limits of "Sex."* New York: Routledge.

———. 1989. *Gender Trouble: Feminism and the Subversion of Identity.* New York: Routledge.

BWHBC [Boston Women's Health Book Collective]. 2005. *Our Bodies, Ourselves: A New Edition for a New Era.* New York: Simon and Schuster.

———. 2000. *Nuestros Cuerpos, Neustras Vidas.* New York: Seven Stories Press.

———. 1998. *Our Bodies, Ourselves for the New Century.* New York: Simon and Schuster.

———. 1992. *The New Our Bodies, Ourselves.* New York: Simon and Schuster.

———. 1984. *The New Our Bodies, Ourselves.* New York: Simon and Schuster.

———. 1979. *Our Bodies, Ourselves.* New York: Simon and Schuster.

———. 1978. *Ourselves, Our Children.* New York: Random House.

———. 1977. *Nuestros Cuerpos, Neustras Vidas.* New York: Simon and Schuster.

———. 1976. *Our Bodies, Ourselves.* New York: Simon and Schuster.

———. 1973. *Our Bodies, Ourselves.* New York: Simon and Schuster.

———. 1970. *Our Bodies, Ourselves: A Course by and for Women.* New York: Simon and Schuster.

Caldeira, Teresa P. R. 1998. "Justice and Individual Rights: Challenges for Women's Movements and Democratization in Brazil." In *Women and Democracy: Latin America and Central and Eastern Europe*, edited by Jane S. Jacquette and Sharon L. Wolchik. 75–103. Baltimore: Johns Hopkins University Press.

Chen, Kuan-Hsing. 1996. "Cultural Studies and the Politics of Internationalization: An Interview with Stuart Hall." In *Stuart Hall: Critical Dialogues in Cultural Studies*, edited by David Morley and Kuan-Hsing Chen, 392–408. London: Routledge.

Chesler, Phyllis. 1973. *Women and Madness.* New York: Avon.

Chodorow, Nancy J. 1978. *The Reproduction of Mothering.* Berkeley: University of California Press.

Clarke, Adele E., and Virginia L. Olesen. 1999a. "Revising, Diffracting, Acting." In *Revisioning Women, Health, and Healing*, edited by Adele E. Clarke and Virginia L. Olesen, 3–48. New York: Routledge.

———. 1999b. *Revisioning Women, Health, and Healing.* New York: Routledge.

Clawson, Dan. 1996. "From the Editor's Desk." *Contemporary Sociology* 25, no. 3: ix.

Code, Lorraine. 1991. *What Can She Know? Feminist Theory and the Construction of Knowledge.* Ithaca: Cornell University Press.

Collins, Patricia Hill. 2000. *Black Feminist Thought: Knowledge, Con-*

sciousness, and the Politics of Empowerment, 2nd ed. New York: Routledge.

———. 1997. "Comment on Hekman's 'Truth and Method: Feminist Standpoint Theory Revisited': Where's the Power?" *Signs* 22, no. 2: 375–81.

Crawford, Robert. 1980. "Healthism and the Medicalization of Everyday Life." *International Journal of Health Services* 10, no. 3: 365–88.

Creager, Angela N. H., Elizabeth A. Lunbeck, and Londa Schiebinger, eds. 2001. *Feminism in Twentieth-Century Science, Technology, and Medicine.* Chicago: University of Chicago Press.

Crenshaw, Kimberlé. 1989. "Demarginalizing the Intersection of Race and Sex: A Black Feminist Critique of Antidiscrimination Doctrine, Feminist Theory, and Antiracist Politics." *University of Chicago Legal Forum*: 139–67.

Daskalova, Krassimira. 1997. "The Women's Movement in Bulgaria after Communism." In *Transitions, Environments, Translations: Feminisms in International Politics*, edited by Joan W. Scott, Cora Kaplan, and Debra Keates, 162–75. New York: Routledge.

Davis, Angela Y. 1981. *Women, Race, and Class.* New York: Random House.

Davis, Flora. 1991. *Moving the Mountain: The Women's Movement in America since 1960.* New York: Simon and Schuster.

Davis, Kathy. 2003. *Dubious Equalities and Embodied Differences.* Lanham, Md.: Rowman and Littlefield.

———. 2002. "Feminist Body/Politics as World Traveller: Translating *Our Bodies, Ourselves.*" *European Journal of Women's Studies* 9, no. 3: 223–47.

———. 1997. "Embody-ing Theory: Beyond Modernist and Postmodernist Readings of the Body." In *Embodied Practices: Feminist Perspectives on the Body*, edited by Kathy Davis, 1–23. London: Sage.

———. 1995. *Reshaping the Female Body.* New York: Routledge.

———. 1988. *Power under the Microscope.* Dordrecht: Foris.

Davis-Floyd, Robbie E. 1994. "Mind over Body: The Pregnant Professional." In *Many Mirrors: Body Image and Social Relations*, edited by Nicole Sault, 204–34. New Brunswick, N.J.: Rutgers University Press.

Diskin, Leah. 1990. "Facts and Fiction of Female Embodiment: *Our Bodies, Ourselves* and the 'Science Question.'" Master's thesis, Stanford University,

Dorkenoo, Efua. 1994. *Cutting the Rose: Female Genital Mutilation.* London: Minority Rights Group.

Duden, Barbara. 2002. *Die Gene im Kopf—der Fötus im Bauch: Historisches zum Frauenkörper.* Hannover: Offizin.

DuPlessis, Rachel Blau, and Ann Snitow, eds. 1998. *Feminist Memoir Project: Voices from Women's Liberation.* New York: Three Rivers.

Eaton, Beverly. 1979. "A Decade of Healthy Feminism." *New Roots* 7: 38–41.

Echols, Alice. 1989. *Daring to be Bad: Radical Feminism in America, 1967–1975*. Minneapolis: University of Minnesota Press.

Ehrenreich, Barbara, and Deirdre English. 2005. *For Her Own Good: Two Centuries on Experts' Advice to Women*, Rev. ed. New York: Anchor.

Einhorn, Barbara. 1993. *Cinderella Goes to Market: Gender, Citizenship, and the Women's Movement in Eastern Europe*. London: Verso.

El Dawla, Aida Seif, Amal Abdel Hadi, and Nadia Abdel Wahab. 1998. "Women's Wit over Men's: Trade-offs and Strategic Accommodations in Egyptian Women's Reproductive Lives." In *Negotiating Reproductive Rights*, edited by Rosalind P. Petchesky and Karen Judd, 69–107. London: Zed.

Enloe, Cynthia. 1989. *Bananas, Beaches, and Bases: Making Feminist Sense of International Politics*, Berkeley: University of California Press.

Ensler, Eve. 1998. *The Vagina Monologues*. New York: Villard.

Evans, Sara. *Tidal Wave: How Women Changed America at Century's End*. New York: Free Press, 2003.

———. 1979. *Personal Politics: The Roots of Women's Liberation in the Civil Rights Movement and the New Left*. New York: Random House.

Faludi, Susan. 1992. *Backlash: The Undeclared War against Women*. London: Chatto and Windus.

Farah, Nadia. 1991. "The Egyptian Women's Health Book Collective." *Middle East Report* 173 (November–December): 16–25.

Fausto-Sterling, Anne. 2005. "The Bare Bones of Sex, Part 1: Sex and Gender." *Signs* 30, no. 2: 1491–1527.

Ferree, Myra Marx, and Patricia Yancey Martin, eds. 1995. *Feminist Organizations: Harvest of the Women's Movement*. Philadelphia: Temple University Press.

Fine, Michelle, Lois Weis, Linda C. Powell, and L. Mun Wong, eds. 1997. *Off White: Readings on Race, Power, and Society*. New York: Routledge.

Firestone, Shulamith. 1970. *The Dialectic of Sex*. New York: Bantam.

Foucault, Michel. 1980. *Power/Knowledge: Selected Interviews and Other Writings, 1972–1977*. Ed. Colin Gordon. Brighton: Harvester.

———. 1978. "Politics and the Study of Discourse." *Ideology and Consciousness* 6: 7–26.

———. 1977. *Discipline and Punish*. Harmondsworth: Peregrine.

———. 1972. *The Archaeology of Knowledge*. London: Tavistock.

Fox, Daniel M. 2005. "Evidence of Evidence-Based Health Policy." *Health Affairs* 24, no. 1 (January–February): 114–23.

Frankenberg, Ruth. 2001. "The Mirage of Unmarked Whiteness." In *The Making and Unmaking of Whiteness*, edited by Birgit Brander

Rasmussen, Eric Klineberg, Irene J. Nexica, and Matt Wray, 72–96. Durham: Duke University Press.

———. 1993. *The Social Construction of Whiteness: White Women, Race Matters*. London: Routledge.

Frankenberg, Ruth, and Lata Mani. 1993. "Crosscurrents, Crosstalk: Race, 'Postcoloniality,' and the Politics of Location." *Cultural Studies* 7, no. 2 (May): 292–310.

Fraser, Marian, and Monica Greco, eds. 2005. *The Body: A Reader*. London: Routledge.

Fraser, Nancy. 1997. *Justice Interruptus: Critical Reflections on the "Postsocialist" Condition*. New York: Routledge.

Freedman, Estelle. 2001. *No Turning Back: The History of Feminism and the Future of Women*. New York: Ballantine.

Freeman, Jo. 1971. *The Women's Liberation Movement: Its Aims, Structures, and Ideas*. Pittsburgh: Know.

Friedman, Susan Stanford. 2001. "Locational Feminism: Gender, Cultural Geographies, and Geopolitical Literacy." In *Feminist Locations: Global and Local, Theory and Practice*, edited by Marianne Dekoven, 13–36. New Brunswick, N.J.: Rutgers University Press.

———. 1998. *Mappings: Feminism and the Cultural Geographies of Encounter*. Princeton: Princeton University Press.

Gabriel, Yiannis. 1993. "Organizational Nostalgia: Reflections on 'The Golden Age.'" In *Emotion in Organizations*, edited by Stephen Fineman, 118–41. London: Sage.

Gal, Susan. 1997. "Feminism and Civil Society." In *Transitions, Environments, Translations: Feminisms in International Politics*, edited by Joan W. Scott, Cora Kaplan, and Debra Keates, 30–45. New York: Routledge.

Gallop, Jane. 1994. "History Is Like Mother." In *The New Historicism*, edited by H. Aram Vesser, 311–41. New York: Routledge.

Gatens, Moira. 1999. "Power, Bodies, and Difference." In *Feminist Theory and the Body*, edited by Janet Price and Margrit Shildrick, 227–34. Edinburgh: Edinburgh University Press.

Geertz, Clifford. 1973. *The Interpretation of Cultures*. New York: Basic Books.

Giddens, Anthony. 1976. *New Rules of Sociological Method*. London: Hutchinson.

Ginsburg, Faye D. 1998. *Contested Lives: The Abortion Debate in an American Community*. Berkeley: University of California Press.

Ginsburg, Faye D., and Rayna Rapp. 1995. *Conceiving the New World Order: The Global Politics of Reproduction*. Berkeley: University of California Press.

Goldfarb, Jeffrey C. 1997. "Why Is There No Feminism after Communism?" *Social Research* 64, no. 2: 235–58.

Goodman, Kenneth W. 2003. *Ethics and Evidence-Based Medicine: Fal-*

libility and Responsibility in Clinical Science. Cambridge: Cambridge University Press.

Goosen, Margaretha, and Barbara Klugman. 1996. "Preface." In *The South African Women's Health Book*, edited by the Women's Health Project. Cape Town: Oxford University Press.

Gordon, Linda. 1988. *Heroes in Their Own Lives: The Politics and History of Family Violence.* New York: Viking.

Gordon, Linda, and Barrie Thorne. 1996. "Women's Bodies and Feminist Subversions." *Contemporary Sociology* 25, no. 3: 322–25.

Grewal, Inderpal, and Caren Kaplan. 2001. "Global Identities: Theorizing Transnational Studies of Sexuality." *glq* 7, no. 4: 663–79.

———. 1994. "Introduction: Transnational Feminist Practices and Questions of Postmodernity." In *Scattered Hegemonies: Postmodernity and Transnational Feminist Practices*, edited by Inderpal Grewal and Caren Kaplan, 1–33. Minneapolis: University of Minnesota Press.

Grosz, Eliabeth. 1994. *Volatile Bodies: Toward a Corporeal Feminism.* Bloomington: Indiana University Press.

Haggis, Jane, and Susanne Schech. 2000. "Meaning Well and Global Good Manners: Reflections on White Western Feminist Cross-Cultural Praxis." *Australian Feminist Studies* 15, no. 33: 387–99.

Hall, Kim Q. 2005. "Queerness, Disability, and *The Vagina Monologues.*" *Hypatia* 20, no. 1 (winter): 99–119.

Hall, Stuart. 1997. "The Local and the Global: Globalization and Ethnicity." In *Culture, Globalization, and the World-System: Contemporary Conditions for the Representation of Identity*, edited by Anthony King, 19–40. Minneapolis: University of Minnesota Press.

———. 1996. "When Was 'The Post-colonial' Thinking at the Limit?" In *The Post-colonial Question: Common Skies, Divided Horizons*, edited by Iain Chambers and Lidia Curti, 242–59. London: Routledge.

———. 1992. "The West and the Rest: Discourse and Power." In *Formations of Modernity*, edited by Stuart Hall and Bram Gieben, 275–320. Cambridge: Polity.

Hantrakul, Sukanya. 1996. "A Woman's Right to Good Health." *Nation* (Thailand), September 11.

Haraway, Donna. 1999. "The Virtual Speculum in the New World Order." In *Revisioning Women, Health, and Healing*, edited by Adele E. Clarke and Virginia L. Olesen, 49–96. New York: Routledge.

———. 1997. *Modest_Witness@Second_Millennium. FemaleMan©_Meets_OncoMouse™: Feminism and Technoscience.* New York: Routledge.

———. 1991a. *Simians, Cyborgs, and Women.* London: Free Association Books.

———. 1991b. "Situated Knowledges: The Science Question in Feminism and the Privilege of Partial Perspective." In *Simians, Cyborgs, and Women*, 183–202. London: Free Association Books.

Harding, Sandra. 1998. *Is Science Multicultural? Postcolonialisms, Feminisms, and Epistemologies*. Bloomington: Indiana University Press.

———. 1997. "Comment on Hekman's 'Truth and Method: Feminist Standpoint Theory Revisited': Whose Standpoint Needs the Regimes of Truth and Reality?" *Signs* 22, no. 2: 382–91.

———. 1991. *Whose Science, Whose Knowledge? Thinking from Women's Lives*. Milton Keynes: Open University Press.

———. 1986. *The Science Question in Feminism*. Ithaca: Cornell University Press.

Hartsock, Nancy. 1998. *The Feminist Standpoint Revisited and Other Essays*. Boulder: Westview.

———. 1997. "Comment on Hekman's 'Truth and Method: Feminist Standpoint Theory Revisited': Truth or Justice?" *Signs* 22, no. 2: 367–74.

———. 1983. "The Feminist Standpoint: Developing the Ground for a Specifically Feminist Historical Materialism." In *Discovering Reality*, edited by Sandra Harding and Merrill B. Hintikka, 283–310. Dordrecht: Reidel.

Hayden, Sara. 1997. "Re-claiming Bodies of Knowledge: An Exploration of the Relationship between Feminist Theorizing and Feminine Style in the Rhetoric of the Boston Women's Health Book Collective." *Western Journal of Communication* 61, no. 2 (spring): 127–63.

———. 1994. *Twenty-Three Years of OBOS: Individualism, Community, and Social Change in the Work of the BWHBC*. Ph.D. diss., University of Minnesota.

Hekman, Susan. 1998. "Material Bodies." In *Body and Flesh: A Philosophical Reader*, edited by Donn Welton, 61–70. Malden, Mass.: Blackwell.

Hekman, Susan. 1997a. "Response to Hartsock, Collins, Harding, and Smith." *Signs* 22, no. 2: 399–402.

———. 1997b. "Truth and Method: Feminist Standpoint Theory Revisited." *Signs* 22, no. 2: 341–65.

Helfland, Mark. 2005. "Using Evidence Reports: Progress and Challenges in Evidence-Based Decision-Making." *Health Affairs* 24, no. 1 (January–February): 123–28.

Hemmings, Clare. 2005. "Telling Feminist Stories." *Feminist Theory* 6, no. 2: 115–39.

Henwood, Karen, Christine Griffin, and Ann Phoenix, eds. 1998. *Standpoints and Differences*. London: Sage.

Hill, Nancy. 1994. "An Egyptian Women's Health Book Inspired by *Our Bodies, Ourselves*: Is Global Sisterhood Possible after All?" Paper presented at a meeting of the Eastern Sociological Society, March 18.

hooks, bell. 2000. *Feminist Theory: From Margin to Center*. Cambridge: South End Press.

————. 1981. *Ain't I a Woman: Black Women and Feminism*. Boston: South End Press.

Huffer, Lynne. 1998. *Maternal Pasts, Feminist Futures: Nostalgia, Ethics, and the Question of Difference*. Palo Alto: Stanford University Press.

Hurtado, Aída. 1998. "*Sitios y Lenguas*: Chicanas Theorize Feminisms." *Hypatia* 13, no. 2 (spring): 134–61.

Ibrahim, Barbara, and Nadia Farah. 1992. "Women's Lives and Health: The Cairo Women's Health Book Collective." *Quality/Calidad/Qualité* 4: 4–11.

Jacobus, Mary, Evelyn Fox Keller, and Sally Shuttleworth, eds. 1990. *Body/Politics: Women and the Discourses of Science*. New York: Routledge.

Jacquette, Jane S., ed. 1994. *The Women's Movement in Latin America*. Boulder: Westview.

Jacquette, Jane S., and Sharon L. Wolchik, eds. 1998. *Women and Democracy: Latin America and Central and Eastern Europe*. Baltimore: Johns Hopkins University Press.

Jaggar, Alison. 1998. "Globalizing Feminist Ethics." *Hypatia* 13, no. 2: 7–31.

James, Stanlie M., and Claire C. Robertson, eds. 2002. *Genital Cutting and Transnational Sisterhood: Disputing U.S. Polemics*. Urbana: University of Illinois Press.

Joeres, Ruth-Ellen Boetcher. 1994. "Sisterhood? Jeder für sich? Gedanken über die heutige feministische Diskussion in den USA." *Feministische Studien* 94, no. 1: 6–16.

John, Mary E. 1996. *Discrepant Dislocations: Feminism, Theory, and Postcolonial Histories*. Berkeley: University of California Press.

Johnston, Jill. 1974. *Lesbian Nation*. New York: Simon and Schuster.

Jordanova, Ludmilla. 1989. *Sexual Visions: Images of Gender in Science and Medicine between the Eighteenth and Twentieth Centuries*. London: Harvester Wheatsheaf.

————. 1999. *Nature Displayed: Gender, Science, and Medicine*. New York: Longman.

Kaplan, Caren. 1996. *Questions of Travel: Postmodern Discourses of Displacement*. Durham: Duke University Press.

Kapsalis, Terri. 1997. *Public Privates: Performing Gynecology from Both Ends of the Speculum*. Durham: Duke University Press.

Kearney, Richard. 2002. *On Stories*. London: Routledge.

Keller, Evelyn Fox. 1992. *Secrets of Life, Secrets of Death: Essays on Language, Gender, and Science*. New York: Routledge.

————. 1985. *Reflections on Gender and Science*. New Haven: Yale University Press.

Khor, Diana. 1999. "Organizing for Change: Women's Grassroots Activism in Japan." *Feminist Studies* 25, no. 3: 633–61.

King, Anthony D., ed. 1997. *Culture, Globalization, and the World-*

System: Contemporary Conditions for the Representation of Identity. Minneapolis: University of Minnesota Press.

King, Deborah. 1988. "Multiple Jeopardy, Multiple Consciousness: The Context of a Black Feminist Ideology." *Signs* 14, no. 1: 42–72.

King, Katie. 1994. *Theory in Its Feminist Travels: Conversations in U.S. Women's Movements.* Bloomington: Indiana University Press.

Kline, Wendy. 2005. "'Please Include This in Your Book': Readers Respond to *Our Bodies, Ourselves.*" *Bulletin of the History of Medicine* 79: 81–110.

Knapp, Gudrun-Axeli. 2005. "Race, Class, Gender: Reclaiming Baggage in Fast Travelling Theories." *European Journal of Women's Studies* 12, no. 3: 249–65.

Kotzeva, Tatyana. 2001. "The Bulgarian *Our Bodies, Ourselves*: Steps in Cultural Adaptation and Its Messages to Bulgarian Women." Paper presented at the conference Crossing Cultural Borders with *Our Bodies, Ourselves*, Utrecht, June.

Kruks, Sonia. 2001. *Retrieving Experience: Subjectivity and Recognition in Feminist Politics.* Ithaca: Cornell University Press.

Kuhlmann, Ellen, and Birgit Babitsch. 2002. "Bodies, Health, Gender: Bridging Feminist Theories and Women's Health." *Women's Studies International Forum* 25, no. 4: 433–42.

Landau, Carol, and Michele G. Cyr. 2003. *The New Truth about Menopause.* New York: St. Martin's Griffin.

Lang, Sabine. 1997. "The NGOization of Feminism." In *Transitions, Environments, Translations: Feminisms in International Politics*, edited by Joan W. Scott, Cora Kaplan, and Debra Keates, 101–20. New York: Routledge.

Laqueur, Thomas W. 2003. *Solitary Sex: A Cultural History of Masturbation.* New York: Zone.

———. 1990. *Making Sex: Body and Gender from the Greeks to Freud.* Cambridge: Harvard University Press.

Lash, Scott. 2002. *Critique of Information.* London: Sage.

Lindemann, Gese. 1997. "The Body of Gender Difference." In *Embodied Practices: Feminist Perspectives on the Body*, edited by Kathy Davis, 73–92. London: Sage.

Lindsey, Elizabeth Sarah. 2005. "Reexamining Gender and Sexual Orientation: Revisioning the Representation of Queer and Trans People in the 2005 Edition of *Our Bodies, Ourselves.*" *NWSA Journal* 17, no. 1 (spring): 184–89.

Lorber, Judith. 1997. *Gender and the Social Construction of Illness.* Thousand Oaks, Calif.: Sage.

Lorde, Audre. 1984. *Sister Outsider.* Trumansburg, N.Y.: Crossing.

Love, Susan. 1990. *Dr. Susan Love's Breast Book.* Reading, Mass.: Addison-Wesley.

Lugones, María. 2003. *Pilgimages/Peregrinajes: Theorizing Coalition against Multiple Oppressions.* Lanham, Md.: Rowman and Little-field.

———. 1990. "Playfullness, 'World'-Travelling, and Loving Perception." In *Making Face, Making Soul: Creative and Critical Perspectives by Feminists of Color,* edited by Gloria Anzaldúa, 390–402. San Francisco: Aunt Lute.

Lugones, María, and Elizabeth V. Spelman. 1983. "Have We Got a Theory for You! Feminist Theory, Cultural Imperialism, and the Demand for 'The Woman's Voice.'" *Women's Studies International Forum* 6, no. 6: 573–81.

Mackie, Vera. 2001. "The Language of Globalization, Transnationality, and Feminism." *International Feminist Journal of Politics* 3, no. 2 (August): 180–206.

Mains, Shelley. 1997. "Our Feminist Institutions, Ourselves." *Sojourner* 23, no. 4: 10–11.

Mani, Lata. 1989. "Multiple Mediations: Feminist Scholarship in the Age of Multinational Reception." *Inscriptions* 5: 1–24.

Mansbridge, Jane, and Aldon Morris. 2001. *Oppositional Consciousness: The Subjective Roots of Social Protest.* Chicago: University of Chicago Press.

Marody, Mira. 1993. "Why I Am Not a Feminist." *Social Research* 60, no. 4: 853–64.

Marshall, Helen. 1996. "Our Bodies, Ourselves: Why We Should Add Old Fashioned Empirical Phenomenology to the New Theories of the Body." *Women's Studies International Forum* 19, no. 3: 253–65.

Martin, Emily. 2001. *The Woman in the Body.* Boston: Beacon.

———. 1991. "The Egg and the Sperm: How Science Has Constructed a Romance Based on Stereotypical Male-Female Roles." *Signs* 16, no. 3: 485–501.

Mayer, Elisabeth. 1996. *"I Am a Woman Giving Birth to Myself": Language, Ownership, and the Body in the Women's Health Movement.* B.A. thesis, Department of Anthropology, Harvard University.

McNay, Lois. 2000. *Gender and Agency: Reconfiguring the Subject in Feminist and Social Theory.* Cambridge: Polity.

———. 1992. *Foucault and Feminism.* Cambridge: Polity.

McPherson, Marianne. 2005. "Breasts, Blood, and the Royal V: Challenges of Revising Anatomy and Periods for the 2005 Edition of *Our Bodies, Ourselves.*" *NWSA Journal* 17, no. 1 (spring): 190–95.

Mediatore, Shari Stone. 2003. *Reading across Borders: Storytelling and Knowledges of Resistance.* New York: Palgrave.

———. 1998. "Chandra Mohanty and the Revaluing of 'Experience.'" *Hypatia* 13, no. 2: 116–33.

Mendoza, Breny. 2002. "Transnational Feminisms in Question." *Feminist Theory* 3, no. 3: 295–314.

Moallem, Minoo. 1991. "Transnationalism, Feminism, and Fundamentalism." In *Between Women and Nation: Nationalisms, Transnational Feminisms, and the State*, edited by Caren Kaplan, Norma Alarcón, and Minoo Moallem, 320–47. Durham: Duke University Press.

Mohanty, Chandra Talpade. 2003. *Feminism without Borders: Decolonizing Theory, Practicing Solidarity*. Durham: Duke University Press.

Mohanty, Chandra Talpade, Ann Russo, and Lourdes Torres, eds. 1991. *Third World Women and the Politics of Feminism*. Bloomington: Indiana University Press.

Moi, Toril. 2002. "While We Wait: The English Translation of *The Second Sex*," *Signs* 27, 4:1005–36.

Moore, Lisa Jean, and Adele E. Clarke. 1995. "Clitoral Conventions and Transgressions: Graphic Representations in Anatomy Texts, c. 1900–1991." *Feminist Studies* 21, no. 2 (summer): 255–301.

Moraga, Cherríe, and Gloria Anzaldúa, eds. 1983. *The Bridge Called My Back: Writing by Radical Women of Color*. New York: Kitchen Table Press.

Morgan, Robin, ed. 1984. *Sisterhood Is Global: The International Women's Movement Anthology*. Garden City, N.Y.: Anchor.

Morgen, Sandra. 2002. *Into Our Own Hands: The Women's Health Movement in the United States, 1969–1990*. New Brunswick, N.J.: Rutgers University Press.

———. 1998. "The Dream of Diversity, the Dilemma of Difference: Race and Class Contradictions in a Feminist Health Clinic." In *Anthropology for the Nineties: Introductory Readings*, edited by Johnnetta B. Cole, 370–80. New York: Free Press.

———. 1995. "'It Was the Best of Times, It Was the Worst of Times': Emotional Discourse in the Work Cultures of Feminist Health Clinics." In *Feminist Organizations: Harvest of the Women's Movement*, edited by Myra Marx Ferree and Patricia Yancey Martin, 234–47. Philadelphia: Temple University Press.

Moss, Kary L., ed. 1996. *Man-Made Medicine: Women's Health, Public Policy, and Reform*. Durham: Duke University Press.

Moya, Paula M. L. 2001. "Chicana Feminism and Postmodernist Theory." *Signs* 26, no. 2: 441–83.

———. "Postmodernism, 'Realism,' and the Politics of Identity: Cherríe Moraga and Chicana Feminism." In *Feminist Genealogies, Colonial Legacies, Democratic Futures*, edited by M. Jacqui Alexander and Chandra Talpade Mohanty, 125–50. New York: Routledge, 1997.

Murphy, Michelle. 2004. "Immodest Witnessing: The Epistemology of Vaginal Self-Examination in the U.S. Feminist Self-Help Movement." *Feminist Studies* 30, no. 1 (spring): 115–47.

Nakanishi, Toyoko. 1997. "Interview." In *Broken Silence: Voices of Japanese Feminism*, edited by Sandra Buckley, 185–225. Berkeley: University of California Press.

Naples, Nancy A., and Manisha Desai, eds. 2002. *Women's Activism and*

Globalization: Linking Local Struggles and Transnational Politics. New York: Routledge.

Narayan, Uma. 1998. "Essence of Culture and a Sense of History: A Feminist Critique of Cultural Essentialism." *Hypatia* 13, no. 2 (spring): 86–106.

———. 1997. *Dislocating Cultures: Identities, Traditions, and Third World Feminism.* New York: Routledge.

Nicholson, Linda. 1994. "Interpreting Gender." *Signs* 20, no. 1: 79–105.

Nikolchina, Miglena. 2002. "The Seminar, *Mode d'emploi*: Impure Spaces in the Light of Late Totalitarianism." *differences* 15, no. 1: 96–127.

Norsigian, Judy. 1996. "The Women's Health Movement in the United States." In *Man-Made Medicine: Women's Health, Public Policy, and Reform,* edited by Kary L. Moss, 79–97. Durham: Duke University Press.

Norsigian, Judy, Vilunya Diskin, Paula Doress-Worters, Jane Pincus, Wendy Coppedge Sanford, and Norma Swenson. 1999. "The Boston Women's Health Book Collective and *Our Bodies, Ourselves*: A Brief History and Reflection." *JAMWA* 54, no. 1 (winter): 35–40.

Norsigian, Judy, and Wendy Coppedge Sanford. 1987. "Ten Years in the 'Our Bodies, Ourselves' Collective." *Women and Therapy* 6, nos. 1–2: 287–92.

Northrup, Christiane. *The Wisdom of Menopause.* New York: Bantam Dell, 2001.

Ogino, Miho. 1997. "About the Japanese Edition." In *Broken Silence: Voices of Japanese Feminism,* edited by Sandra Buckley, 202–12. Berkeley: University of California Press.

Ogino, Miho, with Toyoko Nakanishi and Toshiko Honda. 2001. "From OBOS to SOFL: Why and How We Adapted Them into Japanese Society." Paper presented at the conference Crossing Cultural Borders with *Our Bodies, Ourselves,* Utrecht, June.

Oudshoorn, Nelly. 1994. *Beyond the Natural Body: An Archaeology of Sex Hormones.* New York: Routledge.

Passerini, Luisa. 1996. *Autobiography of a Generation.* Hanover, N.H.: Wesleyan University Press.

———. 1990. "Mythbiography in Oral History." In *The Myths We Live By,* edited by Raphael Samuel and Paul Thompson, 48–60. London: Routledge.

Petchesky, Rosalind P. 2003. *Global Prescriptions: Gendering Health and Human Rights.* London: Zed.

———. 1995. "The Body as Property: A Feminist Re-Vision." In *Conceiving the New World Order,* edited by Faye Ginsburg and Rayna Rapp, 387–406. Berkeley: University of California Press.

Petchesky, Rosalind P., and Karen Judd. 1998. *Negotiating Reproductive Rights: Women's Perspectives across Countries and Cultures.* London: Zed.

Pfeil, Fred. 1994. "No Basta Teorizar: In-Difference to Solidarity in Contemporary Fiction, Theory, and Practice." In *Scattered Hegemonies: Postmodernity and Transnational Feminist Practices*, edited by Inderpal Grewal and Caren Kaplan, 197–230. Minneapolis: University of Minnesota Press.

Phillips, Angela, and Jill Rakusen, eds. 1978. *Our Bodies, Ourselves*. London: Penguin.

Pincus, Jane. 2002. "How a Group of Friends Transformed Women's Health." *Women's e-news*, http://www.womensenews.org/article.cfm/dyn/aid/844 (accessed March 17, 2002).

———. 1998. "Introduction." In *Our Bodies, Ourselves for the New Century*, by Boston Women's Health Collective, 21–23. New York: Simon and Schuster.

Portelli, Alessandro. 1997. *The Battle of Valle Giulia: Oral History and the Art of Dialogue*. Madison: University of Wisconsin Press.

———. 1991. *The Death of Luigi Trastulli and Other Stories: Form and Meaning in Oral History*. Albany: State University of New York Press.

———. 1990. "Uchronic Dreams: Working-Class Memory and Possible Worlds." In *The Myths We Live By*, edited by Raphael Samuel and Paul Thompson, 143–60. London: Routledge.

Rasmussen, Birgit Brander, Eric Klineberg, Irene J. Nexica, and Matt Wray, eds. 2001. *The Making and Unmaking of Whiteness*. Durham: Duke University Press.

Rich, Adrienne. 1986. "Notes toward a Politics of Location." In *Blood, Bread, and Poetry: Selected Prose, 1979–1985*, 210–31. New York: Norton.

Ricoeur, Paul. 1978. *Main Trends in Philosophy*. New York: Holmes and Meier.

Riessman, Catherine K. 1983. "Women and Medicalization: A New Perspective." *Social Policy* 14, no. 1: 3–19.

Riger, Stephanie. 1994. "Challenges of Success: Stages of Growth in Feminist Organizations." *Feminist Studies* 20, no. 2 (summer): 275–300.

Robertson, Roland. 1995. "Glocalization: Time-Space and Homogeneity-Heterogeneity." In *Global Modernities*, edited by Mike Featherstone, Scott Lash, and Roland Robertson, 25–44. London: Sage.

Roof, Judith. 1997. "Generational Difficulties; or, the Fear of a Barren History." In *Generations: Academic Feminists in Dialogue*, edited by Devoney Looser and E. Ann Kaplan, 69–87. Minneapolis: University of Minnesota Press.

———. 1995. "How to Satisfy a Woman 'Every Time.' . . ." In *Feminism Beside Itself*, edited by Diane Elam and Robyn Wiegman, 55–69. London: Routledge.

Rooks, Judith P. 1985. "The Feminist Health Book." *Family Planning Perspectives* 17, no. 5: 238–40. Review of *The New Our Bodies, Ourselves*.

Rosen, Ruth. 2000. *The World Split Open: How the Modern Women's Movement Changed America*. New York: Penguin.

Roy, Parama. 2001. "At Home in the World? The Gendered Cartographies of Globality." *Feminist Studies* 27, no. 3 (fall): 709–31.

Ruiz, Vicki L., and Ellen Carol DuBois, eds. 2000. *Unequal Sisters: A Multicultural Reader in U.S. Women's History*. New York: Routledge.

Ruzek, Sheryl Burt. 1978. *The Women's Health Movement*. New York: Praeger.

Ruzek, Sheryl Burt, and Julie Becker. 1999. "The Women's Health Movement in the United States: From Grass-Roots Activism to Professional Agendas." *JAMWA* 54, no. 1 (winter): 4–8.

Ruzek, Sheryl Burt, Virginia L. Olesen, and Adele E. Clarke. 1997. *Women's Health: Complexities and Differences*. Columbus: Ohio State University Press.

Safa, Helen Icken. 1990. "Women's Social Movements in Latin America." *Gender and Society* 4, no. 3: 354–69.

Said, Edward W. 1994. *Culture and Imperialism*. New York: Vintage.

———. 1983. *The World, the Text, and the Critic*. Cambridge: Harvard University Press.

———. 1978. *Orientalism*. New York: Vintage.

Samuel, Raphael, and Paul Thompson, eds. 1990. *The Myths We Live By*. London: Routledge.

Sandoval, Chela. 2000. *Methodology of the Oppressed*. Minneapolis: University of Minnesota Press.

———. 1991. "U.S. Third World Feminism: The Theory and Method of Oppositional Consciousness in the Postmodern World." *Genders* 10 (spring): 1–24.

Sanford, Wendy Coppedge. 1979. "Working Together, Growing Together: A Brief History of the Boston Women's Health Book Collective." *Heresies* 7, no. 2: 83–92.

Sanford, Wendy Coppedge, and Paula Doress, 1981. "'Our Bodies, Ourselves' and Censorship." *Library Acquisitions: Practice and Theory* 5: 133–42.

Schiebinger, Londa. 2004. *Nature's Body: Gender in the Making of Modern Science*. New Brunswick, N.J.: Rutgers University Press.

Schrager, Cynthia D.1993. "Questioning the Promise of Self-Help: A Reading of *Women Who Love Too Much*." *Feminist Studies* 19, no. 1: 177–92.

Scott, Ellen K. 2000. "Everyone against Racism: Agency and the Production of Meaning in the Anti-racism Practices of Two Feminist Organizations." *Theory and Society* 29: 785–818.

Scott, Joan W. 1992. "Experience." In *Feminists Theorize the Political*, edited by Judith Butler and Joan W. Scott, 22–40. New York: Routledge.

Scott, Joan W., Cora Kaplan, and Debra Keates, eds. 1997. *Transitions,*

Environments, Translations: Feminisms in International Politics. New York: Routledge.

Scudson, Michael. 1997. "Cultural Studies and the Social Construction of 'Social Construction': Notes on 'Teddy Bear Patriarchy.'" In *From Sociology to Cultural Studies,* edited by Elizabeth Long, 379–98. Oxford: Blackwell.

Seaman, Barbara. 2003. *The Greatest Experiment Ever Performed on Women: Exploding the Estrogen Myth.* New York: Hyperion.

Shapiro, Ester R. 2005. "Because Words Are Not Enough: Latina Re-visionings of Transnational Collaborations Using Health Promotion for Gender Justice and Social Change." *NWSA Journal* 17, no. 1: 141–71.

———. 2001. "Gender, Culture, and the Language of Women's Health: Cultural Adaptation in the Spanish Translation of *Our Bodies, Ourselves.*" Paper presented at the conference Crossing Cultural Borders with *Our Bodies, Ourselves,* Utrecht, June.

———. 1999. "Crossing Cultural Borders with North American Feminism: Lessons from the Latin American Translation/Adaptation of *Our Bodies, Ourselves.*" Paper presented at the conference Gender, Culture, and Translation, Budapest, October.

Shih, Shu-Mei. 2002. "Towards an Ethics of Transnational Encounter; or, 'When' Does a 'Chinese' Woman Become a 'Feminist'?" *differences* 15, no. 2: 90–126.

Shreve, Anita. *Women Together, Women Alone: The Legacy of the Consciousness-Raising Movement.* New York: Viking, 1989.

Simonds, Wendy. 1996. *Abortion at Work: Ideology and Practice in a Feminist Clinic.* New Brunswick, N.J.: Rutgers University Press.

Skocpol, Theda. 1979. *States and Social Revolutions.* Cambridge: Cambridge University Press.

Slavova, Kornelia. 2001. "Translating *Our Bodies, Ourselves* into Bulgarian: Texts and Selves." Paper presented at the conference Crossing Cultural Borders with *Our Bodies, Ourselves,* Utrecht, June.

Smith, Barbara, ed. 1983. *Home Girls: A Black Feminist Anthology.* New York: Kitchen Table/Women of Color Press.

Smith, Dorothy E. 1999. *Writing the Social: Critique, Theory, and Investigations.* Toronto: University of Toronto Press.

———. 1997. "Comment on Hekman's 'Truth and Method: Feminist Standpoint Theory Revisited.'" *Signs* 22, no. 2: 392–98.

———. 1990a. *The Conceptual Practices of Power: A Feminist Sociology of Knowledge.* Boston: Northeastern University Press.

———. 1990b. *Texts, Facts, and Femininity: Exploring the Relations of Ruling.* London: Routledge.

———. 1987. *The Everyday World as Problematic: A Feminist Sociology.* Toronto: University of Toronto Press.

Smith, Dorothy E., and Sara J. David, eds. 1975. *Women Look at Psychiatry*. Vancouver: Press Gang.

Smith, Susan Lynn. 1995. *Sick and Tired of Being Sick and Tired: Black Women's Health Activism in America, 1890–1950*. Philadelphia: University of Pennsylvania Press.

Solinger, Rickie, ed. 1998. *Abortion Wars: A Half Century of Struggle, 1950–2000*. Berkeley: University of California Press.

Spelman, Elizabeth. 1988. *Inessential Woman: Problems of Exclusion in Feminist Thought*. Boston: Beacon.

Spivak, Gayatri Chakravorty. 2000. "The Politics of Translation." In *The Translation Studies Reader*, edited by Lawrence Venuti, 397–416. London: Routledge.

———. 1988a. "Can the Subaltern Speak?" In *Marxism and the Interpretation of Culture*, edited by Cary Nelson and Lawrence Grossberg, 271–313. Urbana: University of Illinois Press.

———. 1988b. *In Other Worlds: Essays in Cultural Politics*. New York: Routledge.

———. 1985. "Three Women's Texts and a Critique of Imperialism." *Critical Inquiry* 12, no. 1: 243–61.

Springer, Kimberly, ed. 1999. *Still Lifting, Still Climbing: African American Women's Contemporary Activism*. New York: New York University Press.

Stacey, Judith. 2001. "The empress of feminist Theory is overdressed." *Feminist Theory* 2, no. 1: 99–103.

Stanley, Liz, and Sue Wise. 2000. "But the Empress Has No Clothes! Some Awkward Questions about the 'Missing Revolution' in Feminist Theory." *Feminist Theory* 1, no. 3: 261–88.

———. 1993. *Breaking out Again: Feminist Ontology and Epistemology*. London: Routledge.

Stephenson, Heather. 2005. "*Our Bodies, Ourselves* for a New Generation: Revising a Feminist Classic." *NWSA Journal* 17, no. 1 (spring): 173–74.

Sternbach, Nancy Saporta, Marysa Navarro-Arangueren, Patricia Chuchryk, and Sonia E. Alvarez. 1992. "Feminisms in Latin America: From Bogotá to San Bernardo." *Signs* 17, no. 2: 393–434.

Swann, Catherine. 1997. "Reading the Bleeding Body: Discourses of Premenstrual Syndrome." In *Body Talk: The Material and Discursive Regulation of Sexuality, Madness, and Reproduction*, edited by Jane M. Ussher, 176–98. London: Routledge.

Taylor, Verta. 1999. "Gender and Social Movements: Gender Processes in Women's Self-Help Movements." *Gender and Society* 13, no. 1 (February): 8–33.

Taylor, Verta, and Nancy Whittier. 1995. "Analytical Approaches to Social Movement Culture: The Culture of the Women's Movement." In

Social Movements and Culture, edited by Hank Johnston and Bert Klandermans, 163–87. London: University College London Press.

Thayer, Millie. 2000. "Traveling Feminisms: From Embodied Women to Gendered Citizenship." In *Global Ethnography: Forces, Connections, and Imaginations in a Postmodern World*, edited by Michael Burawoy, Joseph A. Blum, Sheba George, Zsuzsa Gille, Teresa Gowan, Lynne Hanley, Maren Klawiter, Steven H. Lopez, Sean O'Riain, and Millie Thayer, 203–33. Berkeley: University of California Press.

Thompson, Becky. 2002. "Multiracial Feminism: Recasting the Chronology of Second Wave Feminism." *Feminist Studies* 28, no. 2 (summer): 337–55.

Todd, Alexandra Dundas. 1989. *Intimate Adversaries: Cultural Conflict between Doctors and Women Patients*. Philadelphia: University of Pennsylvania Press.

Todorova, Maria. 1994. "Historical Tradition and Transformation in Bulgaria: Women's Issues or Feminist Issues?" *Journal of Women's History* 5, no. 3: 129–43.

Tonkin, Elizabeth. 1992. *Narrating Our Pasts: The Social Construction of Oral History*. Cambridge: Cambridge University Press.

Tsing, Anna Lowenhaupt. 1997. "Transitions as Translations." In *Transitions, Environments, Translations: Feminisms in International Politics*, edited by Joan W. Scott, Cora Kaplan, and Debra Keates, 253–72. New York: Routledge.

Uno, Kathleen S. 1993. "Maternalism in Modern Japan." *Journal of Women's History* 5, no. 2: 126–30.

Vance, Carole S., ed. 1984. *Pleasure and Danger: Exploring Female Sexuality*. Boston: Routledge and Kegan Paul.

Varikas, Eleni. 1995. "Gender, Experience, and Subjectivity: The Tilly-Scott Disagreement." *New Left Review* 211: 89–101.

Venuti, Lawrence. 2000. "Translation, Community, Utopia." In *The Translation Studies Reader*, edited by Lawrence Venuti, 468–88. London: Routledge.

———. 1998. *The Scandals of Translation: Towards an Ethics of Difference*. London: Routledge.

———. 1995. *The Translator's Invisibility: A History of Translation*. London: Routledge.

Wallerstein, Immanuel. 1974. *The Modern World System*. Vol. 1. New York: Academic.

Walters, Shirley, and Linzi Manicom, eds. 1996. *Gender in Popular Education: Methods for Empowerment*. Atlantic Highlands, N.J.: Zed.

Watson, Peggy. 1997. "Civil Society and the Politics of Difference in Eastern Europe." In *Transitions, Environments, Translations: Feminisms in International Politics*, edited by Joan W. Scott, Cora Kaplan, and Debra Keates, 21–29. New York: Routledge.

Wegscheider, Jane Hyman, and Esther Rome. 1996. *Sacrificing Ourselves for Love: Why Women Sacrifice Health and Self-Esteem . . . and How to Stop.* New York: Simon and Schuster.

Weisman, Carol Sachs. 1998. *Women's Health Care: Activist Traditions and Institutional Change.* Baltimore: Johns Hopkins University Press.

Weisser, Susan Ostrov, and Jennifer Fleischner, eds. 1995. *Feminist Nightmares: Women at Odds.* New York: New York University Press.

Wendell, Susan. 1996. *The Rejected Body: Feminist Philosophical Reflections on Disability.* New York: Routledge.

Werner, Elisabeth Yupanqui. 2001. "'Mission Impossible?' Das Konflict potential zwischen Gründerinnen und Newcomern in Frauenprojekten-am Beispiel des Boston Women's Health Book Collective." Master's thesis, Department of Education, Ebenhardz-Karl University, Tübingen, Germany.

Whelan, Sally, and Jane Pincus. 2001. "Crossing Cultural Borders with *Our Bodies, Ourselves*: A Meeting in Utrecht, the Netherlands, June 2001." *BWHC Newsletter*, fall/winter 2001, http://www.ourbodiesour selves.org/programs/network/utrecht.asp (accessed March 23, 2007).

White, Evelyn C., ed. 1990. *The Black Women's Health Book: Speaking for Ourselves.* Seattle: Seal.

Wilson, William J. 1978. *Declining Significance of Race.* Chicago: University of Chicago Press.

Wing, Adrien Katherine, ed. 1997. *Critical Race Feminism: A Reader.* New York: New York University Press.

Women's Health Initiative in Bulgaria. 2003. "Community Outreach: Promoting Women's Health." Report, Sofia, Bulgaria, January.

Woolf, Virginia. 1938. *Three Guineas.* London: Harcourt Brace Jovanovich.

Worters, Paula Doress, and Diana Larkin Siegal. [1987] 1994. *Ourselves Growing Older: Women Aging with Knowledge and Power.* New York: Touchstone.

Yanco, Jennifer J. 1996. "*Our Bodies, Ourselves* in Beijing: Breaking the Silences." *Feminist Studies* 22, no. 3: 511–17.

Young, Iris Marion. 1990a. *Justice and the Politics of Difference.* Princeton: Princeton University Press.

———. 1990b. *"Throwing Like a Girl" and Other Essays in Feminist Philosophy and Social Theory.* Bloomington: Indiana University Press.

Zajicek, Anna M. 2002. "Race Discourses and Antiracist Practices in a Local Women's Movement." *Gender and Society* 16, no. 2: 155–74.

Nuestros Cuerpos, Nuestras Vidas
(Latin American *OBOS*), 5, 15, 19,
64, 66, 68, 77, 174–83

OBOS. See *Our Bodies, Ourselves*
Ogino, Miho (translator of Japanese *OBOS*), 171–73
Olesen, Virginia, 120–21
Oudshoorn, Nelly, 126
Our Bodies, Ourselves (U.S.): as
best seller, 24–27; censorship of,
24–25, 27, 30, 59; continuities and
changes in, 25–30, 36–38, 40–49,
60–69; as course for women,
21–23, 25, 79; differences between
women and the "we" of, 23, 26–
27, 30, 32–33, 37–40, 48–49, 66,
200; editorial control of, 24, 27,
59; as feminist icon, 5–6, 36, 199,
202; feminist theory and, 198–99,
206–7, 209–10; history of, 10–
14, 19–49; letters to, 13, 150–60,
164–65; mainstreaming of, 28–33;
production of, 7, 11–12, 21–22, 24,
28–29, 32–33, 36, 40–41, 44–45,
48–49, 68–69, 100, 160, 200–
201, 211–12; sales of, 2, 24, 208;
significance of, 1–3; as "success
story," 2–3, 5, 14, 20, 27, 43–49,
97–98, 202; as text, 12, 14–15, 142,
161–65; as transnational feminist
project, 5–7, 10–11, 13–15, 51, 77–
81, 118; travels of, 6–7, 9, 11–12, 15,
198–201, 206–7. *See also* Boston
Women's Health Book Collective; Politics; Readers; Translations
Ourselves and Our Children, 21

Passerini, Luisa, 90, 118–9
Petchesky, Rosalind, 203
Pfeil, Fred, 209
Pincus, Jane (founder), 19, 21, 23,
27–28, 33, 39, 90, 95, 103, 105, 112
Politics: of knowledge, 6–8, 12, 15,
21–22, 43, 48, 123–29, 136–41,

160–62, 164–65, 178, 195, 197–98,
202, 204–7, 210, 212; of location,
7–11, 160, 194, 198–200, 202–4,
206; of translation, 70, 173–74,
181–82, 185, 188–95; of women's
health, 1, 3, 15, 27, 29, 38, 44–47,
60, 79–81, 115, 122–25, 140–43,
164, 181, 203, 206. *See also* Epistemology; Feminism; Health;
Our Bodies, Ourselves; Translation
Portelli, Alessandro, 118–9
Potter, Elizabeth, 124
Psychotherapy, 29, 31–32, 67

Racism: feminist organizations
and, 87–88, 95, 109–17; race
and health, 38, 48, 124, 137, 153.
See also Feminism: differences
among women and
Readers, 11–15, 142, 144–54, 161–62,
164–65; active, 161–62; as feminist subjects, 12, 14–15, 142–43,
145–46, 150–51, 161–65, 199; resistant, 149–50, 159, 161, 163–65,
200–201; of translations, 68–70,
180, 185, 191–92, 195. See also *Our
Bodies, Ourselves*: as text
Reproduction, 1–3, 22–23, 25–26,
29, 31, 45, 63–64, 67, 70, 90, 91,
134; reproductive rights, 2, 26–
27, 29, 62, 153, 187, 189, 193, 203,
205–6; technology and, 4, 31, 131
Rich, Adrienne, 7
Ricoeur, Paul, 118
Rome, Esther (founder), 93–94, 99
Rooks, Judith, 151

Said, Edward, 9, 120, 140, 207
Sanford, Wendy (founder), 19, 22,
28, 30, 36–38, 90, 102–5, 107, 111,
153, 160
"Scattered hegemonies" (Grewal
and Kaplan), 10
Schrager, Cynthia, 47
Scott, Joan, 12, 131–32, 134, 199

Kathy Davis * is a senior researcher at the Research
Institute for History and Culture, Utrecht University.
She is the author of *Dubious Equalities and Embodied
Differences: Cultural Studies on Cosmetic Surgery*
(2003) and *Reshaping the Female Body: The Dilemma
of Cosmetic Surgery* (1995).

Library of Congress Cataloging-in-Publication Data

Davis, Kathy.
The making of Our bodies, ourselves: how feminism
travels across borders / Kathy Davis.
p. cm. — (Next wave)
Includes bibliographical references and index.
ISBN-13: 978-0-8223-4045-4 (cloth: alk. paper)
ISBN-13: 978-0-8223-4066-9 (pbk.: alk. paper)
1. Feminism—Cross-cultural studies.
2. Women—Psychology—Cross-cultural studies.
3. Women—Health and hygiene—Cross-cultural studies.
4. Social change—Cross-cultural studies.
5. Boston Women's Health Collective.
I. Our bodies, ourselves. II. Title.
HQ1154.D34 2007
613'.04244—dc22   2007014062

3m